SPEAK CANTONESE WITH CONFIDENCE

ESSENTIAL CANTONESE

PHRASEBOOK & DICTIONARY

Hi, how are you?
Néih hóu ma?

Where are you from?
Néih hái bīn douh làih ga?

I'm an American.
Ngóh haih Méih Gwok yàhn.

Martha Tang

TUTTLE Publishing

Tokyo | Rutland, Vermont | Singapore

Contents

Introduction

●●●

Welcome to the Tuttle Essential Language series, covering all of the most popular Asian languages. These books are basic guides to communicating in the language. They're concise, accessible and easy to understand, and you'll find them indispensable on your trip abroad to get you where you want to go, pay the right prices and do everything you're planning to do.

Each guide is divided into 14 themed sections and starts with a pronunciation guide which explains the phonetic pronunciations of all the words and sentences you'll need to know, and a basic grammar guide which will help you construct basic sentences in the language. At the end of this book is an extensive English–Cantonese dictionary.

Throughout the book you'll come across boxes with a 🖐 beside them. These are designed to help you if you can't understand what your listener is saying to you. Hand the book over to them and encourage them to point to the appropriate answer to the question you are asking.

Other boxes in the book—this time without the 🖐 symbol— give listings of themed words with their English translations beside them.

For extra clarity, we have put all phonetic pronunciations of the Cantonese terms in bold.

This book covers all situations you are likely to encounter during the course of a visit, from reserving a room for the night to ordering food and drinks at a restaurant and what to do if you lose your credit cards and money. With over 2,000 commonly used words and essential sentences at your fingertips you can rest assured that you will be able to get by in all situations, so let **Essential Cantonese** become your passport to learning to communicate with confidence!

Pronunciation guide
· ·

This book adopts the Yale System of Romanization which is the most widely used system in Cantonese language books and dictionaries for English-speaking learners. The pronunciations should be read as if they were English, bearing in mind the following main points:

The Cantonese Consonants

B, ch, d, f, g, h, j, k, l, m, n, p, s, t, w, y are pronounced as in English. Other Cantonese consonants that do not exist in English are the following:

Romanization	Pronunciation
ng	like English **ng** in si**ng**
gw	like the English name **Gw**endolyn
kw	like the English **qu** in **qu**ick with a strong puff of air

Cantonese Vowels

Romanization	Pronunciation
a	like English **u** in '**u**rr'
aa	like English **a** in 'f**a**ther,' but held longer. This long vowel is normally written **aa**. However, it is written **a** when it is used by itself without a consonant.
e	like English **e** in 't**e**n'
i	like English **ee** in 'f**ee**'
o	like English **o** in 'h**o**t'
u	like English **oo** in 'f**oo**l'
eu	like English **e** in 'h**er**'
yu	like English 's**ui**te'

Cantonese Tones

A tone is a variation in pitch. Pronouncing the same syllable at different pitches can dramatically change the meaning of a word, e.g., **si** can mean "silk" or "try" depending on its pronunciation. Here, we use six tones for easy reference, as shown in the tone chart below.

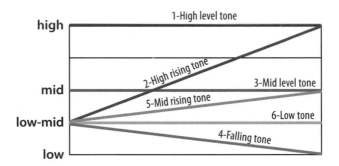

Tone 1 is a high-level tone represented by ——▶. Pronounce this in a higher note than your normal speech.

Tone 2 is a rising tone represented by ——▶. Start off in a mid-low tone and then raise it to the high tone, as if you were asking a question.

Tone 3 has no tone mark and you pronounce it as you would a normal English word, in the mid-tone.

Tone 4 is a falling tone represented by ——▶ + **h**. Start off in a low-mid tone and drop your voice to the low tone.

Tone 5 is a rising tone that starts at the same level as tone 2, but ends at mid-level rather than at the high tone. It is represented by ——▶ + **h.**

Tone 6 is similar to tone 1 and 3, except that it should be pronounced at a lower tone than tone 3, at the low-mid level. It is represented by no tone marking and **h**.

Note: When learning new Cantonese words, it is a good idea to memorize both the word and its tone marking as one unit.

The romanisation of a word, e.g., **si**, has several meanings depending on what tone it is pronounced at, so mispronouncing the tone could change the meaning from "silk" to "time".

For example,

Word	Tone Number	Meaning
絲 **sī**	1	silk
史 **sí**	2	history
試 **si**	3	try
時 **sìh**	4	time
市 **síh**	5	city
事 **sih**	6	matter

Basic grammar

Cantonese grammar is quite simple. There are no verb conjugations, plurals, genders, or articles, and the word order is quite intuitive to English speakers. The following is an outline of Cantonese grammar using parts of speech that are familiar to English speakers.

Word Order

More often than not, Cantonese word order is the same as in English:

Subject — Verb — Object

Ngóh	hohk	Gwóng Dūng wá	我學廣東話。
I	*study*	*Cantonese*	= I study Cantonese.

Nouns and Pronouns

Cantonese nouns are mostly made up of two characters. No distinction is made between singular and plural nouns. When you want to specify the number of items involved, use measure words. For example, the word for 'book' **syū** can be either singular or plural unless it is necessary to indicate that there is more than one object. Thus,

yāt	**bún**	**syū**	一本書
one (measure word for books)	*book*		= one book

léuhng	**bún**	**syū**	兩本書
two (measure word for books)	*books*		= two books

sāam	**bún**	**syū**	三本書
three (measure word for books)	*books*		= three books

In the above examples, the noun **syū** 書'book' is qualified by a number with the appropriate measure word **bún** 本 to indicate its quantity, similar to how we'd say 'one bottle of water' or 'one sheet of paper' in English. Remember to use **léuhng** 兩 'a couple of' instead of **yih** 二 'two' when paired with a measure word.

Like nouns, Cantonese personal pronouns do not change form when used as subjects or objects. Simple personal pronouns are: **ngóh** 我 = 'I/me', **néih** 你 = 'you', **kéuih** 佢 = 'he/him/she/her/it'.

However, Cantonese personal pronouns do have plural forms created by the addition of the suffix **deih** 哋 (plural).

> **ngóh** 我 'I/me' becomes **ngóh deih** 我哋 'we/us'

> **néih** 你 'you' becomes **néih deih** 你哋 'you (plural)'

> **kéuih** 佢 'he/him/she/her/it' becomes **kéuih deih** 佢哋 'they/
> them' (also used for animals or insects)

The demonstrative pronouns **nī** 'this', **gó** 'that' and **bīn** 邊 'which' also have plural forms created by adding **dī** 啲.

> **nī** 呢 'this' becomes **nī dī** 呢啲 'these'

> **gó** 嗰 'that' becomes **gó dī** 嗰啲 'those'

> **bīn** 邊 'which' becomes **bīn dī** 邊啲 'which ones'

Possessives and Measure words

The possessive form of a noun or pronoun is created by adding the particle **ge** 嘅, which is the equivalent of 's in English:

> The tour guide's = **douh yàuh ge** 導遊嘅

> Miss Li's = **Léih síu jé ge** 李小姐嘅

> My or mine = **ngóh ge** 我嘅

> Your or yours = **néih ge** 你嘅

> His or her = **kéuih ge** 佢嘅

> Our = **ngóh deih ge** 我哋嘅

> Your = **néih deih ge** 你哋嘅

> Their = **kéuih deih ge** 佢哋嘅

Measure words

In English we say 'a slice/loaf of bread', 'a piece/ream of paper', 'a school of fish, 'a bottle of water' etc. In Cantonese this usage applies to all nouns in order to specify number. In other words, you cannot just say 'one book' or 'two books' etc., you have to add a 'measure word' for books, which would be **bún** 本, which does not have an English equivalent.

Different types or classes of nouns have different measure words. Each measure word is used for objects with similar characteristics.

Examples:

bún 本 is used for bound books, i.e., 'one (measure word for books) book' **yāt bún syū** 一本書

jēung 張 is used for wide, flat objects including tables, chairs, papers, bedsheets, boards, i.e., 'a (measure word for flat objects) table' **yāt jēung tói** 一張檯

bá 把 is used for objects with handles like knives and forks, i.e., **yāt bá dōu** 一把刀

Fortunately for beginners, there is a general-purpose measure word **go** 個 which can be used in simple phrases like:

nī go   呢個 'this one'

gó go   嗰個 'that one'

bīn go 邊個 'which one?'

géi go 幾個 'how many (items)?'

You can also use this with some nouns, e.g., **yāt go yàhn** 一個人 ('one person'), **yāt go būi** 一個杯 ('one cup/glass'), and be understood.

Verbs

Cantonese verbs are never conjugated, and only have one simple form regardless of the subject or tense. Thus the verb **sihk** 食 'eat' is the same whether the subject is I, you, he/she or they, and whether the action took place yesterday or will happen two days from now. The way to indicate tense in Cantonese sentences is by adding time words like **kàhm yaht** 琴日 'yesterday', **gām yaht** 今日 'today' and **tīng yaht** 聽日 'tomorrow' before the verb. The words **gwo** 過 'passed' and **jó** 咗 'done' indicate past and completed action, and the use of **jauh** 就 'soon' and **wúih** 會 'will/shall' indicates future action. For example,

The use of time words before the verb:

Ngóh kàhm yaht sihk yú. 我琴日食魚。 'I ate fish yesterday.'

Ngóh gām yaht sihk yú. 我今日食魚。 'Today I'm eating fish.'

Ngóh tīng yaht sihk yú. 我聽日食魚。 'I'll eat fish tomorrow.'

The particle **gwo** 過 is used after the verb to indicate that an action occurred on an unspecified time in the past:

Ngóh sihk gwo yú. 我食過魚。 'I've eaten fish before.'

The use of the particle **jó** 咗 after the verb indicates that the action has just been recently completed:

Ngóh sihk jó yú. 我食咗魚。 'I've just eaten (the) fish.'

Aspect particles, **jauh** 就 or **wúih** 會 before the verb, are used to indicate future actions. For example,

Ngóh jauh sihk gó dī yú. 我就食嗰啲魚。 'I'm going to eat (the) fish.'

Ngóh wúih sihk gó dī yú. 我會食嗰啲魚。 'I'll be eating (the) fish.'

Adjectives

Adjectives in Cantonese are simple as they don't need to agree in gender or number with the nouns they modify. They are placed in front of the noun, just like in English, e.g., '**leng** 靚 pretty **sāam** 衫 dress', '**feih** 肥 fat **zai** 仔 boy' or '**gwai** 貴 expensive **fóng** 房 room'.

When an adjective has a single syllable, it can be placed directly in front of the noun it modifies. For example,

sīn cháang jāp 鮮橙汁 'fresh orange juice'

hāk ga fē 黑咖啡 'black coffee'

When adjectives modify nouns in phrases they generally precede the noun, often using the particle **ge** 嘅 in between. For example,

màih yàhn ge fūng gíng	迷人嘅風景	'enchanting scenery'
mìhng gwai ge láih maht	名貴嘅禮物	'expensive gift'
tóu yim ge wū yīng	討厭嘅烏蠅	'annoying flies'

Adverbs

Just as adjectives precede the nouns they modify, adverbs are placed before verbs, adjectives or other adverbs to express time, degree, scope, repetition, possibility, negotiation and tone of speech. Common examples are: **hóu** 好 'very', **dōu** 都 'also', **béi gaau** 比較 'rather', **jauh** 就 'then', **sèhng yaht** 成日 'always'. For example,

Nī   tìuh   louh hóu chèuhng. 呢條路好長。
This (measure word) road very long = 'This road is very long.'

Ngóh dōu séung   máaih. 我都想買。
I   also   want   buy = 'I'm also thinking of buying (this).'

Nī douh hah tīn   béi gaau yiht. 呢度夏天比較熱。
Here   summer rather   hot = 'The summer here is quite hot.'

Néih sīn heui, ngóh jauh   làih. 你先去，我就嚟。
You first go   I'll   then   come = 'Go first, I'll catch up with you.'

Nī douh sèhng yaht lohk yúh. 呢度成日落雨。
Here   always   raining = 'It always rains here.'

The Verb "to be"

In Cantonese, the word for 'to be' is **haih** 係 and cannot be used with adjectives or adverbs as the resulting sentence would become I = very happy. Instead, we use adverbs like **hóu** 好 'very'. Thus, **Ngóh hóu gōu hing** 我好高興 means 'I'm very happy.'

Negatives

Two particles are used to form the negative in Cantonese: **m̀h** 唔 and **móuh** 冇. The former is placed before a verb or adjective to indicate negation in the present while the latter is used to indicate negation of an action that happened in the past. For example,

Seuhng Hói dūng tīn m̀h lohk syut. 上海冬天唔落雪。
Shanghai winter does not snow =
'It does not snow in Shanghai during winter.'

Gauh nín Bāk Gīng móuh lohk syut. 舊年北京冇落雪。
Last year Beijing didn't snow =
'Last year it didn't snow in Beijing.'

Asking a Question

There are three basic ways to ask a question in Cantonese. The most common way is to simply add the particle **ma** 嗎 or **a** 呀 to the end of a sentence, which is like adding a verbal question mark. As in English, it is also accommpanied by a rising tone at the end.

Néih ngoh ma? 你餓嗎？ 'Are you hungry?'

Néih hōi sām ma? 你開心嗎？ 'Are you happy?'

To answer such a question, you use the closest equivalent of 'yes' and 'no' in Cantonese, **haih** 係 and **m̀h haih** 唔係. Repeat the verb used in the question to answer in the affirmative and add the negation word **m̀h** 唔 before the verb in the sentence to answer in the negative. For example,

Question: **Néih ngoh ma?** 你餓嗎？ 'Are you hungry?'
Affirmative: **Ngoh** 餓。 *Hungry* = 'Yes, I'm hungry.'
Negative: **M̀h ngoh** 唔餓。 *Not hungry* = 'No, I'm not hungry.'

Question: **Néih hōi sām ma?** 你開心嗎？ 'Are you happy?'
Affirmative: **Hōi sām** 開心。 *Happy* = 'Yes, I'm happy.'
Negative: **M̀h hōi sām** 唔開心。 *Not happy* = 'No, I'm not happy.'

A second way is to use the positive-negative choice form which presents the listener with two opposite alternatives, e.g., **ngoh m̀h ngoh** 餓唔餓 'hungry not hungry', **hōi m̀h hōi sām** 開唔開心 'happy not happy.'

Néih ngoh m̀h ngoh a? 你餓唔餓呀？
You hungry not hungry (Question marker)
= 'Are you hungry or not?'

13

Néih hōi m̀h hōi sām   **a?**   你開唔開心呀？

You happy not happy (Question marker) = 'Are you happy or not?'

To answer a positive-negative choice question, repeat the positive or negative form of the verb:

Néih ngoh m̀h ngoh a?	你餓唔餓呀？	'Are you hungry or not hungry?'
Ngoh.	餓。	'Hungry.'
M̀h ngoh.	唔餓。	'Not hungry.'
Néih hōi m̀h hōi sām a?	你開唔開心呀？	'Are you happy or not happy?'
Hōi sām.	開心。	'Happy.'
M̀h hōi sām.	唔開心	'Not happy.'

A third way is to use an interrogative pronoun, like **bīn wái** 邊位 'who', **māt yéh** 乜嘢 'what', **dím yéung** 點樣 'how', **bīn** + MW (邊 + measure word)/**bīn dī** 邊啲 'which, **bīn douh/bīn syu** 邊度／邊處 'where', **dím gáai** 點解 'why', **géi dím/géi sìh** 幾點／幾時 'when'.

1. **Néih haih bīn wái**   **a?**   你係邊位呀？
   You are which person (question marker) = 'Who are you?'

2. **Néih giu**   **māt yéh méng**   **a?**   你叫乜嘢名呀？
   You called what   name (question marker)
   = 'What's your name?'

3. **Néih dím yéung fāan gūng**   **ga?**   你點樣番工㗎？
   You how   go to work (question marker)
   = 'How do you get to work?'

4. **Néih hái bīn douh fāan gūng**   **a?**   你喺邊度番工呀？
   You at where   work   (question marker)
   = 'Where do you work?'

5. **Néih dím gáai chìh dou**   **a?**   你點解遲到呀？
   You why   late   (question marker) = 'Why are you late?'

6. **Yìh gā géi dím   la?**   而家幾點喇？
   Now   what time (question marker) = 'What's the time now?'

7. **Néih géi sìh dāk hàahn   a?**   你幾時得閒呀？
   You   when   free   (question marker) = 'When are you free?'

In answering a question involving the interrogative pronoun, follow the grammar of the question and note its word order, changing the subject of the sentence where appropriate, e.g., **néih** 你 'you' becomes **ngóh** 我 'I' when you answer a question. For example, the answers to the questions above can be:

1. **Ngóh haih nī douh ge gīng léih.**   我係呢度嘅經理。
   I   am here   of manager. = 'I'm the manager here.'

2. **Ngóh giu A Sām.**   我叫阿森。
   I   call A Sum = 'My name is Ah Sum.'

3. **Ngóh chóh deih tit.** 我坐地鐵。
   I   take MTR. = 'I take the MTR.'

4. **Ngóh hái Tòhng Lòh Wāan fāan gūng.** 我喺銅鑼灣番工。
   I   in Causeway Bay   work = 'I work in Causeway Bay.'

5. **Ngóh dohng sāt jó louh.** 我蕩失咗路。
   I   lost   just way = 'I lost my way.'

6. **Ngóh m̀h   jī   yìh gā géi dím jūng.** 我唔知而家幾點鐘。
   I   don't know now   what time
   = 'I don't know what the time is now.'

7. **Ngóh tīng yaht dāk hàahn.** 我聽日得閒。
   I   tomorrow free = 'I'm free tomorrow.'

1. The Basics

1.1 Personal details

In Chinese societies, the family name comes first and the given name next. Titles come after the name. For example, Mr Wong is **Wòhng sīn sāang** 黃先生 and Ms Wong is either **Wòhng síu jé** 黃小姐 or **Wòhng néuih sih** 黃女士. The title **taai táai** 太太 is given to married women and is placed after the husband's surname.

Madam	**néuih sih** 女士
Mrs	**taai táai** 太太
Miss	**síu jé** 小姐
Sir/Mr	**sīn sāang** 先生
surname	**sing** 姓
first name	**méng** 名
address	**deih jí** 地址
street	**gāai méng** 街名
number (address)	**mùhn pàaih houh máh** 門牌號碼
postal code	**yàuh kēui houh máh** 郵區號碼
town	**sìhng síh** 城市

sex (gender)	**sing biht** 性別
male	**nàahm** 男
female	**néuih** 女
nationality/citizenship	**gwok jihk** 國籍
date of birth	**chēut sāng yaht kèih** 出生日期
place of birth	**chēut sāng deih dím** 出生地點
occupation	**jīk yihp** 職業
marital status	**fān yān johng fong** 婚姻狀況
married	**yíh fān** 已婚
single	**meih fān** 未婚
widow	**gwá fúh** 寡婦
widower	**gwāan fū** 鰥夫
(number of) children	**yih néuih (sou muhk)** 兒女（數目）
passport	**wuh jiu** 護照
identity card	**sān fán jing** 身分證
driving license number	**ga sái jāp jiu houh máh** 駕駛執照號碼
place of issue	**chīm faat deih dím** 簽發地點
date of issue	**chīm faat yaht kèih** 簽發日期
signature	**chīm méng** 簽名

1.2 Today or tomorrow?

What day is it today?	**Gām yaht haih sīng kèih géi a?** 今日係星期幾呀？
Today is Monday.	**Gām yaht haih sīng kèih yāt.** 今日係星期一。

| Today is Tuesday. | **Gām yaht haih sīng kèih yih.** |
| | 今日係星期二。 |

| Today is Wednesday. | **Gām yaht haih sīng kèih sāam.** |
| | 今日係星期三。 |

| Today is Thursday. | **Gām yaht haih sīng kèih sei.** |
| | 今日係星期四。 |

| Today is Friday. | **Gām yaht haih sīng kèih ńgh.** |
| | 今日係星期五。 |

| Today is Saturday. | **Gām yaht haih sīng kèih luhk.** |
| | 今日係星期六。 |

| Today is Sunday. | **Gām yaht haih sīng kèih yaht.** |
| | 今日係星期日。 |

| in January | **(hái) yāt yuht** (喺) 一月 |

| since February | **yih yuht dou yìh gā** 二月到而家 |

| in spring | **(hái) chēun tīn** (喺) 春天 |

| in summer | **(hái) hah tīn** (喺) 夏天 |

| in autumn | **(hái) chāu tīn** (喺) 秋天 |

| in winter | **(hái) dūng tīn** (喺) 冬天 |

| 2017 | **yih lìhng yāt chāt nìhn** 二零一七年 |

| the twentieth century | **yih sahp sai géi** 二十世紀 |

| the twenty-first century | **yih sahp yāt sai géi** 二十一世紀 |

| What's the date today? | **Gām yaht haih géi houh a?** |
| | 今日係幾號呀？ |

| Today is the 24th. | **Gām yaht haih yih sahp sei houh.** |
| | 今日係二十四號。 |

| Wednesday 3 November | **Sahp yāt yuht sāam houh, sīng kèih sāam** |
| | 十一月三號，星期三 |

| in the morning | **(hái) jīu jóu/jīu tàuh jóu** |
| | (喺) 朝早／朝頭早 |

in the afternoon	**(hái) hah jau** （喺）下晝
in the evening	**(hái) yeh máahn** （喺）夜晚
at night	**(hái) yeh máahn(hāk)** （喺）夜晚〔黑〕
this morning	**gām jīu jóu** 今朝早
this afternoon	**gām yaht hah jau** 今日下晝
this evening	**gām máahn** 今晚
tonight	**gām máahn(hāk)** 今晚〔黑〕
last night	**kàhm/chàhm máahn(hāk)** 琴／尋晚〔黑〕
tomorrow night	**tīng máahn(hāk)** 聽晚〔黑〕
this week	**nī go sīng kèih** 呢個星期
last week	**seuhng go sīng kèih** 上個星期
next week	**hah go sīng kèih** 下個星期
this month	**nī go yuht** 呢個月
last month	**seuhng go yuht** 上個月
next month	**hah go yuht** 下個月
this year	**gām nín/nìhn** 今年
last year	**gauh nín/nìhn** 舊年
next year	**mìhng/chēut nín/nìhn** 明／出年
in…days	**…yaht jī hauh** ⋯日之後
in…weeks	**…sīng kèih jī hauh** ⋯星期之後
in…months	**…yuht jī hauh** ⋯月之後
in…years	**…nìhn jī hauh** ⋯年之後
…weeks ago	**…(go) sīng kèih jī chìhn** ⋯（個）星期之前

two weeks ago	**léuhng go sīng kèih jī chìhn** 兩個星期之前
day off	**fong ga** 放假

1.3 What time is it?

What time is it?	**Yìh gā géi dím a?** 而家幾點呀？
It's nine o'clock.	**Yìh gā gáu dím.** 而家九點。
It's 10:05.	**Yìh gā sahp dím lìhng ngh fān.** 而家十點零五分。
It's five past ten.	**Yìh gā sahp dím (daahp) yāt/sahp dím yāt go jih.** 而家十點(踏)一／十點一個字。
It's 11:15.	**Yìh gā sahp yāt dím sahp ngh fān.** 而家十一點十五分。
It's a quarter past eleven.	**Yìh gā sahp yāt dím (daahp) sāam/sahp yāt dím yāt go gwāt.** 而家十一點(踏)三／十一點一個骨。
It's 12:20.	**Yìh gā sahp yih dím (daahp) sei.** 而家十二點(踏)四。
It's twenty past twelve.	**Yìh gā sahp yih dím sei go jih.** 而家十二點四個字。
It's 1:30.	**Yìh gā yāt dím sāam sahp fān.** 而家一點三十分。
It's half past one.	**Yìh gā yāt dím bun.** 而家一點半。
It's 2:35.	**Yìh gā léuhng dím (daahp) chāt.** 而家兩點(踏)七。
It's twenty-five minutes to three.	**Yìh gā léuhng dím chāt go jih.** 而家兩點七個字。
It's 4:50.	**Yìh gā sei dím (daahp) sahp.** 而家四點(踏)十。

It's ten minutes to five.	**Yìh gā chā léuhng go jih ngh dím.** 而家差兩個字五點。
It's midday (twelve noon).	**Yìh gā haih jūng ngh sahp yih dím.** 而家係中午十二點。
It's midnight.	**Yìh gā haih bun yeh sahp yih dím.** 而家係半夜十二點。
half an hour	**bun go jūng tàuh** 半個鐘頭
What's the time now?	**Géi dím la?/Yìh gā géi dím a?** 幾點喇？／而家幾點呀？
What time can I come by?	**Ngóh géi dím hó yíh gwo làih a?** 我幾點可以過嚟呀？
at...	**hái** 喺…
after...	**...jī hauh** …之後
before...	**...jī chìhn** …之前
between 4:00 and 5:00	**sei dím dou ngh dím jī gāan** 四點到五點之間
from...to...	**chùhng...dou** 從…到
in...minutes	**...fān jūng jī hauh** …分鐘之後
in an hour	**yāt go jūng tàuh jī hauh** 一個鐘頭之後
in two hours	**léuhng go jūng tàuh jī hauh** 兩個鐘頭之後
in a quarter of an hour	**yāt go gwāt jī hauh** 一個骨之後
in three quarters of an hour	**sāam go gwāt jī hauh** 三個骨之後
too early	**taai jóu** 太早
too late	**taai ngaan** 太晏
on time	**jéun sìh** 準時

summertime
(daylight saving)   **hah lihng sìh gaan** 夏令時間

wintertime   **dūng gwai sìh gaan** 冬季時間

1.4 One, two, three...

0 **lìhng** 零

1 **yāt** 一

2 **yih** 二

3 **sāam** 三

4 **sei** 四

5 **ńgh** 五

6 **luhk** 六

7 **chāt** 七

8 **baat** 八

9 **gáu** 九

10 **sahp** 十

11 **sahp yāt** 十一

12 **sahp yih** 十二

13 **sahp sāam** 十三

14 **sahp sei** 十四

15 **sahp ńgh** 十五

16 **sahp luhk** 十六

17 **sahp chāt** 十七

18 **sahp baat** 十八

19 **sahp gáu** 十九

20 **yih sahp** 二十

21 **yih sahp yāt** 二十一

22 **yih sahp yih** 二十二

30 **sāam sahp** 三十

31 **sāam sahp yāt** 三十一

32 **sāam sahp yih** 三十二

40 **sei sahp** 四十

50 **ńgh sahp** 五十

60 **luhk sahp** 六十

70 **chāt sahp** 七十

80 **baat sahp** 八十

90 **gáu sahp** 九十

100 **yāt baak** 一百

101 **yāt baak lìhng yāt** 一百零一

110 **yāt baak yāt sahp** 一百一十

200 **léuhng baak/yih baak** 兩百／二百

300 **sāam baak** 三百

400 **sei baak** 四百

500 **ńgh baak** 五百

600 **luhk baak** 六百

700 **chāt baak** 七百

800 **baat baak** 八百

900 **gáu baak** 九百

1,000 **yāt chīn** 一千

1,100 **yāt chīn yāt baak** 一千一百

2,000 **léuhng chīn/yih chīn** 兩千／二千

10,000 **yāt maahn** 一萬

100,000 **sahp maahn** 十萬

1,000,000 **(yāt) baak maahn** （一)百萬

10,000,000 **(yāt) chin maahn** （一)千萬

1st **daih yāt** 第一

2nd **daih yih** 第二

3rd **daih sāam** 第三

once **yāt chi** 一次

twice **léuhng chi** 兩次

double **léuhng púih** 兩倍

triple **sāam púih** 三倍

half **yāt bun** 一半

a quarter **sei fahn jī yāt** 四分之一

a third **sāam fahn jī yāt** 三分之一

some **yāt dī** 一啲

a few **géi go** 幾個

2 + 4 = 6 **yih gā sei dáng yùh luhk** 二加四等如六

4 – 2 = 2 **sei gáam yih dáng yùh yih** 四減二等如二

2 x 4 = 8 **yih sìhng sei dáng yùh baat** 二乘四等如八

4 ÷ 2 = 2 **yih chèuih sei dáng yùh yih** 二除四等如二

even number **sēung sou** 雙數

odd number **dāan sou** 單數

total **yāt guhng** 一共

What is your office telephone number, please?	**Chíng mahn néih gūng sī dihn wá géi dō houh a?** 請問你公司電話幾多號呀？
What is your home telephone number, please?	**Chíng mahn néih ngūk kéi dihn wá géi dō houh a?** 請問你屋企電話幾多號呀？
What is your mobile number, please?	**Chíng mahn néih sáu tàih dihn wá géi dō houh a?** 請問你手提電話幾多號呀？
My mobile number is 9326 4819. And yours?	**Ngóh sáu tàih dihn wá haih gáu sāam yih luhk sei baat yāt gáu, néih nē?** 我手提電話係9326 4819，你呢？
What is the telephone number for emergencies in Hong Kong?	**Hēung Góng gán gāp dihn wá haih géi dō houh a?** 香港緊急電話係幾多號呀？
Hong Kong's emergency telephone number is 999.	**Hēung Góng gán gāp dihn wá haih gáu gáu gáu.** 香港緊急電話係999。
What's the Telephone Directory's number?	**Chàh sēun dihn wá houh máh dá géi dō houh a?** 查詢電話號碼打幾多號呀？
Dial 1081.	**Dá yāt lìhng baat yāt.** 打1081。

1.5 The weather

Is the weather going to be good?	**Tīn hei wúih hóu ma?** 天氣會好嗎？
Yes, it should be fine.	**Tīn hei wúih hóu.** 天氣會好。
Is it going to get cold?	**Tīn hei wúih m̀h wúih dung a?** 天氣會唔會凍呀？
Is it going to get hot?	**Tīn hei wúih m̀h wúih yiht a?** 天氣會唔會熱呀？
Yes, it will get cold. Bring a coat.	**Tīn hei wúih dung. Daai lāu a.** 天氣會凍。 帶褸呀。
What temperature is it going to be?	**Gām yaht hei wān géi dō douh a?** 今日氣溫幾多度呀？

About 10 degrees.	**Daaih yeuk sahp douh.** 大約十度。	
Is it going to rain?	**Wúih m̀h wúih lohk yúh a?** 會唔會落雨呀？	
Yes, bring an umbrella.	**Wúih, gei dāk daai jē.** 會，記得帶遮。	
Is there going to be a storm?	**Wúih m̀h wúih dá fūng a?** 會唔會打風呀？	
Is it going to snow?	**Wúih m̀h wúih lohk syut a?** 會唔會落雪呀？	
Is it going to freeze?	**Wúih m̀h wúih duhng dou git bīng a?** 會唔會凍到結冰呀？	
Yes, don't go out.	**Wúih a, m̀h hóu chēut gāai.** 會呀，唔好出街。	
Is it going to be foggy?	**Wúih m̀h wúih daaih mouh a?** 會唔會大霧呀？	
Yes, drive carefully.	**Wúih a, síu sām jā chē.** 會呀，小心揸車。	
Is there going to be a thunderstorm?	**Wúih m̀h wúih yáuh lèuih yúh a?** 會唔會有雷雨呀？	
The weather is changing.	**Tīn hei bin la.** 天氣變喇。	
What's the weather going to be like today?	**Gām yaht tīn hei wúih dím a?** 今日天氣會點呀？	
Tomorrow the weather is going to be cold.	**Tīng yaht tīn hei wúih dung.** 聽日天氣會凍。	

frost **lohk sēung** 落霜	sweltering/muggy **muhn yiht** 悶熱	fine/clear **chìhng lóhng** 晴朗	very hot **hóu yiht** 好熱
rain **lohk yúh** 落雨	overnight frost **yeh gāan lohk sēung** 夜間落霜	heavy rain **lohk daaih yúh** 落大雨	heatwave **yiht lohng** 熱浪

sunny **chìhng lóhng** 晴朗	downpour **bouh yúh/kīng pùhn daaih yúh** 暴雨／傾盆大雨	hail **lohk bīng bohk** 落冰雹	fog **mouh** 霧
clear skies **làahm tīn** 藍天	cold and damp **yauh dung yàuh chìuh sāp** 又凍又潮濕	moderate **mèih fūng** 微風	foggy **daaih mouh** 大霧
overcast **yām tīn** 陰天	bleak **yauh yām yauh dung** 又陰又凍	strong **kèung fūng** 强風	humid **chìuh sāp** 潮濕
gusts of wind **fāan fūng** 翻風	typhoon **tòih fūng/dá fūng** 颱風／打風	mild **wòh nyúhn** 和暖	cool **lèuhng sóng** 涼爽
wind **fūng** 風	cloudy **maht wàhn/dō wàhn** 密雲／多雲	frost **sēung** 霜	snow **lohk syut** 落雪
windy **daaih fūng** 大風	…degrees (Celsius) **(sip sih) douh** (攝氏)…度	frosty **hòhn láahng** 寒冷	storm **bouh fūng yúh** 暴風雨
ice/icy **bīng dung/bīng láahng** 冰凍／冰冷	…degrees (below zero) **lìhng hah…douh** 零下…度	very strong winds **kwòhng fūng** 狂風	hurricane **geuih fūng** 颶風

1.6 Here, there...

See also 5.1 Asking directions

here, over here	**nī douh**	呢度
there, over there	**gó douh**	嗰度
somewhere	**máuh go deih fōng**	某個地方
everywhere	**dou chyu**	到處
far away	**hóu yúhn**	好遠
nearby	**fuh gahn**	附近
(on the) right	**(hái) yauh bihn/bīn**	(喺)右邊
(on the) left	**(hái) jó bihn/bīn**	(喺)左邊

to the right of	**kaau yauh bihn/bīn** 靠右邊
to the left of	**kaau jó bihn/bīn** 靠左邊
straight ahead	**yāt jihk heung chìhn jáu** 一直向前走
via	**gīng gwo** 經過
in	**(hái)…yahp bihn/bīn** (喺)…入邊
on	**(hái)…seuhng bihn/bīn** (喺)…上邊
under	**(hái)…hah bihn/bīn** (喺)…下邊
against	**ngāai jyuh** 挨住
opposite/facing	**deui mihn** 對面
facing	**deui jyuh** 對住
next to	**hái…pòhng bīn** 喺…旁邊
near	**gahn jyuh** 近住
in front of	**hái…chìhn mihn** 喺…前面
in the center	**hái…jūng gāan** 喺…中間
forward	**heung chìhn** 向前
down	**heung hah** 向下
up	**heung seuhng** 向上
inside	**yahp mihn** 入面
outside	**ngoih mihn** 外面
behind	**hauh mihn** 後面
at the front of…	**hái…chìhn mihn** 喺…前面
at the back of…	**hái…hauh mihn** 喺…後面
to the north of…	**hái…bāk mihn** 喺…北面
to the south of…	**hái…nàahm mihn** 喺…南面
from the west	**hái sāi mihn làih** 喺西面嚟
from the east	**hái dūng mihn làih** 喺東面嚟

1.7 What does that sign say?

See 5.2 Traffic signs

路牌
Louh Páai
Traffic Signs

出租
Chēut Jōu
For Hire

出租
Chēut Jōu
For Rent

預留
Yuh Làuh
Reserved

賣完
Maaih Yùhn
Sold Out

推
Tēui
Push

開
Hōi
Open

入口
Yahp Háu
Entrance

洗手間
Sái Sáu Gāan
Bathrooms

冇人
Móuh Yàhn
Vacant

有人
Yáuh Yàhn
Engaged

出售
Chēut Sauh
For Sale

郵局
Yàuh Gúk
Post Office

警察局
Gíng Chaat Gúk
Police Station

消防局
Sīu Fòhng Gúk
Fire Department

醫院
Yī Yún
Hospital

售票處
Sauh Piu Chyu
Ticket Office

收銀處
Sāu Ngàhn Chyu
Cashier

時間表
Sìh Gaan Bíu
Timetable

交通警察
Gāau Tūng Gíng Chaat
Traffic Police

此路不通
Chí Louh Bāt Tūng
No Access

禁止入內
Gam Jí Yahp Noih
No Entry

候機室／候車室
Hauh Gēi Sāt/Hauh Chē Sāt
Waiting Lounge (for flight and
bus/train)

安全出口／消防通道
**Ngōn Chyùhn Chēut Háu/Sīu Fòhng
Tūng Douh**
Fire Escape

急救室／急症室
Gāp Gaau Sāt/Gāp Jing Sāt
First Aid/Accident and
Emergency/Casualty (Hospital)

旅遊咨詢處
Léuih Yàuh Jī Sēun Chyu
Tourist Information Bureau

酒店／旅館
Jáu Dim/Léuih Gún
Hotel

熱／凍水
Yiht/Dung Séui
Hot/Cold Water

非飲用水
Fēi Yám Yuhng Séui
Water (Not for Drinking)

提防惡狗
Tàih Fòhng Ngok Gáu
Beware of the Dog

(免費)入場
(Míhn Fai) Yahp Chèuhng
Entrance (Free)

請勿吸煙
Chíng Maht Kāp Yīn
No Smoking

The Basics

1

29

行人	緊急煞掣	請勿騷擾／觸摸
Hàhng Yàhn	**Gán Gāp Saat Jai**	**Chíng Maht Sōu Yíu/Jūk Mó**
Pedestrians	Emergency Brake	Please Do Not Disturb/Touch

停用	(緊急)出口	請勿隨地拋棄垃圾
Tìhng Yuhng	**(Gán Gāp) Chēut Háu**	**Chíng Maht Chèuih Deih Pāau Hei Laahp Saap**
Not in Use	(Emergency) Exit	No Littering

停(止)	待維修	油漆未乾
Tìhng (Jí)	**Doih Wàih Sāu**	**Yàuh Chāt Meih Gōn**
Stop	Out Of Order	Wet Paint

危險	高壓電	休假／裝修期內 停止營業
Ngàih Hím	**Gōu Ngaat Dihn**	**Yāu Ga/Jōng Sāu Kèih Noih Tìhng Jí Yìhng Yihp**
Danger	High Voltage	Closed (for Holiday/Refurbishment)

致命	易燃物品	
Ji Mihng	**Yih Yìhn Maht Bán**	
Danger To Life	Fire Hazard	

兌換	客滿／滿座	禁止打獵／釣魚
Deui Wuhn	**Haak Múhn/Múhn Joh**	**Gam Jí Dá Lihp/Diu Yú**
Exchange	Full	No Hunting/Fishing

1.8 Public holidays

In Hong Kong, both the Western and Chinese New Years are celebrated, along with Christmas and Easter.

The six Chinese festivals follow the Lunar calendar, identified as the first month, the second month and so on. During Chinese New Year, people flock to temples to pray for good fortune, try their luck at the racecourse in Happy Valley, visit relatives to give lucky red packets to children and enjoy stunning fireworks over the Victoria Harbour. The Ching Ming Festival and the Chung Yeung Festival are dedicated to the ancestors, and families clean the tombs and pay their respects. Legend has it that nine dragons sprayed water to bathe the baby Buddha at birth, thus believers gather at Buddhist temples on the Buddha's Birthday to bathe the baby Buddha statues and purify their soul.

The Dragon Boat Festival commemorates the death of Qu Yuan who drowned himself in a river in a protest against corrupt rulers. To scare away fish from eating his body, his supporters rowed boats, beat drums and threw glutinous rice dumplings into the river. Families, relatives and friends get together to enjoy seasonal fruits and mooncakes during the Mid-Autumn Festival. Colorful lanterns can be seen everywhere, and the biggest lantern exhibition is held in Victoria Park.

Since 1997, three other public holidays have been added—National Day on October 1, Hong Kong Special Administrative Region Establishment Day on July 1 and Labor Day on May 1. On these occasions, most government offices, public utilities and banks are closed. Major tourist attractions, theme parks, shopping malls, restaurants and public transport and convenience chain stores operate as usual.

New Year's Day (1st January) **Sāi lihk sān nìhn/Yùhn dāan** 西曆新年/元旦

Lunar New Year (1st day of the 1st lunar month, usually in January/February) **Nùhng lihk sān nìhn** 農曆新年

Easter (a Sunday in March/April) **Fuhk wuht jit** 復活節

Ching Ming Festival (4th/5th day of April) **Chīng mìhng jit** 清明節

Labor Day (1st May) **Lòuh duhng jit** 勞動節

The Buddha's Birthday (8th day of 4th lunar month) **Faht daan** 佛誕

Tuen Ng Festival/Dragon Boat Festival (5th day of the 5th lunar month) **Dyūn ńgh jit** 端午節

Hong Kong Special Administrative Region Establishment Day (1st July) **Hēung Góng dahk biht hàhng jing kēui sìhng laahp géi nihm yaht** 香港特別行政區成立紀念日

Mid-Autumn Festival (15th day of the 8th lunar month) **Jūng chāu jit** 中秋節

National Day (1st October) **Gwok hing yaht** 國慶日

Chung Yeung Festival (9th day of the 9th lunar month) **Chùhng yèuhng jit** 重陽節

Christmas Day (25th December) **Sing daan jit** 聖誕節

2. Meet and Greet

It is common in Hong Kong to shake hands on meeting and parting company. The strength of the handshake is determined by the level of acquaintance (that is, a strong handshake for business meetings or when you want to impress the other party) and the importance of the occasion. Generally one should refrain from giving a strong handshake to male or female acquaintances. Hugging is reserved for relatives and kissing on the cheeks is now more common among Cantonese-speaking Chinese communities in different parts of the world, like Sydney, London and Vancouver etc.

2.1   Greetings

Good morning, Mr Williams.	**Jóu sàhn, Wāi Lìhm sīn sāang.** 早晨，威廉先生。
Good morning, Mrs Jones.	**Jóu sàhn, Jūng Sih taai táai.** 早晨，鍾士太太。
Hello, Peter.	**Néih hóu, Béi Dāk.** 你好，彼德。
Hi, Helen.	**Néih hóu, Hói Lùhng.** 你好，海倫。
Good morning, madam.	**Jóu sàhn, taai táai/fū yàhn!** 早晨，太太／夫人。
Good morning, sir!	**Jóu sàhn, sīn sāang!** 早晨，先生！
Good afternoon!	**Ńgh on!** 午安！

Good evening!	**Máahn on!** 晚安！
How are you?	**Néih jeui gahn dím a?** 你最近點呀？
Fine, thank you, and you?	**Géi hóu, yáuh sām, néih nē?** 幾好，有心，你呢？
Very well, and you?	**Géi hóu, néih nē?** 幾好，你呢？
In excellent health.	**Jīng sàhn hóu.** 精神好。
In great shape.	**Sān tái hóu.** 身體好。
So-so	**Gwo dāk heui lā/Màh má déi lā** 過得去啦／麻麻哋啦
Not very well	**M̀h haih gam hóu** 唔係咁好
Not bad	**M̀h cho/Syun haih gám lā** 唔錯／算係咁啦
I'm going to leave.	**Ngóh jáu sīn.** 我走先。
I have to go, someone's waiting for me.	**Ngóh yiu jáu la, yáuh yàhn dáng gán ngóh.** 我要走喇，有人等緊我。
Good-bye!	**Bāai baai!** 拜拜！
See you later!	**Joi gin!** 再見！
See you soon!	**Daih yaht gin!** 第日見！
See you in a little while!	**Yāt jahn gāan gin!** 一陣間見！
Sweet dreams!	**Faat go hóu muhng!** 發個好夢！
Good night!	**Jóu táu!** 早抖！
All the best/Good luck!	**Jūk néih hóu wahn!** 祝你好運！
Have fun!	**Wáan dāk hōi sām dī!** 玩得開心啲！
Have a nice vacation!	**Ga kèih yuh faai!** 假期愉快！
Bon voyage!	**Yāt louh seuhn fūng!** 一路順風！
Have a good trip.	**Léuih tòuh yuh faai!** 旅途愉快！

Thank you, the same to you.	**Dō jeh néih, daaih ga gám wah.** 多謝你，大家咁話。
Give my regards to… (formal).	**Chíng doih ngóh mahn hauh…** 請代我問候…
Say hello to… (informal).	**Bōng ngóh mahn hauh…** 幫我問候…

2.2 Asking a question

Who?	**Bīn go?** 邊個？
Who? (polite)	**Bīn wái?** 邊位？
What?	**Māt yéh?** 乜嘢？
What is there to see?	**Yáuh māt yéh tái a?** 有乜嘢睇呀？
What category of hotel is it?	**Nī gāan jáu dim haih géi sīng kāp ga?** 呢間酒店係幾星級㗎？
Where?	**Bīn douh/Bīn chyu?** 邊度？／邊處？
Where's the bathroom?	**Sái sáu gāan hái bīn douh a?** 洗手間喺邊度呀？
Where are you going?	**Néih heui bīn douh/bīn chyu a?** 你去邊度／邊處呀？
Where are you from?	**Néih hái bīn douh làih ga?** 你喺邊度嚟㗎？
What?	**Māt yéh?** 乜嘢？
How?	**Dím yéung?** 點樣？
What's your family name?	**Gwai sing a?** 貴姓呀？
What's your given name?	**Néih giu māt yé méng a?** 你叫乜嘢名呀？
How far is it?	**Yáuh géi yúhn a?** 有幾遠呀？
How long does it take?	**Yiu géi noih a?/Yiu géi chèuhng sìh gaan a?** 要幾耐呀？／要幾長時間呀？

How long is the trip?	**Nī chi léuih hàhng heui géi noih a?/Heui géi chèuhng sìh gaan a?** 呢次旅行去幾耐呀？／去幾長時間呀？
How much?	**Géi dō chín a?** 幾多錢呀？
How much is this?	**Nī go géi dō chín a?** 呢個幾多錢呀？
What time is it?	**Yìh gā géi dím a?** 而家幾點呀？
Which one?	**Bīn go?** 邊個？
Which ones?	**Bīn dī?** 邊啲？
Which glass is mine?	**Bīn go būi haih ngóh ga?** 邊個杯係我㗎？
When?	**Géi sìh a?** 幾時呀？
When are you leaving?	**Néih géi sìh/géi dím chēut faat a?** 你幾時／幾點出發呀？
Why?	**Dím gáai a?** 點解呀？
Could you...?	**Hó m̀h hó yíh...a?/M̀h gōi...** 可唔可以…呀？／唔該…
Could you help me please?	**Hó m̀h hó yíh bōng ngóh...a?** 可唔可以幫我…呀？
Could you give me a hand please?	**M̀h gōi bōng ngóh...** 唔該幫我…
Could you point that out to me please?	**M̀h gōi jí béi ngóh tái háh.** 唔該指俾我睇吓。
Could you show me please?	**M̀h gōi ló béi ngóh tái háh.** 唔該攞俾我睇吓。
Could you come with me, please?	**M̀h gōi gān ngóh làih.** 唔該跟我嚟。
Could you reserve some tickets for me, please?	**M̀h gōi bōng ngóh yuh dehng géi jēung fēi.** 唔該幫我預訂幾張飛。

Could you recommend another hotel?	**M̀h gōi néih tēui jin daih yih gāan jáu dim béi ngóh.** 唔該你推薦第二間酒店俾我。
Do you know…?	**Néih jī m̀h jī…a?** 你知唔知⋯呀？
Do you know whether…?	**Haih m̀h haih…a?** 係唔係⋯呀？
Do you have…?	**Néih (deih) yáuh móuh…a?** 你(哋)有冇⋯呀？
Do you have a vegetarian dish, please?	**Nī douh yáuh móuh jāai sihk a?** 呢度有冇齋食呀？
I would like (one of)…	**Ngóh séung yiu (yāt go)…** 我想要(一個)⋯
I'd like a kilo of apples, please.	**M̀h gōi béi yāt gōng gān pìhng gwó ngóh.** 唔該俾一公斤蘋果我。
Can/May I?	**Ngóh hó yíh…ma?** 我可以⋯嗎？
Can/May I take this away?	**Ngóh hó yíh līng jáu ma?** 我可以拎走嗎？
Can I smoke here?	**Ngóh hó yíh hái nī douh sihk yīn ma?** 我可以喺呢度食煙嗎？
Could I ask you something?	**Ngóh hó yíh mahn néih dī yéh ma?** 我可以問你啲嘢嗎？

2.3 How to Reply

My family name is…	**Ngóh sing…** 我姓⋯
My given name is…	**Ngóh giu…** 我叫⋯
Yes, of course.	**Haih, dōng yìhn lā.** 係，當然啦。
No, I'm sorry.	**M̀h haih, deui m̀h jyuh!** 唔係，對唔住！
What can I do for you?	**Yáuh dī māt yéh hó yíh bōng dóu néih nē?** 有啲乜嘢可以幫到你呢？

Just a moment, please.	**M̀h gōi dáng yāt jahn.** 唔該等一陣。
No, I don't have time now.	**Deui m̀h jyuh, ngóh yìh gā m̀h dāk hàahn.** 對唔住，我而家唔得閒。
No, that's impossible.	**Deui m̀h jyuh, ngóh jouh m̀h dóu.** 對唔住，我做唔到。
I agree.	**Ngóh tùhng yi.** 我同意。
I don't agree.	**Ngóh m̀h tùhng yi.** 我唔同意。
I hope so too.	**Ngóh dōu hēi mohng haih gám.** 我都希望係咁。
No, not at all.	**M̀h haih, m̀h haih gám yéung.** 唔係，唔係咁樣。
Absolutely not.	**Jyuht deui m̀h haih.** 絕對唔係。
No, no one.	**Móuh, móuh yàhn.** 冇，冇人。
No, nothing.	**Móuh, māt yéh dōu móuh.** 冇，乜嘢都冇。
That's right.	**Móuh cho.** 冇錯。
Something's wrong.	**Yáuh dī m̀h tóh/mahn tàih.** 有啲唔妥／問題。
OK/it's fine.	**Dāk laak, móuh mahn tàih.** 得嘞，冇問題。
OK, all right.	**Dāk laak, gáau dihm.** 得嘞，搞掂。
Perhaps/maybe	**Waahk jé haih/yáuh hó nàhng** 或者係／有可能
I don't know.	**Ngóh m̀h jī(dou).** 我唔知(道)。

2.4 Thank you

| You're welcome. | **M̀h sái haak hei.** 唔駛客氣。 |
| Thank you very much. | **M̀h gōi saai.** 唔該晒。 |

Many thanks.	**Dō jeh saai.** 多謝晒。
Very kind of you.	**Néih taai haak hei la.** 你太客氣喇。
My pleasure.	**Yīng gōi gé.** 應該嘅。
I enjoyed it very much. (food)	**Hóu hóu sihk, ngóh sihk jó hóu dō.** 好好食，我食咗好多。
I enjoyed it very much.	**Wáan dāk hóu hōi sām.** 玩得好開心。
Thank you for...	**Dō jeh néih béi ngóh ge...** 多謝你俾我嘅…
You shouldn't have/That was very kind of you.	**Néih jān haih taai haak hei laak.** 你真係太客氣嘞。
Don't mention it.	**Bāt/m̀h sìhng ging yi.** 不／唔成敬意。
That's all right.	**Síu síu yi si jē.** 少少意思啫。

2.5 I'm sorry

Sorry	**Deui m̀h jyuh** 對唔住
Sorry, I didn't know that.	**Deui m̀h jyuh, ngóh m̀h jī dou...** 對唔住，我唔知道…
Excuse me (Can I ask...?)	**Chíng mahn** 請問
Pardon me	**M̀h hóu yi si** 唔好意思
I apologize sincerely.	**Ngóh jān sìhng douh hip.** 我真誠道歉。
I do apologize.	**Jān haih deui m̀h jyuh laak.** 真係對唔住嘞。
I didn't mean it. It was an accident.	**Ngóh m̀h haih gu yi ga. Nī go haih yi ngoih.** 我唔係故意㗎。呢個係意外。
That's all right. Don't worry about it.	**M̀h gán yiu. Móuh só waih.** 唔緊要。冇所謂。
Never mind. Forget it.	**Móuh sih. Syun la.** 冇事。算啦。

| It could happen to anyone. | **Nī gihn sih hó nàhng faat sāng hái yahm hòh yàhn sān seuhng.** 呢件事可能發生喺任何人身上。 |

2.6 What do you think?

Which do you like best?	**Néih jeui jūng yi bīn go a?** 你最鍾意邊個呀？
What do you think?	**Néih gok dāk dím a?** 你覺得點呀？
Don't you like dancing?	**Néih m̀h jūng yi tiu móuh mē?** 你唔鍾意跳舞咩？
I don't mind.	**Ngóh m̀h gaai yi.** 我唔介意。
Well done!	**Jouh dāk hóu hóu!** 做得好好！
Not bad!	**M̀h cho ā!** 唔錯吖！
Great!/Marvelous!	**Hóu jeng a!** 好正呀！
Wonderful!	**Fēi sèuhng hóu!** 非常好！
How lovely!	**Hóu leng a!** 好靚呀！
I am pleased for you.	**Ngóh dahng néih hōi sām.** 我戥你開心。
I'm delighted to...	**Ngóh hóu gōu hing...** 我好高興⋯
It's really nice here!	**Nī douh jāu wàih dō hóu leng!** 呢度周圍都好靚！
How nice!	**Jān hóu!** 真好！
I'm very happy with...	**Ngóh deui...hóu múhn yi.** 我對⋯好滿意。
I'm (not) very happy with...	**Ngóh deui...m̀h múhn yi.** 我對⋯唔滿意。
I'm glad that...	**Ngóh hóu hōi sām...** 我好開心⋯

I'm having a great time.	**Ngóh wáan dāk hóu hōi sām.** 我玩得好開心。
I can't wait till tomorrow.	**Ngóh jān haih séung tīng yaht faai dī làih.** 我真係想聽日快啲嚟。
I'm looking forward to tomorrow.	**Ngóh kèih mohng tīng yaht ge lòih làhm.** 我期望聽日嘅來臨。
I hope it works out.	**Ngóh hēi mohng yāt chai jeun hàhng seuhn leih.** 我希望一切進行順利。
How awful!	**Taai chā gihng la!** 太差勁喇！
It's horrible.	**Taai húng bou la!** 太恐怖喇！
That's ridiculous!	**Taai hó siu la!** 太可笑喇！
That's terrible!	**Taai hó pa la!** 太可怕喇！
What a pity/shame!	**Jān haih hó sīk!** 真係可惜！
How disgusting!	**Jān haih lihng yàhn fáan waih!** 真係令人反胃！
What nonsense!	**Jān haih fai wá!** 真係廢話！
How silly!	**Jān haih wùh naauh!** 真係胡鬧！
I don't like it.	**Ngóh m̀h jūng yi gó go.** 我唔鐘意嗰個。
I don't like them.	**Ngóh m̀h jūng yi gó dī.** 我唔鐘意個啲。
I'm bored to death.	**Muhn dou fēi héi.** 悶到飛起！
I'm fed up.	**Fàahn séi yàhn la.** 煩死人喇！
This is no good.	**Gám yéung m̀h hóu.** 咁樣唔好！
This is not what I expected.	**Ngóh móuh nám dou wúih gám yéung.** 我冇諗到會咁樣！

3. Small Talk

3.1 Introductions

May I introduce myself?	**Dáng ngóh gaai siuh jih géi.** 等我介紹自己。
My name's…	**Ngóh giu…** 我叫…
I'm…	**Ngóh haih…** 我係…
What's your name? (formal)	**Chíng mahn gwai sing a?** 請問貴姓呀？
What's your name? (informal)	**Néih giu māt yéh méng a?** 你叫乜嘢名呀？
May I introduce…?	**Ngóh làih gaai siuh, nī wái haih…, nī wái haih…** 我嚟介紹，呢位係…，呢位係…
This is my wife.	**Nī go haih ngoh taai táai.** 呢個係我太太。
This is my husband.	**Nī go haih ngóh sīn sāang.** 呢個係我先生。

This is my daughter.	**Nī go haih ngóh go néui.** 呢個係我個女。
This is my son.	**Nī go haih ngóh go jái.** 呢個係我個仔。
This is my mother.	**Nī go haih ngóh màh mā.** 呢個係我媽媽。
This is my father.	**Nī go haih ngóh bàh bā.** 呢個係我爸爸。
This is my fiancée.	**Nī go haih ngóh meih fān chāi.** 呢個係我未婚妻。
This is my fiancé.	**Nī go haih ngóh meih fān fū.** 呢個係我未婚夫。
This is my girlfriend.	**Nī go haih ngóh néuih pàhng yáuh.** 呢個係我女朋友。
This is my boyfriend.	**Nī go haih ngóh nàahm pàhng yáuh.** 呢個係我男朋友。
This is my friend.	**Nī go haih ngóh pàhng yáuh.** 呢個係我朋友。
How do you do?	**Néih jeui gahn dím a?** 你最近點呀？
Hi, pleased to meet you.	**Néih hóu!** 你好！
Pleased to meet you (formal).	**Hóu gōu hing yihng sīk néih.** 好高興認識你。
Where are you from?	**Néih hái bīn douh làih ga?** 你喺邊度嚟㗎？
I'm American.	**Ngóh haih Méih Gwok yàhn.** 我係美國人。
I'm Australian.	**Ngóh haih Ou Daaih Leih A yàhn.** 我係澳大利亞人。
I'm British.	**Ngóh haih Yīng Gwok yàhn.** 我係英國人。
I'm Canadian.	**Ngóh haih Gā Nàh Daaih yàhn.** 我係加拿大人。
I'm Singaporean.	**Ngóh haih Sān Ga Bō yàhn.** 我係新加坡人。

What city do you live in?	**Néih jyuh hái bīn go sìhng síh a?** 你住喺邊個城市呀？
In…	**Hái…** 喺
Near…	**Kaau gahn…** 靠近⋯
Have you been here long?	**Néih làih jó nī douh géi noih a?** 你嚟咗呢度幾耐呀？
A few days	**Géi yaht** 幾日
How long are you staying here?	**Néih dá syun hái nī douh jyuh géi noih a?** 你打算喺呢度住幾耐呀？
We'll be leaving tomorrow.	**Ngóh deih tīng yaht jáu.** 我哋聽日走。
We'll be leaving in two weeks.	**Ngóh deih léuhng go sīng kèih hauh jáu.** 我哋兩個星期後走。
Where are you staying?	**Néih jyuh hái bīn douh a?** 你住喺邊度呀？
I'm staying in a hotel.	**Ngóh jyuh hái jáu dim.** 我住喺酒店。
I'm staying with friends.	**Ngóh jyuh hái pàhng yáuh ngūk kéi.** 我住喺朋友屋企。
I'm staying with relatives.	**Ngóh jyuh hái chān chīk ngūk kéi.** 我住喺親戚屋企。
Are you here on your own?	**Néih jih géi yāt go yàhn làih àh?** 你自己一個人嚟呀？
Are you here with your family?	**Néih tùhng gā yàhn làih àh?** 你同家人嚟呀？
I'm on my own.	**Ngóh jih géi yāt go yàhn làih.** 我自己一個人嚟。
I'm with my wife.	**Ngóh tùhng ngóh taai táai yāt chàih làih.** 我同我太太一齊嚟。
I'm with my husband.	**Ngóh tùhng ngóh sīn sāang yāt chàih làih.** 我同我先生一齊嚟。
I'm with my family.	**Ngóh tùhng gā yàhn làih.** 我同家人嚟。
I'm with my relatives.	**Ngóh tùhng chān chīk làih.** 我同親戚嚟。

I'm with my friend.	**Ngóh tùhng yāt go pàng yáuh làih.** 我同一個朋友嚟。
I'm with my friends.	**Ngóh tùhng géi go pàng yáuh làih.** 我同幾個朋友嚟。
Are you married?	**Néih git jó fān meih a?** 你結咗婚未呀？
Do you have a steady girlfriend?	**Néih yáuh néuih pàhng yáuh meih a?** 你有女朋友未呀？
Do you have a steady boyfriend?	**Néih yáuh nàahm pàhng yáuh meih a?** 你有男朋友未呀？
I'm married.	**Ngóh git jó fān.** 我結咗婚。
I'm single.	**Ngóh haih dāan sān ge.** 我係單身嘅。
I'm not married.	**Ngóh juhng meih git fān.** 我仲未結婚。
I'm separated.	**Ngóh fān jó gēui.** 我分咗居。
I'm divorced.	**Ngóh lèih jó fān.** 我離咗婚。
I'm a widow.	**Ngóh jeuhng fū gwo jó sāng.** 我丈夫過咗身。
I'm a widower.	**Ngóh taai táai gwo jó sāng.** 我太太過咗身。
I live alone.	**Ngóh jih géi yāt go yàhn jyuh.** 我自己一個人住。
Do you have any children?	**Néih yáuh móuh sai mān jái a?** 你有冇細蚊仔呀？
Do you have any grandchildren?	**Néih yáuh móuh syūn a?** 你有冇孫呀？
How old are you?	**Néih géi daaih nìhn géi la?** 你幾大年紀喇？
How old is she/he?	**Kéuih géi daaih nìhn géi la?** 佢幾大年紀喇？
I'm…(years old).	**Ngóh gām nìhn…seui.** 我今年…歲。
She/he is…(years old).	**Kéuih gām nìhn…seui.** 佢今年…歲。

What do you do for a living?	**Néih jouh māt yéh gūng jok ga?** 你做乜嘢工作㗎？
I work in an office.	**Ngóh hái sé jih làuh jouh sih ge.** 我喺寫字樓做事嘅。
I'm a student.	**Ngóh haih hohk sāang.** 我係學生。
I'm unemployed.	**Ngóh sāt jó yihp.** 我失咗業。
I'm retired.	**Ngóh teui jó yāu.** 我退咗休。
I'm on a disability pension.	**Ngóh yìh gā líhng sēung chàahn fú sēut gām.** 我而家領傷殘撫恤金。
I'm a housewife.	**Ngóh haih gā tìhng jyú fúh.** 我係家庭主婦。
Do you like your job?	**Néih jūng yi néih ge gūng jok ma?** 你鍾意你嘅工作嗎？
Most of the time.	**Daaih bouh fahn sìh gaan dòu jūng yi.** 大部份時間都鍾意。
Mostly I do, but I prefer vacations.	**Sēui yìhn ngóh m̀h gaai yi jouh yéh, bāt gwo dōu haih fong ga hóu.** 雖然我唔介意做嘢，不過都係放假好。

3.2 I beg your pardon?

I don't speak any...	**Ngóh m̀h sīk góng...** 我唔識講…
I speak a little...	**Ngóh sīk góng síu síu...** 我識講少少…
Do you speak English?	**Néih sīk m̀h sīk góng Yīng Mán a?** 你識唔識講英文呀？
Is there anyone who speaks...?	**Nī douh yáuh móuh yàhn sīk góng...a?** 呢度有冇人識講…呀？
I beg your pardon/What?	**Mē wá?** 咩話？
I don't understand.	**Ngóh tēng m̀h mìhng.** 我聽唔明。
Do you understand me?	**Néih mìhng m̀h mìhng ngóh góng māt yéh a?** 你明唔明我講乜嘢呀？

3

Could you repeat that, please?	**M̀h gōi (néih) joi góng yāt chi.** 唔該(你)再講一次。
Could you speak more slowly, please?	**M̀h gōi (néih) góng maahn dī.** 唔該(你)講慢啲。
What does this/that mean?	**Dím gáai a?** 點解呀？
It's more or less the same as…	**Tùhng…chā m̀h dō yi sī.** 同…差唔多意思。
Could you write that down for me, please?	**M̀h gōi bōng ngóh sé dāi.** 唔該幫我寫低。
Could you spell that for me, please?	**M̀h gōi yuhng jih móuh ping chēut làih.** 唔該用字母拼出嚟。
Could you point to the phrase in this book, please?	**M̀h gōi hái nī bún syū (nī) douh jí béi ngóh tái.** 唔該喺呢本書(呢)度指俾我睇。
Just a minute, I'll look it up.	**M̀h gōi dáng yāt jahn, ngóh chàh yāt háh.** 唔該等一陣，我查一吓。
I can't find the word/ the sentence.	**Ngóh wán m̀h dóu nī go chìh/nī geui wah.** 我搵唔到呢個詞／呢句話。
How do you say that in…?	**Yuhng…dím gong a?** 用…點講呀？
How do you pronounce that word?	**Nī go jih dím duhk a?** 呢個字點讀呀？

3.3 Starting/ending a conversation

Could I ask you something?	**Ngóh hó yíh mahn néih dī yéh ma?** 我可以問你啲嘢嗎？
Excuse/Pardon me	**Chíng mahn…** 請問…
Could you help me please?	**Néih hó m̀h hó yíh bōng ngóh a?** 你可唔可以幫我呀？
Yes, what's the problem?	**Dāk, māt yéh sih a?** 得，乜嘢事呀？
What can I do for you?	**Yáuh māt yéh (ngóh) hó yíh bōng dóu néih ga?** 有乜嘢(我)可以幫到你㗎？

Sorry, I don't have time now.	**M̀h hóu yi si, ngóh yìh gā hóu mòhng.** 唔好意思，我而家好忙。
Do you have a light?	**M̀h gōi je go fó?** 唔該借個火。
May I join you?	**Ngóh hó yíh gā yahp (néih deih) ma?** 我可以加入(你哋)嗎？
Can I take a picture?	**Ngóh hó yíh yíng jēung séung ma?** 我可以影張相嗎？
Could you take a picture of me/us?	**Hó yíh bōng ngóh/ngóh deih yíng jēung séung ma?** 可以幫我／我哋影張相嗎？
Leave me alone.	**M̀h hóu fàahn ngóh.** 唔好煩我。
Get lost.	**Hàahng hōi/Jáu hōi.** 行開／走開。
Go away or I'll scream.	**Néih joi m̀h jáu, ngóh jauh ngaai ga la.** 你再唔走，我就嗌㗎喇。

3.4 A chat about the weather

See also 1.5 The weather

It's so hot today!	**Gām yaht hóu yiht!** 今日好熱！
It's so cold today!	**Gām yaht hóu dung!** 今日好凍！
Isn't it a lovely day?	**Gām yaht jān haih yèuhng gwōng póu jiu!** 今日真係陽光普照！
It's so windy!	**Hóu daaih fūng a!** 好大風呀！
What a storm!	**Fūng taai daaih la!** 風太大喇！
All that rain!	**Lohk gam daaih yúh!** 落咁大雨！
All that snow!	**Lohk gam daaih syut!** 落咁大雪！
It's so foggy!	**Hóu daaih mouh a!** 好大霧呀！
Has the weather been like this for long?	**Gám ge tīn hei haih m̀h haih yíh gīng hóu noih la?** 咁嘅天氣係唔係已經好耐喇？
Is it always this hot here?	**Nī douh ge tīn hei sèhng yaht dōu gam yiht gàh?** 呢度嘅天氣成日都咁熱㗎？

Is it always this cold here?	**Nī douh ge tīn hei sèhng yaht dōu gam dung gàh?** 呢度嘅天氣成日都咁凍㗎?
Is it always this dry here?	**Nī douh ge tīn hei sèhng yaht dōu gam gōn cho gàh?** 呢度嘅天氣成日都咁乾燥㗎?
Is it always this humid here?	**Nī douh ge tīn hei sèhng yaht dōu gam chìuh sāp gàh?** 呢度嘅天氣成日都咁潮濕㗎?

3.5 Hobbies

to sing (karaoke)	**cheung gō (kā lāai OK)** 唱歌 (卡啦OK)
to play computer games	**dá gēi** 打機
to play golf	**dá gōu yíh fū kàuh** 打高爾夫球
to play bridge	**dá kìuh páai** 打橋牌
to play mahjong	**dá màh jéuk** 打麻雀
to play ball games	**dá bō** 打波
to go shopping	**hàahng gāai** 行街
to go hiking	**hàahng sāan** 行山
to travel	**heui léuih hàhng** 去旅行
to read newspapers	**tái bou jí** 睇報紙
to read books/a novel	**tái syū/síu syut** 睇書/小說
to read online articles	**tái móhng seuhng màhn jēung** 睇網上文章
to read comics	**tái lihn wàahn tòuh** 睇連環圖
to read manga	**tái maahn wá** 睇漫畫
to watch television	**tái dihn sih** 睇電視
to do rock-climbing	**pāan sehk** 攀石
to swim	**yàuh séui** 游水
to go for a boat trip/cruise	**yàuh syùhn hó** 遊船河

to go diving	**heui chìhm séui** 去潛水
to fish	**heui diu yú** 去釣魚
Do you have any hobbies?	**Néih yáuh māt yéh si hou a?** 你有乜嘢嗜好呀？
I enjoy listening to music.	**Ngóh jūng yi tēng yām ngohk.** 我鍾意聽音樂。
I enjoy playing the guitar.	**Ngóh jūng yi tàahn git tā.** 我鍾意彈結他。
I enjoy playing the piano.	**Ngóh jūng yi tàahn gong kàhm.** 我鍾意彈鋼琴。
I enjoy playing the ukelele.	**Ngóh jūng yi tàahn hah wāi yìh síu git tā.** 我鍾意彈夏威夷小結他。
What do you enjoy doing in your spare time?	**Néih dāk hàahn jūng yi jouh dī māt yéh a?** 你得閒鍾意做啲乜嘢呀？
I like knitting, reading and photography.	**Ngóh jūng yi jīk lāang sāam, tái syū tùhng yíng séung.** 我鍾意織冷衫，睇書同影相。
I like knitting and reading too but I don't like photography.	**Ngóh dōu jūng yi jīk lāang sāam tùhng tái syū, bāt gwo ngóh m̀h jūng yi yíng séung.** 我都鍾意織冷衫同睇書，不過我唔鍾意影相。
I like the cinema.	**Ngóh jūng yi tái hei/dihn yíng.** 我鍾意睇戲／電影。
I like playing sports.	**Ngóh jūng yi wahn duhng.** 我鍾意運動。

3.6 Invitations

What do you want to do tonight?	**Gām máahn néih séung jouh māt yéh a?** 今晚你想做乜嘢呀？
Do you have any plans for today?	**Gām yaht néih yáuh māt yéh wuht duhng a?** 今日你有乜嘢活動呀？

Let's go out, okay?	**Ngóh deih chēut gāai hàhng háh, hóu ma?** 我哋出街行吓，好嗎？
Would you like to go out?	**Yáuh móuh hing cheui chēut gāai hàhng háh a?** 有冇興趣出街行吓呀？
Let's go dancing, okay?	**Ngóh deih heui tiu móuh, hóu ma?** 我哋去跳舞，好嗎？
Would you like to go dancing?	**Yáuh móuh hing cheui heui tiu móuh a?** 有冇興趣去跳舞呀？
Let's go to lunch, okay?	**Ngóh deih chēut heui sihk ngaan, hóu ma?** 我哋出去食晏，好嗎？
Would you like to have dinner outside?	**Yáuh móuh hing cheui chēut gāai sihk máahn faahn a?** 有冇興趣出街食晚飯呀？
Let's go to the beach, okay?	**Ngóh deih heui hói tāan wáan, hóu ma?** 我哋去海灘玩，好嗎？
Would you like to go to the beach with me?	**Yáuh móuh hing cheui tùhng ngóh heui hói tāan wáan a?** 有冇興趣同我去海灘玩呀？
We are meeting our friends. Do you want to join us?	**Ngóh deih heui taam pàhng yáuh, néih séung m̀h séung yāt chàih heui a?** 我哋去探朋友，你想唔想一齊去呀？
	Yáuh móuh hing cheui tùhng ngóh deih heui taam pàhng yáuh a? 有冇興趣同我哋去探朋友呀？
Shall we sit at the bar?	**Heui jáu bā chóh háh, hóu m̀h hóu a?** 去酒吧坐吓，好唔好呀？
Would you like something to drink?	**Yám dī māt yéh a?** 飲啲乜嘢呀？
Shall we go for a walk?	**Chēut heui hàhng háh, hóu m̀h hóu a?** 出去行吓，好唔好呀？
Shall we go for a drive?	**Heui yàuh chē hó, hóu m̀h hóu a?** 去遊車河，好唔好呀？
Yes, all right.	**Hóu a!** 好呀！

Good idea!	**Hóu jyú yi!** 好主意！
No thank you.	**M̀h hóu la, dō jeh laak.** 唔好喇，多謝嘞！
Maybe later.	**Chìh dī sīn lā.** 遲啲先啦。
I don't feel like it.	**Ngóh móuh sām chìhng.** 我冇心情。
I don't have time.	**Ngóh m̀h dāk hàahn.** 我唔得閒。
I already have a date.	**Ngóh yí gīng yeuk jó yàhn.** 我已經約咗人。
I'm not very good at dancing.	**Ngóh m̀h haih hóu sīk tiu móuh.** 我唔係好識跳舞。
I'm not very good at volleyball.	**Ngóh m̀h haih hóu sīk dá pàaih kàuh.** 我唔係好識打排球。
I'm not very good at swimming.	**Ngóh m̀h haih hóu sīk yàuh séui.** 我唔係好識游水。

3.7 Giving a compliment

You look great!	**Néih tái héi làih jān sàhn hei!** 你睇起嚟真神氣！
Your car looks great!	**Néih ga chē jān haih jeng!** 你架車真係正！
Your ski outfit looks great!	**Néih gihn waaht syut jōng jān haih jeng!** 你件滑雪裝真係正！
You are a nice person!	**Néih deui yàhn jān hóu!/Néih jān haih hóu yàhn!** 你對人真好！／你真係好人！
You're a good dancer.	**Néih tiu móuh tiu dāk hóu hóu.** 你跳舞跳得好好。
You're a very good cook.	**Néih jyú sung jyú dāk hóu hóu meih.** 你煮餸煮得好好味。
You're a good soccer player.	**Néih tek bō tek dāk jān haih gihng.** 你踢波踢得真係勁。

3.8 Intimate comments/questions

I like being with you.
Ngóh jūng yi tùhng néih hái yāt chàih.
我鍾意同你喺一齊。

I've missed you so much.
Ngóh hóu gwa jyuh néih a.
我好掛住你呀。

I dreamt about you.
Ngóh faat muhng dōu nám jyuh néih.
我發夢都諗住你。

I think about you all day.
Ngóh yāt yaht dou hāk dōu nám jyuh néih.
我一日到黑都諗住你。

I've been thinking about you all day.
Ngóh sèhng yaht dōu nám jyuh néih.
我成日都諗住你。

You have such a sweet smile.
Néih siu dāk jān haih tìhm.
你笑得真係甜。

You have such beautiful eyes.
Néih deui ngáahn jān haih màih yàhn.
你對眼真係迷人。

I'm fond of you.
Ngóh jūng yi néih. 我鍾意你。

I'm in love with you.
Ngóh ngoi séuhng néih. 我愛上你。

I love you too.
Ngóh dōu ngoi néih. 我都愛你。

I don't feel as strongly about you.
Ngóh deui néih móuh dahk biht ge gám chìhng. 我對你冇特別嘅感情。

I already have a girlfriend.
Ngóh yíh gīng yáuh néuih pàhng yáuh.
我已經有女朋友。

I already have a boyfriend.
Ngóh yíh gīng yáuh nàahm pàhng yáuh.
我已經有男朋友。

I'm not ready for that.
Ngóh deui néih ge gám chìhng juhng meih dou nī yāt bouh.
我對你嘅感情仲未到呢一步。

I don't want to rush into it.
Ngóh m̀h séung gam faai jauh gám yéung.
我唔想咁快就咁樣。

Take your hands off me.   **Ló hōi néih jek sáu!** 攞開你隻手!

Okay, no problem.   **Dāk, móuh mahn tàih.** 得,冇問題。

Will you spend the night with me?   **Néih háng m̀h háng pùih ngóh fan yāt máahn?** 你肯唔肯陪我瞓一晚?

I'd like to go to bed with you.   **Ngóh séung tùhng néih fan yāt máahn.** 我想同你瞓一晚。

Only if we use a condom.   **Bāt gwo yāt dihng yiu yuhng beih yahn tou.** 不過一定要用避孕套。

We have to be careful about AIDS.   **Ngóh deih yiu síu sām ngoi jī behng.** 我哋要小心愛滋病。

That's what they all say.   **Dī yàhn dōu haih gám wah.** 啲人都係咁話。

We shouldn't take any risks.   **Ngóh deih m̀h yīng gōi mouh nī go hím.** 我哋唔應該冒呢個險。

Do you have a condom?   **Néih yáuh móuh beih yahn tou a?** 你有冇避孕套呀?

No? Then the answer is no.   **Móuh à? Móuh jauh m̀h hó yíh.** 冇呀?冇就唔可以。

3.9 Congratulations and condolences

Happy birthday!   **Sāang yaht faai lohk!** 生日快樂!

Many happy returns!   **Yāt chai seuhn leih!** 一切順利!

Please accept my condolences.   **Chíng jip sauh ngóh ge wai mahn.** 請接受我嘅慰問。

My deepest sympathy.   **Chíng jip sauh ngóh jeui sām chit ge tùhng chìhng.** 請接受我最深切嘅同情。

3.10 Arrangements

When will I see you again?	**Ngóh géi sìh joi gin dóu néih a?** 我幾時再見到你呀？
Are you free over the weekend?	**Nī go jāu muht néih dāk m̀h dāk hàahn a?** 呢個週末你得唔得閒呀？
What's the plan, then?	**Néih yáuh māt yé gai waahk a?** 你有乜嘢計劃呀？
Where shall we meet?	**Ngóh deih hái bīn douh gin mihn a?** 我哋喺邊度見面呀？
Will you pick me/us up?	**Néih haih m̀h haih làih jip ngóh/ngóh deih a?** 你係唔係嚟接我／我哋呀？
Shall I pick you up?	**Haih m̀h haih ngóh làih jip néih/néih deih a?** 係唔係我嚟接你／你哋呀？
I have to be home by…	**Ngóh…chìhn yāt dihng yiu fāan dou ngūk kéi.** 我…前一定要返到屋企。
I don't want to see you anymore.	**Ngóh m̀h séung joi gin dóu néih.** 我唔想再見到你。

3.11 Being the host(ess)

See also 4 Eating out

What would you like to drink?	**Néih séung yám dī māt yéh a?** 你想飲啲乜嘢呀？
Something non-alcoholic, please.	**Móuh jáu jīng ge yéh la.** 冇酒精嘅嘢喇。
Would you like a cigarette/cigar?	**Néih séung m̀h séung sihk jī yīn/syut gā a?** 你想唔想食枝煙／雪茄呀？
I don't smoke.	**Ngóh m̀h sihk yīn ga.** 我唔食煙㗎。

3.12 Saying goodbye

Can I send you home?
Ngóh hó yíh sung néih fāan ngūk kéi ma?
我可以送你返屋企嗎？

Can I email you?
Ngóh hó yíh sé dihn yàuh béi néih ma?
我可以寫電郵俾你嗎？

Will you call me?
Néih wúih m̀h wúih dá dihn wá béi ngóh a?
你會唔會打電話俾我呀？

Can I have your address?
Néih hó yíh béi néih go deih jí ngóh ma?
你可以俾你個地址我嗎？

Thanks for everything.
Dō jeh néih waih ngóh jouh ge yāt chai.
多謝你為我做嘅一切。

It was a lot of fun.
Ngóh deih wáan dāk hóu hōi sām.
我哋玩得好開心。

Say hello to…
Bōng ngóh mahn hauh… 幫我問候…

All the best!
Jūk néih maahn sih yùh yi!
祝你萬事如意！

Good luck!
Jūk néih hóu wahn! 祝你好運！

When will you be back?
Néih géi sìh fāan làih a? 你幾時返嚟呀？

I'd like to see you again.
Ngóh séung joi gin dóu néih.
我想再見到你。

I hope we meet
again soon.
Ngóh hēi mohng hóu faai jauh joi gin dóu néih. 我希望好快就再見到你。

Here's my address.
If you're ever in the
United States,
you must call on me.
Nī go haih ngóh ge deih jí. Daih yaht néih làih Méih Gwok, yāt dihng yiu làih wán ngóh. 呢個係我嘅地址。
第日你嚟美國，一定要嚟搵我。

You'd be more than
welcome.
Néih géi sìh làih, ngóh dōu hóu fūn yìhng. 你幾時嚟，我都好歡迎。

4. Eating Out

Hong Kong is home to a wide variety of food, ranging from the most-lauded Michelin-starred restaurants to the humble **cha chan teng** serving everyday comfort food. When you are in Hong Kong, there are certain dishes you must try. Top of the must-eat list is **yumcha** (**yám chàh** 飲茶), literally 'drinking tea', a wide selection of snack-sized portions of steam, pan-fried, and deep-fried **dimsums** (**dím sām** 點心) served in bamboo containers and paired with Chinese tea. For lunch, many locals go to Chinese barbecue restaurants, which offer a fast and hearty meal of barbecued pork and roast goose with rice or noodles. Otherwise, treat yourself and friends to a seafood feast in the popular restaurants in Sai Kung and Lei Yu Mun. You can pick your live seafood—charged by weight, with a cooking fee—from the tanks.

Poon choi (**pùhn choi** 盆菜) is a traditional rustic cuisine served at village gatherings. Nine to twelve layers of ingredients such as pork, beef, lamb, abalone, chicken, duck, shrimp, crab, tofu, radish and mushrooms are piled in a large wooden or metal bowl for communal consumption.

If you are traveling on a shoestring budget, **cha chan teng** (**chàh chāan tēng** 茶餐廳) foods such as beef-brisket rice (**ngàuh nàahm fahn** 牛腩飯), cart noodles (**chē jái mihn** 車仔麵), wonton noodles (**wàhn tān mihn** 雲吞麵), Cantonese-style congee (**sāang gwán jūk** 生滾粥) are inexpensive and delicious.

Mealtimes

In Hong Kong people usually have three meals:

1. **jóu chāan** 早餐 (breakfast), is eaten sometime between 7.30 and 10 a.m. It generally consists of buns, eggs, assorted dim-sums known collectively in the West as 'yamcha food', congee and fried cruller known locally as **yauh tiu** 油條.

2. **ńgh chāan** 午餐 (lunch), eaten between 12 and 2 p.m., usually includes a hot dish. Lunch usually consists of rice or noodles with vegetables, stir-fried meats or seafood on top.

3. **máahn faahn** 晚飯 (dinner) is considered to be the most important meal of the day, at around 7 or 8 p.m. It often includes a clear soup and a few meat and vegetable dishes.

 At the restaurant

I'd like to reserve a table for seven o'clock, please.	**Ngóh séung dehng jēung chāt dím ge tói.** 我想訂張七點嘅檯。
A table for two, please.	**Léuhng wái, m̀h gōi.** 兩位，唔該。
We've reserved.	**Ngóh deih dehng jó tói.** 我哋訂咗檯。
We haven't reserved.	**Ngóh deih móuh dehng tói.** 我哋冇訂檯。

你哋有冇訂檯呀？ **Néih deih yáu móuh dehng tói a?**	Do you have a reservation?
你用乜嘢名訂檯呀？ **Néih yuhng māt yéh méng dehng tói a?**	What name is it reserved under, please?
請跟我過嚟呢邊。 **Chíng gān ngóh gwo làih nī bihn.**	This way, please.
呢張檯已經有人訂咗。 **Nī jēung tói yíh gīng yáuh yàhn dehng jó.**	This table is reserved.
十五分鐘後就有檯。 **Sahp ńgh fān jūng hauh jauh yáuh tói.**	We'll have a table free in fifteen minutes.
你介唔介意等一陣呀？ **Néih gaai m̀h gaai yi dáng yāt jahn a?**	Would you mind waiting?

Is the restaurant open yet?	**Chāan tēng hōi jó mùhn meih a?** 餐廳開咗門未呀？
What time does the restaurant open?	**Chāan tēng géi sìh hōi mùhn a?** 餐廳幾時開門呀？
What time does the restaurant close?	**Chāan tēng géi sìh sāan mùhn a?** 餐廳幾時閂門呀？
Can we wait for a table?	**Yùh gwó ngóh deih dáng yāt jahn, yáuh móuh tói a?** 如果我哋等一陣，有冇檯呀？
Do we have to wait long?	**Sái m̀h sái dáng hóu noih a?** 駛唔駛等好耐呀？
Is this seat taken?	**Nī go wái yáuh yàhn chóh ma?** 呢個位有人坐嗎？
Could we sit here?	**Ngóh deih hó yíh chóh hái nī douh ma?** 我哋可以坐喺呢度嗎？
Can we sit by the window?	**Ngóh deih hó yíh chóh chēung háu wái ma?** 我哋可以坐窗口位嗎？
Are there any tables outside?	**Chēut bihn yáuh móuh hūng tói a?** 出邊有冇空檯呀？
Do you have another chair for us?	**M̀h gōi béi dō jēung dang ngóh deih ā.** 唔該俾多張凳我哋吖。
Do you have a high chair?	**M̀h gōi béi jēung gōu dang ngóh deih ā.** 唔該俾張高凳我哋吖。
Is there a socket for this bottle-warmer?	**Yáuh móuh chaap nī go nyúhn pìhng hei ge chaap sōu a?** 有冇插呢個暖瓶器嘅插蘇呀？
Could you warm up this bottle/jar for me? (in the microwave)	**M̀h gōi bōng ngóh yuhng mèih bō lòuh nyúhn háh go náaih jēun.** 唔該幫我用微波爐暖下個奶樽。
Not too hot, please.	**M̀h hóu taai yiht, m̀h gōi.** 唔好太熱，唔該。

Is there somewhere I can change the baby's diaper? **Yáuh móuh deih fōng wuhn bìh bī jái niuh bou a?** 有冇地方換BB仔尿布呀？

Where are the restrooms? **Sái sáu gāan hái bīn douh a?** 洗手間喺邊度呀？

4.2 Ordering

Waiter/Waitress **Fó gei/sih ying sāng/fuhk mouh yùhn** 伙記／侍應生／服務員

We'd like something to eat/drink. **Ngóh deih séung sihk/yám dī yéh.** 我哋想食／飲啲嘢。

What is the quickest dish (to order and eat)? **Yáuh dī māt yéh chāan haih jeui faai ga?** 有啲乜嘢餐係最快㗎？

We don't have much time. **Ngóh deih gón sìh gaan.** 我哋趕時間。

We'd like to have a drink first. **Ngóh deih séung yám būi yéh sīn.** 我哋想飲杯嘢先。

Could we see the menu, please? **M̀h gōi béi ngóh deih tái háh choi páai.** 唔該俾我哋睇吓菜牌。

Could we see the wine list, please? **M̀h gōi béi ngóh deih tái háh jáu páai.** 唔該俾我哋睇吓酒牌。

Do you have a menu in English? **Yáuh móuh Yīng Mán ge choi páai a?** 有冇英文嘅菜牌呀？

Do you have a dish of the day? **Gām yaht yáuh móuh dahk biht ge choi a?** 今日有冇特別嘅菜呀？

Do you have a tourist menu? **Yáuh móuh béi yàuh haak tái ge choi páai a?** 有冇俾遊客睇嘅菜牌呀？

We haven't decided yet. **Ngóh deih juhng meih nám dóu sihk māt yéh.** 我哋仲未諗到食乜嘢。

What do you recommend? **M̀h gōi gaai siuh dī hóu choi.** 唔該介紹啲好菜。

What are the local specialties? **Néih deih yáuh dī māt yéh fūng meih choi a?** 你哋有啲乜嘢風味菜呀？

What are your specialities?	**Néih deih yáuh dī māt yéh jīu pàaih choi a?** 你哋有啲乜嘢招牌菜呀？
I like fish.	**Ngóh jūng yi sihk yú.** 我鍾意食魚。
I don't like meat.	**Ngóh m̀h jūng yi sihk yuhk.** 我唔鍾意食肉。
What's this?	**Nī dī haih māt yéh làih ga?** 呢啲喺乜嘢嚟㗎？
Does it have…in it?	**Yahp bihn yáuh móuh…a?** 入邊有冇…呀？
What does it taste like?	**Māt yéh meih douh ga?** 乜嘢味道㗎？
Is this a hot or a cold dish?	**Nī go choi yiht dihng dung ga?** 呢個菜熱定凍㗎？
Is this sweet?	**Nī go choi haih m̀h haih tìhm ga?** 呢個菜係唔係甜㗎？
Is this spicy?	**Nī go choi laaht m̀h laaht ga?** 呢個菜辣唔辣㗎？

(你/你哋)想食啲乜嘢呢？ **(Néih/Néih deih) séung sihk dī māt yéh nē?**	What would you like?
(你/你哋)諗定食乜嘢未呀？ **(Néih/Néih deih) nám dihng sihk māt yéh meih a?**	Have you decided?
(你/你哋)想唔想飲啲嘢先呀？ **(Néih/Néih deih) séung m̀h séung yám dī yéh sīn a?**	Would you like a drink first?
(你/你哋)飲啲乜嘢呢？ **(Néih/Néih deih) yám dī māt yéh nē?**	What would you like to drink?
菜嚟齊喇，請慢用。 **Choi làih chàih la, chíng maahn yuhng.**	Enjoy your meal.
飯菜做得好唔好食呀？ **Faahn choi jouh dāk hóu m̀h hóu sihk a?**	Is everything all right?
收得檯未呀？ **Sāu dāk tói meih a?**	May I clear the table?

Do you have anything else, by any chance?	**Juhng yáuh móuh choi meih làih a?** 仲有冇菜未嚟呀？
I'm on a salt-free diet.	**Ngóh m̀h sihk dāk yìhm.** 我唔食得鹽。
I can't eat pork.	**Ngóh m̀h sihk dāk jyū yuhk.** 我唔食得豬肉。
I can't have sugar.	**Ngóh m̀h sihk dāk tòhng.** 我唔食得糖。
I'm on a fat-free diet.	**Ngóh m̀h sihk dāk yàuh neih ge yéh.** 我唔食得油膩嘅嘢。
I can't have spicy food.	**Ngóh m̀h sihk dāk laaht ge choi.** 我唔食得辣嘅菜。
We'll have what those people are having.	**Ngóh deih yiu kéih deih sihk gó dī choi.** 我哋要佢哋食嗰啲菜。
We don't want to eat shark's fin.	**Ngóh deih m̀h séung sihk yùh chi.** 我哋唔想食魚翅。
We're not having Peking Duck.	**Ngóh deih m̀h yiu Bāk Gīng ngaap.** 我哋唔要北京鴨。
A cup of coffee please.	**Yāt būi ga fē, m̀h gōi.** 一杯咖啡，唔該。
A cup of milk tea please.	**Yāt būi náaih chàh, m̀h gōi.** 一杯奶茶，唔該。
A glass of jasmine tea, please.	**Yāt būi hēung pín, m̀h gōi.** 一杯香片，唔該。
A glass of beer, please.	**Yāt būi bē jáu, m̀h gōi.** 一杯啤酒，唔該。
A glass of orange juice, please.	**Yāt būi cháang jāp, m̀h gōi.** 一杯橙汁，唔該。
Could I have some more rice, please?	**M̀h gōi béi dō dī baahk faahn.** 唔該俾多啲白飯。
Could I have another bottle of mineral water, please?	**M̀h gōi béi dō yāt jēun kwong chyùhn séui.** 唔該俾多一樽礦泉水。
Could I have another bottle of wine, please?	**M̀h gōi béi dō yāt jēun jáu.** 唔該俾多一樽酒。

Could I have another portion of…, please?	**M̀h gōi béi dō yāt fahn…** 唔該俾多一份…
Could I have the salt and pepper, please?	**M̀h gōi béi dī yìhm tùhng wùh jīu fán ngóh.** 唔該俾啲鹽同胡椒粉我。
Could I have a napkin, please?	**M̀h gōi béi tìuh chāan gān ngóh.** 唔該俾條餐巾我。
Could I have a teaspoon, please?	**M̀h gōi béi go chàh gāng ngóh.** 唔該俾個茶羹我。
Could I have an ashtray, please?	**M̀h gōi béi go yīn fūi jūng ngóh.** 唔該俾個煙灰盅我。
Could I have a box of matches, please?	**M̀h gōi béi hahp fó chàaih ngóh.** 唔該俾盒火柴我。
Could I have some toothpicks, please	**M̀h gōi béi dī ngàh chīm ngóh.** 唔該俾啲牙簽我。
Could I have a glass of boiled water, please?	**M̀h gōi béi būi gwán séui ngóh.** 唔該俾杯滾水我。
Could I have a straw please?	**M̀h gōi béi jī yám túng ngóh.** 唔該俾枝飲筒我。
Please give me a pair of chopsticks.	**M̀h gōi béi yāt deui faai jí ngóh.** 唔該俾一對筷子我。
Please give me a fork.	**M̀h gōi béi yāt go chā ngóh.** 唔該俾一個叉我。
Please give me a knife.	**M̀h gōi béi yāt bá dōu ngóh.** 唔該俾一把刀我。
Please give me a plate.	**M̀h gōi béi yāt go díp ngóh.** 唔該俾一個碟我。
Please give me a bowl.	**M̀h gōi béi yāt go wún ngóh.** 唔該俾一個碗我。
Please give me a spoon.	**M̀h gōi béi yāt go chìh gāng ngóh.** 唔該俾一個匙羹我。
Cheers!	**Yám sing!** 飲勝！

| The next round is on me. | **Hah chi ngóh chéng.** 下次我請。 |
| Could we have a doggy bag, please? | **M̀h gōi bōng ngóh dá bāau.** 唔該幫我打包。 |

4.3 The bill

See also 8.2 Settling the bill

How much is this dish?	**Nī dihp choi géi dō chin a?** 呢碟菜幾多錢呀？
The bill, please.	**M̀h gōi màaih dāan.** 唔該埋單。
All together	**Júng guhng...** 總共…
Everyone pays separately.	**Ngóh deih gok jih màaih dāan.** 我哋各自埋單。
Let's go Dutch.	**Ngóh deih fān jó nī jēung dāan.** 我哋分咗呢張單。
Could we have the menu again, please?	**Màh fàahn néih joi béi go choi páai ngóh deih.** 麻煩你再俾個菜牌我哋。
The...is not on the bill.	**Jēung dāan seuhng mihn móuh nī go choi.** 張單上面冇呢個菜。

4.4 Complaints

It's taking a very long time.	**Ngóh yíh gīng dáng jó hóu noih la.** 我已經等咗好耐喇。
We've been here an hour already.	**Ngóh deih làih jó yíh gīng yāt go jūng la.** 我哋嚟咗已經一個鐘喇。
This must be a mistake.	**Ngóh nám néih deih gáau cho la.** 我諗你哋搞錯喇。
This is not what I ordered.	**Ngóh deih móuh giu nī dihp choi.** 我哋冇叫呢碟菜。
I ordered...	**Ngóh giu gó dihp choi haih...** 我叫嗰碟菜係…

There's a dish missing.	**Síu jó yāt dihp choi.** 少咗一碟菜。
The plate is broken.	**Nī go díhp bāng jó.** 呢個碟崩咗。
The plate is not clean.	**M̀h gōn jehng.** 唔乾淨。
The food's cold.	**Nī dihp choi dung jó.** 呢碟菜凍咗。
The food's not fresh.	**Nī dihp choi m̀h sān sīn.** 呢碟菜唔新鮮。
The food's too salty.	**Nī dihp choi taai hàahm la.** 呢碟菜太鹹喇。
The food's too sweet.	**Nī dihp choi taai tihm la.** 呢碟菜太甜喇。
The food's too spicy.	**Nī dihp choi taai laaht la.** 呢碟菜太辣喇。
The food is off/has gone bad.	**Nī dihp choi yáuh dī sūk meih.** 呢碟菜有啲餿味。
Could I have something else instead of this?	**Wuhn dihp daih yih dī ge choi, dāk m̀h dāk a?** 換碟第二啲嘅菜，得唔得呀？
The bill/this amount is not right.	**Nī jēung dāan hóu chíh gā cho jó.** 呢張單好似加錯咗。
We didn't have this.	**Ngóh deih móuh giu nī dihp choi.** 我哋冇叫呢碟菜。
There's no toilet paper in the restroom.	**Sái sáu gāan yahp bihn móuh chi jí.** 洗手間入邊冇廁紙。
Will you call the manager, please?	**M̀h goi giu néih deih ge gīng léih làih.** 唔該叫你哋嘅經理嚟。

4.5 Giving a compliment

That was a sumptuous meal.	**Dī choi hóu fūng fu.** 啲菜好豐富。
The food was excellent.	**Dī choi jyú dāk hóu sihk.** 啲菜煮得好食。
The…in particular was delicious.	**Dahk biht haih…, jān haih taai hóu sihk la.** 特別係…，真係太好食喇。

4.6 Drinks

coffee	**ga fē** 咖啡
cold cocoa	**dung jyū gū līk** 凍朱古力
hot milk	**yiht ngàuh náaih** 熱牛奶
black tea	**hùhng chàh (m̀h gā náaih)** 紅茶(唔加奶)
English tea (with milk)	**náaih chàh** 奶茶
Hong Kong-style milk tea	**góng sīk náaih chàh** 港式奶茶
Hong Kong-style milk tea and coffee	**yīn yēung** 鴛鴦
freshly squeezed orange juice	**sīn ja cháang jāp** 鮮榨橙汁
mineral water	**kwong chyùhn séui** 礦泉水
soda water	**sō dá séui** 梳打水
Coca-Cola	**Hó háu hó lohk** 可口可樂
brandy	**baahk lāan déi** 白蘭地
whisky	**wāi sih géi** 威士忌
champagne	**hēung bān** 香檳
red wine	**hùhng jáu** 紅酒
white wine	**baahk jáu** 白酒
water, boiled	**gwán séui** 滾水
water, cold	**dung séui** 凍水
water, ice	**bīng séui** 冰水
ice, to add	**gā bīng** 加冰
Puer (Yunnan tea)	**Póu néi** 普洱
Puer with chrysanthemum tea	**Gūk póu** 菊普
Saumei tea	**Sauh méi** 壽眉

Some popular Cantonese dishes

Barbecued goose (**sīu ngó** 燒鵝) is seasoned and roasted in a char-coal oven, producing tender meat and crispy skin and served with plum sauce.

Barbecued pork (**chā sīu** 叉燒) is pork seasoned with honey, spices, fermented tofu and rice wine and barbecued over an open fire.

Barbecued pork bun (**chā sīu bāau** 叉燒包) is a soft bun with sweet, slow-roasted pork inside.

Cantonese-style congee (**sāang gwán jūk** 生滾粥) is a rice porridge with fish, beef or chicken.

Claypot rice (**bōu jái faahn** 煲仔飯), where juicy meats and fresh vegetables are placed on top of rice in a clay pot and slow-cooked over a coal-lit fire.

Dimsums (**dím sām** 點心) are snack-sized portions of steam, pan-fried, and deep-fried items served in bamboo containers. These include *shao mai* (**sīu máai** 燒賣), a popular Chinese dumpling with pork, shrimp, mushrooms, green onions and ginger, and topped with some crab roe and steamed shrimp dumpling (**hā gáau** 蝦餃).

Egg tart (**daahn tāat** 蛋撻) is a sweet baked pastry-crust filled with egg custard.

Hotpot (**fó wō** 火鍋) is a delicious mixture of seafood, meats and vegetables cooked in a steamboat pot.

Pineapple bun with butter (**bō ló yàuh** 菠蘿油) has a pineapple-like top (hence the name) but contains no pineapple. It is sweet with a slice of butter inside a warm bun.

Steamed fish (**jīng yùh** 蒸魚) is a must in all Hong Kong seafood menus. The fresh fish is seasoned with ginger, shallots and soy sauce.

Wonton noodles (**wàhn tān mihn** 雲吞麵) are shrimp and pork dumplings served in an aromatic stock with egg noodles.

5. Getting Around

 Asking directions

Excuse me, could I ask you something?	**M̀h gōi, ngóh hó yíh mahn néih dī yéh ma?** 唔該，我可以問你啲嘢嗎？
I've lost my way.	**Ngóh dohng sāt jó.** 我蕩失咗。
Is there a…around here?	**Fuh gahn yáuh móuh…?** 附近有冇…
Excuse me, what direction is…?	**Chíng mahn…hái bīn go fōng heung?** 請問…喺邊個方向？
Excuse me, am I going in the right direction for the bus stop?	**Chíng mahn heui bā sí jaahm haih m̀h haih hàahng nī go fōng heung a?** 請問去巴士站係唔係行呢個方向呀？
Excuse me, am I going in the right direction for the mini-bus stop?	**Chíng mahn heui síu bā jaahm haih m̀h haih hàahng nī go fōng heung a?** 請問去小巴站係唔係行呢個方向呀？
Excuse me, am I going in the right direction for the railway station?	**Chíng mahn heui fó chē jaahm haih m̀h haih hàahng nī go fōng heung a?** 請問去火車站係唔係行呢個方向呀？
Excuse me, am I going in the right direction for the subway station?	**Chíng mahn heui deih tit jaahm haih m̀h haih hàahng nī go fōng heung a?** 請問去地鐵站係唔係行呢個方向呀？

Could you tell me how to get to…?	**Chíng mahn…dím heui a?** 請問…點去呀？
How many kilometers is it to…?	**Heui…yáuh géi dō gūng léih a?** 去…有幾多公里呀？
Is it far?	**Yúhn m̀h yúhn a?** 遠唔遠呀？
Can I walk there?	**Hàahng m̀h hàahng dóu heui a?** 行唔行到去呀？
Is it difficult to find?	**Yùhng m̀h yùhng yih wán a?** 容唔容易搵呀？

唔清楚喎，我呢度啲路唔熟。
M̀h chīng chó wo, ngóh nī douh dī louh m̀h suhk.

I'm not sure; I don't know my way around here.

你行錯咗喇。
Néih hàahng cho jó la.

You're going the wrong way.

你要行返轉頭。
Néih yiu hàahng fāan jyun tàuh.

You have to go back.

由呢度開始，跟住路牌行。
Yàuh nī douh hōi chí, gān jyuh louh páai hàahng.

From here, just follow the signs.

到咗之後再問人。
Dou jó jī hauh joi mahn yàhn.

When you get there, ask again.

一直行 **Yāt jihk hàahng**	Go straight ahead
行到盡頭 **Hàahng dou jeuhn tàuh**	Go till the end of the road
跟住 **Gān jyuh**	Follow
過 **Gwo**	Cross
轉右 **Jyun yauh**	Turn right
轉左 **Jyun jó**	Turn left

---

road/street **louh/gāai** 路／街	overpass **gōu ga kìuh** 高架橋	building **láu** 樓
river **hòh** 河	tunnel **seuih douh** 隧道	road signs **louh páai** 路牌

traffic lights
hùhng luhk dāng/gāau tūng dāng
紅綠燈／交通燈

bridge
kìuh
橋

street corner
gāai háu/gok lōk táu
街口／角落頭

grade crossing
**tit louh tùhng gūng louh ge gāau
  chā háu**
鐵路同公路嘅交叉口

arrow
jin jéui
箭嘴

intersection/crossroads
sahp jih louh háu
十字路口

5.2 Traffic signs

交通訊號
Gāau Tūng Seun Houh
Traffic Signs

油站
Yàuh Jaahm
Service Station

不准堵塞
Bāt Jéun Dóu Sāk
Do Not Obstruct

小心
Síu Sām
Beware

前面修路
Chìhn Mihn Sāu Louh
Road Works

道路封閉
Douh Louh Fūng Bai
Road Closed

緊急車道
Gán Gāp Chē Douh
Emergency Lane

收費泊車
Sāu Fai Paak Chē
Paying Carpark

專用車位
Jyūn Yuhng Chē Wái
Reserved Parking

入隧道請開着車頭燈
**Yahp Seuih Douh Chíng Hōi Jeuhk
  Chē Tàuh Dāng**
Turn On Headlights (In The
Tunnel)

十字路口
Sahp Jih Louh Háu
Intersection/Crossroads

靠右／左行駛
Kaau Yauh/Jó Hàhng Sái
Keep Right/Left

路面損壞／不平
Louh Mihn Syún Waaih/Bāt Pìhng
Broken/Uneven Surface

汽車故障服務處
Hei Chē Gu Jeung Fuhk Mouh Chyu
Road Assistance (Breakdown
Service)

限時停車
Haahn Sìh Tìhng Chē
Stopping for a Limited Period

監控停車場
Gāam Hung Tìhng Chē Chèuhng
Supervised Garage/Parking Lot

(鐵路／公路)交叉口
(Tit Louh/Gūng Louh) Gāau Chā Háu
Grade Crossing

停(車)
Tìhng (Chē)
Stop

出口
Chēut Háu
Exit

路不開放
Louh Bāt Hōi Fong
Road Closed

載重貨車
Joi Chúhng Fo Chē
Heavy Trucks

通行費
Tūng Hàhng Fai
Toll Payment

道路阻塞
Douh Louh Jó Sāk
Road Blocked

換車道
Wuhn Chē Douh
Change Lanes

不准駛入
Bāt Jéun Sái Yahp
No Entry

慢駛
Maahn Sái
Slow Down

最高速度
Jeui Gōu Chūk Douh
Maximum Speed

不准搭順風車
Bāt Jéun Daap Seuhn Fūng Chē
No Hitchhiking

此路不通
Chí Louh Bāt Tūng
No Access

不准轉右／左
Bāt Jéun Jyun Yauh/ Jó
No Right/Left Turn

前面急彎
Chìhn Mihn Gāp Wāan
Curves Ahead

危險
Ngàih Hím
Danger(ous)

繞道行駛
Yíu Douh Hàhng Sái
Detour

淨空高度
Jihng Hūng Gōu Douh
Maximum Headroom…

下一段路多雨或雪
Hah Yāt Dyuhn Louh Dō Yúh Waahk Syut
Rain or Ice for…Kms

行人不准通過
Hàhng Yàhn Bāt Jéun Tūng Gwo
No Pedestrian Access

必須顯示泊車票
Bīt Sēui Hín Sih Paak Chē Piu
Display the Parking Receipt

優先使用車道權
Yāu Sīn Sí Yuhng Chē Douh Kyùhn
Right of Way

前面路窄
Chìhn Mihn Louh Jaak
Narrowing in the Road

不能通行嘅路肩
Bāt Nàhng Tūng Hàhng Ge Louh Gīn
Impassible Shoulder

小心山上滑落石頭
Síu Sām Sāan Seuhng Waahk Lohk Sehk Tàuh
Beware, Falling Rocks

不准超車
Bāt Jéun Chīu Chē
No Passing

不准泊車
Bāt Jéun Paak Chē
No Parking

單程路
Dāan Chìhng Louh
One Way Road

拖車地帶
Tō Chē Deih Daai
Tow-Away Area

隧道
Seuih Douh
Tunnel

車道口
Chē Douh Háu
Driveway

安全島
Ngōn Chyùhn Dóu
Traffic Island

行人道
Hàhng Yàhn Douh
Pedestrian Walk

5.3 The car

See the diagram on page 75

The speed limits for different vehicles vary in different districts and on different roads. Generally speaking for cars and motorcycles, the limit is 80 to 100 km/h on non-urban highways and 50 km/h on main roads and built-up areas. Otherwise speed limits on certain roads are clearly marked. Bicycles are commonplace in the New Territories with special bicycle lanes. Unlike China, vehicles in Hong Kong has right-hand drive and travel on the left side of the road.

The parts of a car
(the diagram shows the numbered parts)

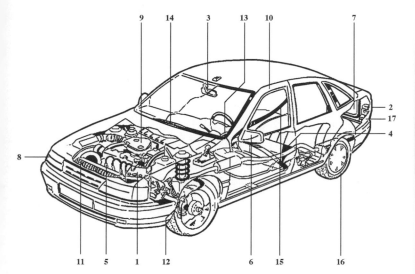

1	battery	**dihn chìh**	電池
2	rear light	**méih dāng**	尾燈
3	rear-view mirror	**dou hauh geng**	倒後鏡
4	gas tank	**yàuh sēung**	油箱
5	spark plugs	**fó jéui**	火嘴
6	side mirror	**jó/yauh dou hauh geng**	左/右倒後鏡
7	trunk	**chē méih sēung**	車尾箱
8	headlight	**chē tàuh dāng**	車頭燈
9	air filter	**hei gaak**	氣隔
10	door	**chē mùhn**	車門
11	radiator	**séui sēung**	水箱
12	brake disc	**dihp yìhng saat chē jai**	碟形煞車掣
13	indicator	**yauh/jó jáam dāng**	右/左㦈燈
14	windshield wiper	**dóng fūng bō lēi séui buht**	擋風玻璃 水撥
15	seat belt	**ngōn chyùhn dáai**	安全帶
16	wheel	**chē lūk**	車轆
17	spare wheel	**sih bē tāai**	士啤呔

5.4 The gas station

How far is it to the next gas station, please?	**Dou hah go yàuh jaahm yáuh géi yúhn a?** 到下個油站有幾遠呀？
I would like 50 liters of Premium unleaded petrol.	**Ngóh yahp ńgh sahp gūng sīng chīu kāp mòuh yùhn hei yàuh.** 我入五十公升超級無鉛汽油。
I would like 50 liters of Standard unleaded petrol.	**Ngóh yahp ńgh sahp gūng sīng mòuh yùhn hei yàuh.** 我入五十公升無鉛汽油。
I would like 50 liters of LPG gas.	**Ngóh yahp ńgh sahp gūng sīng sehk yàuh hei.** 我入五十公升石油氣。
I would like 50 liters of diesel.	**Ngóh yahp ńgh sahp gūng sīng chàaih yàuh/yàuh jā.** 我入五十公升柴油／油渣。
I would like 500 dollars of gas.	**Ngóh yahp ńgh baak mān ge hei yàuh.** 我入五百蚊嘅汽油。
Fill her up, please.	**Yahp múhn kéuih, m̀h gōi.** 入滿佢，唔該。
Could you check the oil level?	**M̀h gōi bōng ngóh gím chàh yāt háh gēi yáu.** 唔該幫我檢查一吓機油。
Could you check the tyre pressure?	**M̀h gōi bōng ngóh gím chàh yāt háh chē tāai hei ngaat.** 唔該幫我檢查一吓車呔氣壓。
Could you change the oil, please?	**M̀h gōi bōng ngóh wuhn gēi yáu.** 唔該幫我換機油。
Could you clean the windshield, please?	**M̀h gōi bōng ngóh chaat gōn jehng dóng fūng bō lēi.** 唔該幫我擦乾淨擋風玻璃。
Could you wash the car, please?	**M̀h gōi bōng ngóh sái háh ga chē.** 唔該幫我洗吓架車。

5.5 Breakdowns and repairs

My car has broken down, could you help me?
Ngóh ga chē waaih jó, hó yíh bōng yāt bōng ngóh ma?
我架車壞咗，可以幫一幫我嗎？

My motorbike has run out of gas.
Ngóh ga dihn dāan chē móuh saai yáu.
我架電單車冇晒油。

I've locked myself outside the car.
Ngóh ge só sìh só jó hái chē yahp bihn.
我嘅鎖匙鎖咗喺車入邊。

The motorbike won't start.
Ngóh ga dihn dāan chē tāat m̀h jeuhk fó.
我架電單車撻唔著火。

Could you contact the breakdown service for me, please?
M̀h gōi bōng ngóh dá dihn wá giu gán gāp fuhk mouh.
唔該幫我打電話叫緊急服務。

Could you call a garage for me, please?
M̀h gōi bōng ngóh dá dihn wá wán chē fòhng sī fú.
唔該幫我打電話搵車房師傅。

Could you give me a lift to the nearest garage?
Néih hó m̀h hó yíh sung ngóh heui jeui káhn ge chē fòhng?
你可唔可以送我去最近嘅車房？

Can we take my motorcycle?
Néih hó yíh wahn ngóh ga dihn dāan chē ma? 你可以運我架電單車嗎？

Could you tow me to a garage?
Hó m̀h hó yíh tō ngóh gā chē heui chē fòhng a? 可唔可以拖我架車去車房呀？

There's probably something wrong with...(See 5.6)
... hó nàhng yáuh dī waaih
… 可能有啲壞

Can you fix it?
Jíng m̀h jíng dāk fāan a?
整唔整得番呀？

Could you fix my tyre?
M̀h gōi bōng ngóh bóu tāai.
唔該幫我補呔。

Could you change this wheel?
M̀h gōi bōng ngóh wuhn go chē lūk.
唔該幫我換個車轆。

Can you fix it so it'll get me to…?	**M̀h gōi bōng ngóh sāu léih yāt háh, ngóh yiu jā heui…** 唔該幫我修理一下，我要揸去…
Which garage can help me?	**Bīn gāan chē fòhng hó yíh bōng dóu ngóh a?** 邊間車房可以幫到我呀？
When will my car/bicycle be ready?	**Ngóh ga chē géi sìh jíng hóu a?** 我架車幾時整好呀？
Have you already finished?	**Jíng hóu meih a?** 整好未呀？
Can I wait for it here?	**Ngóh hó yíh hái (nī) douh dáng néih jíng ma?** 我可以喺(呢)度等你整嗎？
How much will it cost?	**Yiu géi dō chín a?** 要幾多錢呀？
Could you itemize the bill?	**M̀h gōi néih liht chēut yiu sāu léih ge hohng muhk.** 唔該你列出要修理嘅項目。
Could you give me a receipt for insurance purposes?	**M̀h gōi béi jēung sāu geui ngóh jouh bóu hím yuhng tòuh.** 唔該俾張收據我做保險用途。

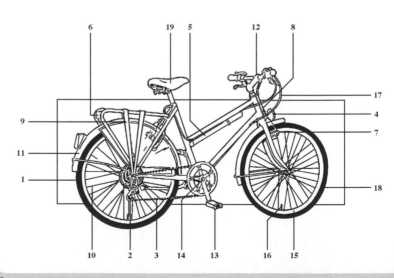

5.6 Bicycles/mopeds

The parts of a bicycle

1	rear wheel	hauh lūk	後轆
2	gear change	bihn chūk hei	變速器
3	chain	dāan chē lín	單車鏈
4	headlight	chē tàuh dāng	車頭燈
5	pump	hei bām	氣泵
6	reflector	fáan gwōng geng	反光鏡
7	brake shoe	saat chē péi	煞車皮
8	brake cable	saat chē wāi yá	煞車威也
9	carrier straps	wahn joi bou dáai	運載布帶
10	spoke	gong sín	鋼線
11	mudguard	sā báan	沙板
12	handlebar	dāan chē bá sáu/táaih	單車把手／鈦
13	toe clip	geuk daahp kau	腳踏扣
14	drum brake	gú saat chē	鼓煞車
15	valve	wuht mùhn	活門
16	valve tube	hei jéui	氣嘴
17	gear cable	bō sēung wāi yá	波箱威也
18	front wheel	chìhn lūk	前轆
19	seat	joh wái	座位

我冇你要嘅零件。
Ngóh móuh néih yiu ge lìhng gín.

I don't have the parts that you want.

我要去第二度幫你配零件。 **Ngóh yiu heui daih yih douh bōng néih pui lìhng gín.**

I have to get the parts from somewhere else.

需要半日時間。 **Sēui yiu bun yaht sìh gaan.**

That'll take half a day.

需要一日時間。 **Sēui yiu yāt yaht sìh gaan.**

That'll take a day.

需要幾日時間。 **Sēui yiu géi yaht sìh gaan.**

That'll take a few days.

需要一個星期嘅時間。
Sēui yiu yāt go sìng kèih ge sìh gaan.

That'll take a week.

修理費貴過架車。
Sāu léih fai gwai gwo ga chē.

The repair cost is more expensive than the bike.

你架單車/電單車整唔番。
Néih ga dāan chē/dihn dāan chē jíng m̀h fāan.

Your bicycle/motorbike can't be repaired.

你架電單車⋯點就整好。
Néih ga dihn dāan chē... dím jauh jíng hóu.

Your motorbike will be ready at...o'clock.

5.7 Renting a vehicle

Do I need an international driving licence for that? **Ngóh sái m̀h sái yiu gwok jai chē pàaih a?**
我駛唔駛要國際車牌呀？

I'd like to rent a car. **Ngóh yiu jōu yāt ga chē.**
我要租一架車。

How much does it cost to hire (a car) per day? **Jōu yāt yaht yiu géi dō chín a?**
租一日要幾多錢呀？

How much does it cost to hire (a car) for two days? **Jōu léuhng yaht yiu géi dō chín a?**
租兩日要幾多錢呀？

How much does it cost to hire per kilometer? **Jōu múih gūng léih yiu géi dō chín a?**
租每公里要幾多錢呀？

How many kilometers per day do I get for the basic fee? **Yāt yaht ge sāu fai hó yíh hàhng géi dō gūng léih a?**
一日嘅收費可以行幾多公里呀？

Does the price include gas? **Ga chìhn bāau m̀h bāau kut hei yàuh a?**
價錢包唔包括汽油呀？

How much is the deposit? **Ngon gām yiu géi dō chín a?**
按金要幾多錢呀？

Could I have a receipt for the deposit? **M̀h gōi béi jēung ngon gām sāu geui ngóh?**
唔該俾張按金收據我？

Does that include insurance? **Sāu fei bāau kut bóu hím fai ma?**
收費包括保險費嗎？

What time can I pick the car up? **Ngóh géi sìh hó yíh làih ló chē a?**
我幾時可以嚟攞車呀？

When does the car have to be back? **Géi sìh yiu wàahn chē a?**
幾時要還車呀？

Where's the gas tank? **Yàuh sēung hái bīn douh a?**
油箱喺邊度呀？

What sort of fuel does it take? **Yuhng māt yéh yìhn líu ga?**
用乜嘢燃料㗎？

Does it come with a GPS?	**Yáuh móuh bāau douh hòhng hei a?** 有冇包導航器呀？

5.8 Getting a lift

Where are you heading?	**Néih heui bīn go fōng heung a?** 你去邊個方向呀？
Can you give me a lift?	**Hó m̀h hó yíh daap néih ga chē heui a?** 可唔可以搭你架車去呀？
Can my friend come too?	**Ngóh pàhng yáuh hó m̀h hó yíh làih màaih a?** 我朋友可唔可以嚟埋呀？
I'd like to go to...	**Ngóh séung heui...** 我想去…
Is that on the way to...?	**Nī tìuh louh haih m̀h haih heui...?** 呢條路係唔係去…？
Could you drop me off here?	**Néih hó m̀h hó yíh hái nī douh fong dāi ngóh a?** 你可唔可以喺呢度放低我呀？
Could you drop me off at the intersection to the highway?	**Néih hó m̀h hó yíh hái gūng louh ge yahp háu fong dāi ngóh a?** 你可唔可以喺公路嘅入口放低我呀？
Could you drop me off at the next intersection?	**Néih hó m̀h hó yíh hái hah go sahp jih louh háu fong dāi ngóh a?** 你可唔可以喺下個十字路口放低我呀？
Could you stop here, please?	**Néih hó m̀h hó yíh hái nī douh tìhng a?** 你可唔可以喺呢度停呀？
I'd like to get out here.	**Ngóh séung hái nī douh lohk chē.** 我想喺呢度落車。
Thanks for the lift.	**Hóu dō jeh néih béi ngóh daap néih ga chē.** 好多謝你俾我搭你架車。

6. Arrival and Departure

General

Public transport is very efficient and accessible in Hong Kong. People usually commute by subway, trains, buses, trams and ferries. In addition, there are mini-buses and taxis and a light rail system in the New Territories, so there is no real need for private cars. For example, the airport is well-serviced by the airport express, air-conditioned buses, taxis and ferries. More affordable alternatives might include ride-sharing apps like Gobee and Uber.

How do I get to the Peak Tram station?	**Chíng mahn dím heui laahm chē jaahm a?** 請問點去纜車站呀？
You can take the bus.	**Néih hó yíh daap bā sí.** 你可以搭巴士。
You can take the minibus.	**Néih hó yíh daap síu bā.** 你可以搭小巴。
You can take the ferry.	**Néih hó yíh daap syùhn.** 你可以搭船。
You can take the tram.	**Néih hó yíh daap dihn chē.** 你可以搭電車。
You can take the MTR. (Mass Transit Railway)	**Néih hó yíh daap góng tit.** 你可以搭港鐵。
You can take the taxi.	**Néih hó yíh daap dīk sí.** 你可以搭的士。

Where does this train go to?	**Nī bāan fó chē heui bīn douh a?** 呢班火車去邊度呀？
Does this boat go to Macau?	**Nī jek syùhn haih m̀h haih heui Ngou Mún a?** 呢隻船係唔係去澳門呀？
Can I take this bus to Mongkok?	**Hó m̀h hó yíh chóh nī ga bā sí heui Wohng Gok a?** 可唔可以坐呢架巴士去旺角呀？
Does this train stop at Tsim Sha Tsui?	**Nī bāan fó chē tìhng m̀h tìhng Jīm Sā Jéui a?** 呢班火車停唔停尖沙嘴呀？
Is this seat taken?	**Nī go wái yáuh móuh yàhn chóh a?** 呢個位有冇人坐呀？
I've reserved...	**Ngóh yuh dehng jó...** 我預定咗…
Where do I have to get off for Mongkok?	**Heui Wohng Gok hái bīn douh lohk chē a?** 去旺角喺邊度落車呀？
Please let me know when we get to Tsim Sha Tsui.	**Dou Jīm Sā Jéui m̀h gōi wah bēi ngóh jī.** 到尖沙嘴唔該話俾我知。
Could you stop at the next stop, please?	**M̀h gōi hah go jaahm yáuh lohk.** 唔該下個站有落。
Where are we?	**Ngóh deih yìh gā hái bīn douh a?** 我哋而家喺邊度呀？
Do I have to get off here?	**Ngóh haih m̀h haih hái nī douh lohk chē a?** 我係唔係喺呢度落車呀？
Have you already passed Tsim Sha Tsui?	**Néih gwo jó Jīm Sā Jéui meih a?** 你過咗尖沙嘴未呀？
How long does this train stop here?	**Nī bāan fó chē wúih hái nī douh tìhng géi noih a?** 呢班火車會喺呢度停幾耐呀？
Can I come back on the same ticket?	**Hó m̀h hó yíh yuhng nī jēung fēi chóh fāan làih a?** 可唔可以用呢張飛坐返嚟呀？
Can I change on this ticket?	**Ngóh hó m̀h hó yíh yuhng nī jēung fēi jyun chē a?** 我可唔可以用呢張飛轉車呀？

| How long is this ticket valid for? | **Nī jēung fēi hó yíh yuhng géi noih a?** 呢張飛可以用幾耐呀? |

6.2 Immigration and customs

你嘅護照,唔該。 **Néih ge wuh jiu, m̀h gōi.**	Your passport, please.
你嘅綠咭,唔該。 **Néih ge luhk kāat, m̀h gōi.**	Your green card, please.
你嘅身份証,唔該。 **Néih ge sān fán jing, m̀h gōi.**	Your identity card, please.
你嘅駕駛執照,唔該。 **Néih ge ga sái jāp jiu, m̀h gōi.**	Your driving licence, please.
你嘅汽車文件,唔該。 **Néih ge hei chē màhn gính, m̀h gōi.**	Your vehicle documents, please.
你嘅簽証,唔該。 **Néih ge chīm jing, m̀h gōi.**	Your visa, please.
你去邊度呀? **Néih heui bīn douh a?**	Where are you going?
你打算留幾耐呀? **Néih dá syun làuh géi noih a?**	How long are you planning to stay?
有冇嘢要報關呀? **Yáuh móuh yéh yiu bou gwāan a?**	Do you have anything to declare?
唔該打開佢。 **M̀h gōi dá hōi kéuih.**	Open this, please.

My children are entered on this passport.	**Ngóh dī sai louh jái dōu sé jo hái wuh jiu léuih mihn.** 我啲細路仔都寫咗喺護照裏面。
I'm traveling through...	**Ngóh wúih gīng gwo...** 我會經過…。
I'm going on vacation to...	**Ngóh heui...léuih hàhng.** 我去…旅行。
I'm on a business trip.	**Ngóh haih làih gūng gon.** 我係嚟公幹。
I don't know how long I'll be staying.	**Ngóh m̀h jī dou ngóh wúih làuh géi noih.** 我唔知道我會留幾耐。
I'll be staying here for a weekend.	**Ngóh wúih hái douh gwo jāu muht.** 我會喺度過周末。
I'll be staying here for a few days.	**Ngóh wúih hái douh làuh géi yaht.** 我會喺度留幾日。

I'll be staying here for a week. | **Ngóh wúih hái douh làuh yāt go sīng kèih.** 我會喺度留一個星期。

I'll be staying here for two weeks. | **Ngóh wúih hái douh làuh léuhng go sīng kèih.** 我會喺度留兩個星期。

I've got nothing to declare. | **Ngóh móuh yéh bou gwāan.** 我無嘢報關。

I have a carton of cigarettes. | **Ngóh yáuh yāt tìuh hēung yīn.** 我有一條香煙。

I have a bottle of whisky. | **Ngóh yáuh yāt jēun wāi sih géi.** 我有一樽威士忌。

I have some souvenirs. | **Ngóh yáuh yāt dī géi nihm bán.** 我有一啲紀念品。

These are personal items. | **Nī dī haih sī yàhn maht bán.** 呢啲係私人物品。

These are not new. | **Nī dī m̀h haih sān ge.** 呢啲唔係新嘅。

Here's the receipt. | **Nī jēung haih sāu geui.** 呢張係收據。

This is for private use. | **Haih sī yàhn yuhng bán.** 係私人用品。

How much import duty do I have to pay? | **Ngóh yiu béi géi dō yahp háu seui a?** 我要俾幾多入口稅呀？

May I go now? | **Yī gā jáu dāk meih a?** 依家走得未呀？

6.3 Luggage

Porter! | **Būn wahn yùhn!** 搬運員！

Could you take this luggage to...? | **M̀h gōi bōng ngóh jēung hàhng léih būn heui...** 唔該幫我將行李搬去…。

This is a small tip for you. | **Nī douh síu síu tīp sí haih béi néih ge.** 呢度少少貼士係俾你嘅。

Where can I find a cart? | **Bīn douh yáuh sáu tēui chē a?** 邊度有手推車呀？

Could you store this luggage for me?	Ṁh gōi bōng ngóh chyùhn fong nē gin hàhng léih. 唔該幫我存放呢件行李。
Where are the luggage lockers?	Hàhng léih gwaih hái bīn douh a? 行李櫃喺邊度呀？
I can't get the locker open.	Ngóh hōi ṁh dóu hàhng léih gwaih. 我開唔到行李櫃。
How much is it per item per day?	Chyùhn fong yāt gihn hàhng léih yāt yaht yiu géi dō chín a? 存放一件行李一日要幾多錢呀？
This is not my bag/ suitcase.	Nī go ṁh haih ngóh ge léuih hàhng dói/ léuih hàhng gīp. 呢個唔係我嘅旅行袋／旅行喼。
There's a missing bag/ suitcase.	Ngóh ṁh gin jó go léuih hàhng dói/léuih hàhng gīp. 我唔見咗個旅行袋／旅行喼。
My suitcase is damaged.	Ngóh go léuih hàhng gīp béi yàhn jíng waaih jó. 我個旅行喼俾人整壞咗。
My luggage has not arrived.	Ngóh ge hàhng léih juhng meih dou. 我嘅行李仲未到。
When do you think my luggage will arrive?	Ngóh ge hàhng léih wúih géi sìh dou? 我嘅行李會幾時到？
Will I be compensated for my lost luggage?	Ngóh ṁh gin jó ge hàhng léih yáuh móuh dāk pùih a? 我唔見咗嘅行李有冇得賠呀？
Can you please send my luggage to this address?	Néih hó ṁh hó yíh sung ngóh ge hàhng léih dou nī go deih jí a? 你可唔可以送我嘅行李到呢個地址呀？
The lock has been broken.	Bá só waaih jó. 把鎖壞咗。
Where can I find the luggage forwarding service?	Bīn douh yáuh hàhng léih tok wahn a? 邊度有行李托運呀？
How soon will I get my luggage?	Ngóh géi sìh wúih ló dou hàhng léih a? 我幾時會攞到行李呀？

Does it cost more for same-day delivery?	**Jīk yaht sung wahn haih màih gwai dī a?** 即日送運係咪貴啲呀?

6.4 Questions to passengers

Ticket types

One Octopus card, please.	**M̀h gōi yāt jēung Baat Daaht Tūng.** 唔該一張八達通。
Two train tickets, please.	**M̀h gōi léuhng jēung fó chē fēi.** 唔該兩張火車飛。
Single or return?	**Dāan chìhng dihng haih lòih wùih a?** 單程定係來回呀?
Smoking or non-smoking?	**Kāp yīn chē sēung dihng haih mòuh yīn chē sēung a?** 吸煙車廂定係無煙車廂呀?
Window seat?	**Chēung háu wái a?** 窗口位呀?
Front or back (of train)?	**(Fó chē) chìhng bihn dihng haih hauh bihn a?** (火車)前邊定係後邊呀?
Seat or berth?	**Joh wái dihng haih ngoh pōu a?** 座位定係臥舖呀?
How many are traveling?	**Yáuh géi wái sìhng haak a?** 有幾位乘客呀?

Destination

Where are you going to?	**Néih heui bīn douh a?** 你去邊度呀?
When are you leaving?	**Néih géi sìh jáu a?** 你幾時走呀?
Your train leaves at 10 a.m.	**Néih bāan fó chē seung jau sahp dím hōi chē.** 你班火車上晝十點開車。
You have to get off at Admiralty station.	**Néih yiu hái Gām Jūng lohk chē.** 你要喺金鐘落車。
You get to Mongkok via Admiralty station.	**Néih yiu gīng Gām Jūng heui Wohng Gok.** 你要經金鐘去旺角。

The outward journey is on Tuesday, 10 a.m.	**Heui chìhng hái sīng kèih yih sahp dím.** 去程喺星期二十點。
The return journey is on Friday, 2 p.m.	**Wùih chìhng hái sīng kèih ńgh léuhng dím.** 回程喺星期五兩點。
You have to be on board by 1 p.m.	**Néih yiu hái yāt dím jī chìhn séuhng chē/gēi.** 你要喺一點之前上車／機。

Inside the vehicle

Tickets, please.	**Chē fēi ā, m̀h gōi.** 車飛吖，唔該。
Your reservation, please.	**M̀h gōi béi ngóh tái háh néih jēung dehng fēi dāan.** 唔該俾我睇吓你張訂飛單。
Your passport, please	**M̀h gōi béi ngóh tái háh néih bún wuh jiu.** 唔該俾我睇吓你本護照。
You're in the wrong seat.	**Néih chóh cho wái la.** 你坐錯位喇。
You have made a mistake.	**Néih gáau cho jó la.** 你搞錯咗喇。
This seat is reserved.	**Nī go wái yáuh yàhn dehng jó la.** 呢個位有人訂咗喇。
You have to pay extra.	**Néih sēui yiu béi dō dī chín.** 你需要俾多啲錢。
The…has been delayed by…minutes.	**…jēung wúih yìhn chìh…fān jūng.** …將會延遲…分鐘。

6.5 Tickets

Where can I buy a ticket?	**Ngóh heui bīn douh máaih fēi a?** 我去邊度買飛呀？
Where can I reserve a seat?	**Ngóh heui bīn douh dehng wái a?** 我去邊度訂位呀？
Could I have two tickets to Beijing please?	**M̀h gōi béi léuhng jēung heui Bāk Gīng ge chē fēi.** 唔該俾兩張去北京嘅車飛。
A single ticket to Beijing, please.	**M̀h gōi béi yāt jēung heui Bāk Gīng ge dāan chìhng piu.** 唔該俾一張去北京嘅單程票。

A return ticket to Beijing, please.	**M̀h gōi béi yāt jēung heui Bāk Gīng ge lòih wùih piu.** 唔該俾一張去北京嘅來回票。
A first class ticket please.	**M̀h gōi béi yāt jēung tàuh dáng chōng piu.** 唔該俾一張頭等艙票。
A business class ticket, please.	**M̀h gōi béi yāt jēung sēung mouh chōng piu.** 唔該俾一張商務艙票。
An economy class ticket, please.	**M̀h gōi béi yāt jēung gīng jai chōng piu.** 唔該俾一張經濟艙票。
I'd like to reserve a seat.	**Ngóh séung dehng go joh wái.** 我想訂個座位。
I'd like to reserve a berth.	**Ngóh séung dehng go ngoh pōu.** 我想訂個臥舖。
I'd like to reserve a cabin.	**Ngóh séung dehng go chē sēung.** 我想訂個車廂。
I'd like to reserve a top berth in the sleeping car.	**Ngóh séung dehng go seuhng pōu.** 我想訂個上舖。
I'd like to reserve a bottom berth in the sleeping car.	**Ngóh séung dehng go hah pōu.** 我想訂個下舖。
Where's the information desk?	**Sēun mahn chyu hái bīn douh a?** 詢問處喺邊度呀？

6.6 Information

Where can I find a schedule?	**Bīn douh yáuh sìh gaan bíu a?** 邊度有時間表呀？
Do you have a city map with the bus routes on it?	**Yáuh móuh bā sí louh sin tòuh a?** 有冇巴士路線圖呀？
Do you have a city map with the subway routes?	**Yáuh móuh deih tit louh sin tòuh a?** 有冇地鐵路線圖呀？
Will I get my money back?	**Hó m̀h hó yíh ló fāan chín a?** 可唔可以攞番錢呀？

I'd like to confirm my reservation for Shenzhen.	**Ngóh séung kok yihng ngóh yùh dihng heui Sām Jan ge léuih chìhng.**
	我想確認我預定去深圳嘅旅程。
I'd like to cancel my trip to Shenzhen.	**Ngóh séung chéui sīu ngóh yùh dihng heui Sām Jan ge léuih chìhng.**
	我想取消我預定去深圳嘅旅程。
I'd like to change my reservation for Shenzhen.	**Ngóh séung gói bin ngóh yùh dihng heui Sām Jan ge léuih chìhng.**
	我想改變我預定去深圳嘅旅程。
I'd like to go to Guangzhou.	**Ngóh séung heui Gwóng Jāu.**
	我想去廣州。
What is the quickest way to get to Shenzhen?	**Heui Sām Jan jeui faai ge louh chìhng haih bīn tìuh a?**
	去深圳最快嘅路程係邊條呀？
How much is a single/ return to Guangzhou?	**Heui Gwóng Jāu ge dāan chìhng/lòih wùih haih géi dō chín a?**
	去廣州嘅單程／來回係幾多錢呀？
Do I have to pay extra?	**Sái m̀h sái béi dō dī chín a?**
	駛唔駛俾多啲錢呀？
How much luggage am I allowed?	**Hó yíh daai géi dō hàhng léih a?**
	可以帶幾多行李呀？
Is this a direct train?	**Haih m̀h haih jihk tūng chē a?**
	係唔係直通車呀？
Do I have to change buses?	**Sái m̀h sái jyun bā sí a?**
	駛唔駛轉巴士呀？
Do I have to change trains?	**Sái m̀h sái jyun fó chē a?**
	駛唔駛轉火車呀？
Do I have to change flights?	**Sái m̀h sái jyun fēi gēi a?**
	駛唔駛轉飛機呀？
Where do I change buses?	**Hái bīn douh jyun bā sí a?**
	喺邊度轉巴士呀？
Where do I change trains?	**Hái bīn douh jyun fó chē a?**
	喺邊度轉火車呀？

Where do I go to transfer flights?	**Hái bīn douh jyun fēi gēi a?** 喺邊度轉飛機呀？
Will there be any stopovers?	**Jūng tòuh yiu tìhng làuh ma?** 中途要停留嗎？
Does the boat stop at any other ports on the way?	**Syùhn jūng tòuh yiu tìhng kèih tā máh tàuh ma?** 船中途要停其他碼頭嗎？
Does the train stop at Tsim Sha Tsui?	**Fó chē hái Jīm Sā Jéui tìhng ma?** 火車喺尖沙嘴停嗎？
Where do I get off? (train, bus/boat)	**Hái bīn douh lohk chē/syùhn a?** 喺邊度落車／船呀？
Is there a connection to Tsim Sha Tsui?	**Yáuh móuh chē jip bok heui Jīm Sā Jéui a?** 有冇車接駁去尖沙嘴呀？
How long is the wait?	**Yiu dáng géi noih a?** 要等幾耐呀？
When does the bus leave?	**Nī bāan bā sí géi dím hōi chē a?** 呢班巴士幾點開車呀？
When does the train leave?	**Nī bāan fó chē géi dím hōi chē a?** 呢班火車幾點開車呀？
Where does the boat to Macau leave from?	**Heui Ngou Mún ge syùhn hái bīn douh hōi chēut a?** 去澳門嘅船喺邊度開出呀？
Where does the plane to Beijing leave from?	**Heui Bāk Gīng ge fēi gēi hái bīn douh héi fēi a?** 去北京嘅飛機喺邊度起飛呀？
Is this the bus to Tsim Sha Tsui?	**Nē bāan bā sí heui Jīm Sā Jéui ma?** 呢班巴士去尖沙嘴嗎？

Airports

You will find the following signs at the Hong Kong International Airport (**Hēung Góng Gwok Jai Gēi Chèuhng** 香港國際機場):

| 登機處 **Dāng Gēi Chyu** Check-In | 入境 **Yahp Gíng** Arrivals | 出境 **Chēut Gíng** Departures | 國際 **Gwo Jai** International | 國內航班 **Gwok Noih Hòhng Bāan** Domestic Flights |

6.8 Long-distance trains

The Kowloon-Canton Railway—from Hung Hom (**Hùhng Ham** 紅磡) to Lo Wu (**Lòh Wùh** 羅湖)—provides inter-city train services to and from Shenzhen, Guangzhou, Shanghai and Beijing. You will need valid travel documents for entering the China Mainland.

The train to…is now arriving at platform…	**Hōi wóhng…ge liht chē, yìh gā dou daaht…houh yuht tòih.** 開往⋯嘅列車,而家到達⋯號月臺。
The train from…is now arriving at platform…	**Yàuh…hōi chēut ge liht chē, yìh gā dou daaht…houh yuht tòih.** 由⋯開出嘅列車而家到達⋯號月臺。
The train to…will leave from platform…	**Hōi wóhng…ge liht chē, yìh gā hái…houh yuht tòih hōi chēut.** 開往⋯嘅列車,而家喺⋯號月臺開出。
Today the [time] train to…will leave from platform…	**Gām yaht…dím hōi wóhng…ge liht chē, yìh gā hái…houh yuht tòih hōi chēut.** 今日⋯點開往⋯嘅列車,而家喺⋯號月臺開出。
Where does this train go to?	**Nī bāan fó chē heui bīn douh a?** 呢班火車去邊度呀?
Please don't stand too close to the train doors.	**Chíng maht kaau gahn chē mùhn.** 請勿靠近車門。
Mind the gap between the train and the platform.	**Chíng síu sām yuht tòih gāan jī hūng kwīk.** 請小心月臺間之空隙。
The next station is…	**Hah go jaahm haih…** 下個站係⋯
Please let passengers get off the train first.	**Chíng sīn yeuhng sìhng haak lohk chē.** 請先讓乘客落車。
Please alight from the left door of the train.	**Chíng hái jó bīn chē mùhn lohk chē.** 請喺左邊車門落車。
Please go to the opposite platform to change trains.	**Chíng dou deui mihn yuht tòih jyun chē.** 請到對面月臺轉車。

Could you let me know when we get to...?	**Dou...sìh, m̀h gōi néih wah béi ngoh jī.** 到⋯時，唔該你話俾我知。
Could you stop at the next stop, please?	**M̀h gōi, ngóh hah go jaahm lohk chē.** 唔該，我下個站落車。
Where are we?	**Ngóh deih yìh gā hái bīn douh a?** 我哋而家喺邊度呀？
Can I get off the train for a while?	**Ngóh hó m̀h hó yíh lohk fó chē yāt jahn a?** 我可唔可以落火車一陣呀？
Do I have to get off here?	**Ngóh haih m̀h haih yiu hái nī douh lohk chē a?** 我係唔係要喺呢度落車呀？

Taxis

Taxis provide a reasonably priced and efficient means of getting about in Hong Kong. You can pick up your taxi at hotels, taxi stands or hail on the street. Most taxi drivers speak English.

出租 **chēut jōu** for hire	有人 **yáuh yàhn** occupied	的士站 **dīk sí jaahm** taxi stand	的士 **dīk sí** taxi

Could you take a different route?	**Hó yíh hàahng daih yih tìuh louh ma?** 可以行第二條路嗎？
I'd like to get out here, please	**Ngóh hái nī douh lohk chē.** 我喺呢度落車。
Go	**Hàahng dāk** 行得
You have to go...here	**Hái nī douh...heui** 喺呢度⋯去
Go straight ahead	**Yāt jihk heui** 一直去
Go till end of road	**Hàahng dou jeuhn tàuh** 行到盡頭
Turn left	**Jyun jó** 轉左
Turn right	**Jyun yauh** 轉右
This is it/We're here.	**Nī douh jauh haih./Dou la.** 呢度就係。／到喇。

| Could you wait a minute for me, please? | **Hó yíh dáng ngóh yāt jahn ma?** 可以等我一陣嗎？ |
| How much do I owe you? | **Géi dō chín a?** 幾多錢呀？ |

6.10 Traveling out of Hong Kong

You can take the hydrofoil.	**Néih hó yíh daap séui yihk syùhn.** 你可以搭水翼船。
You can take the catamaran.	**Néih hó yíh daap sēung tái syùhn.** 你可以搭雙體船。
How much is the hydrofoil ticket?	**Séui yihk syùhn fēi géi dō chín a?** 水翼船飛幾多錢呀？
How much does it cost to go by train?	**Daap fó chē géi dō chín a?** 搭火車幾多錢呀？
What are the places of interest in Shenzhen/Macau?	**Sām Jan/Ngou Mún yáuh dī māt yéh deih fōng hóu wáan ā?** 深圳／澳門有啲乜嘢地方好玩呀？
In Shenzhen, there are…	**Sām Jan yáuh…** 深圳有⋯
–OCT East	**Dūng Bouh Wàh Kìuh Sìhng** 東部華僑城
–Splendid China	**Gám Sau Jung Wàh** 錦繡中華
–Window of the World	**Sai Gaai Jī Chēung** 世界之窗
–Lowu Commercial Center	**Lòh Wùh Sēung Yihp Sìhng** 羅湖商業城
In Macau, there are…	**Ngou Mún yáuh…** 澳門有⋯
–Lisbon Casino	**Pòuh Gīng Dóu Chèuhng** 葡京賭場
–Ruins of St. Paul's Cathedral	**Daaih Sāam Bā Pàaih Fōng** 大三巴牌坊
–Temple of Mahjou	**Mā Jóu Míu** 媽祖廟

7. A Place to Stay

7.1 General

Hong Kong offers accommodations for every budget, ranging from five-star hotels of international brands to backpacker-style of shared bunker-type rooms with common bathroom and toilet facilities. The YMCA, the YWCA, and the HKYHA offer accommodation similar to a three-star hotel, and price-conscious travelers can also find comfortable and clean rooms in guesthouses in Mong Kok (**Wohng Gok** 旺角), Yau Ma Tei (**Yàuh Màh Déi** 油麻地), Jordan (**Jó Dēun** 佐敦) and Tsuen Wan (**Chyùhn Wāan** 荃灣). You can also rent an entire apartment in the city from Airbnb or book your accommodation in advance via online booking sites.

My name is…	**Ngóh go méng giu...** 我個名叫…
I've made a reservation.	**Ngóh yíh gīng dehng jó fóng.** 我已經訂咗房。
How much is it per night?	**Nī gāan fóng jyuh yāt máahn géi dō chín a?** 呢間房住一晚幾多錢呀？
We'll be staying for a week.	**Ngóh deih dá syun jyuh yāt go sīng kèih.** 我哋打算住一個星期。
Is there any mail for me?	**Ngóh yáuh móuh seun a?** 我有冇信呀？
How long will you be staying?	**Néih wúih jyuh géi noih a?** 你會住幾耐呀？
I'm not sure how long I'm staying.	**Ngóh m̀h jī wúih jyuh géi noih.** 我唔知會住幾耐。

唐該你填呢張表格。	Fill out this form, please.
M̀h gōi néih tìhn nī jēung bíu gaak.	
唐該俾我睇吓你本護照。	Could I see your passport?
M̀h gōi béi ngóh tái háh néih bún wuh jiu.	
你需要俾按金。	You'll need to pay a deposit.
Néih sēui yiu béi ngon gām.	
你需要先俾錢。	You'll have to pay in advance.
Néih sēui yiu sīn béi chín.	

7.2 Hotels/hostels/budget accommodations

Booking

Do you have a single room available?	**Yáuh móuh yāt gāan dāan yàhn fóng a?** 有冇一間單人房呀？
I'd like a double room.	**Ngóh yiu yāt gāan sēung yàhn fóng.** 我要一間雙人房。
I'd like a room with twin beds.	**Ngóh yiu yāt gāan yáuh léuhng jēung dāan yàhn chòhng ge fóng.** 我要一間有兩張單人床嘅房。
I'd like a room with a bath tub.	**Ngóh yiu yāt gāan yáuh yuhk gōng ge fóng.** 我要一間有浴缸嘅房。
I'd like a room with a shower.	**Ngóh yiu yāt gāan yáuh fā sá ge fóng.** 我要一間有花洒嘅房。
I'd like a room with a balcony.	**Ngóh yiu yāt gāan yáuh yèuhng tòih ge fóng.** 我要一間有陽臺嘅房。
I'd like a suite.	**Ngóh yiu yāt gāan tou fóng.** 我要一間套房。
Does that include breakfast?	**Fòhng ga haih m̀h haih bāau kut jóu chāan a?** 房價係唔係包括早餐呀？
Does that include all three meals?	**Fòhng ga haih m̀h haih bāau kut sāam chāan a?** 房價係唔係包括三餐呀？

Does that include service charge?	**Fòhng ga haih m̀h haih bāau kut fuhk mouh fai a?** 房價係唔係包括服務費呀？
Could we have two adjoining rooms?	**Yáuh móuh léuhng gāan hái yāt chàih ge fóng a?** 有冇兩間喺一齊嘅房呀？
Could we have a room facing the front?	**Yáuh móuh yāt gāan deui jing chìhn mihn ge fóng a?** 有冇一間對正前面嘅房呀？
Could we have a room at the back?	**Yáuh móuh yāt gāan deui jing hauh mihn ge fóng a?** 有冇一間對正後面嘅房呀？
Could we have a room with a street view?	**Yáuh móuh yāt gāan deui jing daaih gāai ge fóng a?** 有冇一間對正大街嘅房呀？
Could we have a room with a river view?	**Yáuh móuh yāt gāan deui jing hòh ge fóng a?** 有冇一間對正河嘅房呀？
Could we have a room with a sea view?	**Yáuh móuh yāt gāan deui jing hói ge fóng a?** 有冇一間對正海嘅房呀？
Is there air conditioning in the room?	**Fóng yahp mihn yáuh móuh láahng hei a?** 房入面有冇冷氣呀？
Is there heating in the room?	**Fóng yahp mihn yáuh móuh nyún hei a?** 房入面有冇暖氣呀？
Is there a TV in the room?	**Fóng yahp mihn yáuh móuh dihn sih a?** 房入面有冇電視呀？
Is there a refrigerator in the room?	**Fóng yahp mihn yáuh móuh syut gwaih a?** 房入面有冇雪櫃呀？
Is there an electric water kettle in the room?	**Fóng yahp mihn yáuh móuh dihn séui wú a?** 房入面有冇電水壺呀？
Is there free Internet in the room?	**Fóng yahp mihn yáuh móuh míhn fai séuhng móhng a?** 房入面有冇免費上網呀？

Hotels

Is there an elevator in the hotel?	**Jáu dim yáuh móuh dihn tāi a?** 酒店有冇電梯呀？
Do you have room service?	**Yáuh móuh sung chāan ge fuhk mouh a?** 有冇送餐嘅服務呀？
When does the gate open?	**Géi dím hōi mùhn a?** 幾點開門呀？
When does the door close?	**Géi dím sāan mùhn a?** 幾點閂門呀？
Could I see the room?	**Ngóh hó yíh tái háh gāan fóng ma?** 我可以睇吓間房嗎？
I'll take this room.	**Ngóh jauh yiu nī gāan fóng.** 我就要呢間房。
We don't like this one.	**Ngóh m̀h jūng yi nī gāan.** 我唔鐘意呢間。
Do you have a larger room?	**Yáuh móuh daaih dī ge fóng a?** 有冇大啲嘅房呀？
Do you have a less expensive room?	**Yáuh móuh pèhng dī ge fóng a?** 有冇平啲嘅房呀？
What time is breakfast?	**Géi dím sihk jóu chāan a?** 幾點食早餐呀？
Where's the dining room?	**Chāan tēng hái bīn douh a?** 餐廳喺邊度呀？
Can I have breakfast in my room?	**Hó yíh hái fóng yahp mihn sihk jóu chāan ma?** 可以喺房入面食早餐嗎？
Where's the emergency exit/fire escape?	**Gán gāp/sīu fòhng tūng douh hái bīn douh a?** 緊急／消防通道喺邊度呀？
Where can I park my car?	**Hái bīn douh paak chē a?** 喺邊度泊車呀？
The key to room…, please.	**M̀h gōi béi…houh fóng ge só sìh ngóh.** 唔該俾…號房嘅鎖匙我。
Could you put this in the safe, please?	**M̀h gōi fong hái gaap maahn yahp mihn.** 唔該放喺夾萬入面。
Could you wake me at…tomorrow?	**M̀h gōi tīng yaht…dím giu séng ngóh.** 唔該聽日…點叫醒我。

Could you find a babysitter for me?	**Hó m̀h hó yíh bōng ngóh wán go bóu móuh a?** 可唔可以幫我搵個保姆呀？
Could you put in a cot?	**Hó m̀h hó yíh gā yāt jēung yīng yìh chòhng a?** 可唔可以加一張嬰兒床呀？
Could I have an extra blanket?	**M̀h gōi béi dō yāt jēung jīn ngóh.** 唔該俾多一張氈我。
What days does Housekeeping come in?	**Bīn yaht jāp fóng a?** 邊日執房呀？
When are the sheets/ towels changed?	**Dī chòhng dāan/mòuh gān géi sìh wuhn a?** 啲床單／毛巾幾時換呀？

唔該跟我嚟吖。 **M̀h gōi gān ngóh làih ā.**	This way please.
你(哋)間房…喺…樓，…號房 **Néih (deih) gāan fóng hái…láu,…houh fóng.**	Your room is on the… floor, number…
冇喇, 都住滿喇。 **Móuh la, dōu jyuh múhn la.**	No, they are all occupied.
廁所同沖涼房喺同一層／喺埋一間房。 **Chi só tùhng chūng lèuhng fóng hái tùhng yāt chàhng/hái màaih yāt gāan fóng.**	The toilet and shower are on the same floor/in the room.

7.3 Complaints

It's too noisy and we can't sleep.	**Taai chòuh la, ngóh deih fan m̀h jeuhk.** 太嘈喇，我哋瞓唔着。
Could you turn the radio down, please?	**M̀h gōi jēung sāu yām gēi gaau dāi yāt dī.** 唔該將收音機較低一啲。
We're out of toilet paper.	**Chi jí yuhng yùhn la.** 廁紙用完喇。
There aren't any…	**Móuh…la** 冇…喇
There's not enough…	**M̀h gau…** 唔夠…
The bed sheet is dirty.	**Chòhng dāan haih wū jōu ge.** 床單係污糟嘅。
The room hasn't been cleaned.	**Gāan fóng móuh jāp gwo.** 間房冇執過。

The heating isn't working.	**Nyúhn hei yáuh mahn tàih, dōu m̀h yiht gé.** 暖氣有問題，都唔熱嘅。
There's no hot water/ electricity.	**Móuh yiht séui/dihn la.** 冇熱水／電喇。
…doesn't work/is broken	**…m̀h yūk/waaih jó.** …唔郁／壞咗。
Could you fix that, please?	**M̀h gōi néih wán yàhn jíng háh.** 唔該你搵人整吓。
Could I have another room?	**Ngóh hó m̀h hó yíh yiu daih yih gāan fóng a?** 我可唔可以要第二間房呀？
The bed creaks terribly.	**Jēung chòhng hóu daaih sēng.** 張床好大聲。
The bed sags.	**Jēung chòhng nāp jó lohk heui.** 張床凹咗落去。
Could I have a board under the mattress?	**Hó m̀h hó yíh fong faai bán hái chòhng din hah mihn?** 可唔可以放塊板喺床墊下面？
This place is full of mosquitos/cockroaches.	**Nī douh jāu wàih dōu yáuh mān/gaaht jáat.** 呢度周圍都有蚊／甲由。

7.4 Departure

See also 8.2 Settling the bill

I'm leaving tomorrow.	**Ngóh tīng yaht jáu.** 我聽日走。
Where can I pay my bill, please?	**Chíng mahn heui bīn douh jáau sou a?** 請問去邊度找數呀？
My room number is…	**Ngóh gāan fóng ge houh máh haih…** 我間房嘅號碼係…
What time should we check out?	**Ngóh yīng gōi géi sìh teui fóng a?** 我應該幾時退房呀？
Could I have my deposit back, please?	**M̀h gōi béi fāan dehng gām ngóh.** 唔該俾番訂金我。
We're in a big hurry.	**Ngóh deih hóu gón sìh gaan.** 我哋好趕時間。

Could we leave our luggage here until we leave?	**Hó m̀h hó yíh fong dī hàhng léih hái douh, ngóh yāt jān fāan làih ló a?** 可唔可以放啲行李喺度，我一陣返嚟攞呀？
Thanks for your hospitality.	**Dō jeh néih deih ge yiht chìhng jīu doih.** 多謝你地嘅熱情招待。

7.5 Camping/Backpacking

Campsites in Hong Kong (including Big Wave Bay, Lantau Island and Tai Mo Shan Rotary Park campgrounds) are often free. Some of these also rent out tents and surfboards, and have restaurants, shower and toilet facilities and barbecue grills.

You can pick your own site.	**Néih hó yíh gáan néih jih géi ge yìhng deih.** 你可以揀你自己嘅營地。
You'll be allocated a site.	**Néih jēung wúih fān dóu yāt go yìhng deih.** 你將會分到一個營地。
This is your site number.	**Nī go haih néih ge yìhng deih houh máh.** 呢個係你嘅營地號碼。
Please stick this to your car.	**Chíng néih jēung nī jēung jing tip saht hái ga chē douh.** 請你張呢張證貼實喺架車度。
You must not lose this card.	**Néih yāt dihng m̀h hó yíh m̀h gin nī jēung jing.** 你一定唔可以唔見呢張證。
Where's the manager?	**Gīng léih hái bīn douh a?** 經理喺邊度呀？
Are we allowed to camp here?	**Ngóh deih hó m̀h hó yíh hái nī douh louh yìhng a?** 我哋可唔可以喺呢度露營呀？
There are three of us and we have two tents.	**Ngóh deih yáuh sāam go yàhn tùhng màaih léuhng go jeung pùhng.** 我哋有三個人同埋兩個帳篷。
Can we pick our own site?	**Ngóh deih hó m̀h hó yíh jih géi gáan yìhng deih a?** 我哋可唔可以自己揀營地呀？
Do you have any other sites available?	**Néih yáuh móuh kèih tā yìhng deih a?** 你有冇其他營地呀？

Do you have a quiet spot for us?	**Néih hó m̀h hó yíh béi go ngōn jihng ge yìhng deih ngóh deih a?** 你可唔可以畀個安靜嘅營地我哋呀?
It's too windy/sunny here.	**Nī douh taai daaih fūng/taai saai.** 呢度太大風／太曬。
It's too crowded here.	**Nī douh taai bīk.** 呢度太迫。
The ground's too hard/uneven.	**Go deih hah taai ngaahng/taai nāp daht.** 嗰地下太硬／太凹凸。
Do you have a more level spot?	**Yáuh móuh pìhng dī ge deih fōng a?** 有冇平啲嘅地方呀?
Could we have adjoining sites?	**Yáuh móuh sēung lìhn ge yìhng deih a?** 有冇相連嘅營地呀?
How much is it per person/tent/car?	**Múih go yàhn/go jeung pùhng/ga chē géi dō chín a?** 每個人／個帳篷／架車幾多錢呀?
Do you have chalets for hire?	**Néih yáuh móuh ngūk jái jōu a?** 你有冇屋仔租呀?
Are there any hot showers?	**Yáuh móuh yiht séui chūng lèuhng a?** 有冇熱水沖涼呀?
Are there any washing machines?	**Yáuh móuh sái yī gēi a?** 有冇洗衣機呀?
Is there a children's play area on the site?	**Nī go yìhng deih yáuh móuh yìh tùhng yàuh lohk chèuhng a?** 呢個營地有冇兒童遊樂場呀?
Are there covered cooking facilities on the site?	**Nī go yìhng deih yáuh móuh jyú sihk yuhng geuih a?** 呢個營地有冇煮食用具呀?
Are we allowed to barbecue here?	**Ngóh deih hó m̀h hó yíh hái douh sīu hāau a?** 我哋可唔可以喺度燒烤呀?
Are there any power outlets?	**Yáuh móuh dihn yùhn a?** 有冇電源呀?
Is there drinking water?	**Yáuh móuh yám yuhng séui a?** 有冇飲用水呀?

When's the garbage collected?	**Géi sìh sāu laahp saap a?** 幾時收垃圾呀?
Do you sell gas bottles?	**Néih deih yáuh móuh maaih jēun jōng hei a?** 你哋有冇賣樽裝氣呀?

Camping/backpacking equipment

(the diagram shows the numbered parts)

1	tool bag	**gūng geuih dói**	工具袋
2	gas cooker	**sehk yàuh hei lòuh**	石油氣爐
3	groundsheet	**deih bou**	地布
4	gas can	**sehk yàuh hei gun**	石油汽罐
5	folding chair	**jip dang**	摺凳
6	insulated picnic box	**bóu wān léui hàhng háp**	保溫旅行盒
7	airbed	**hei chòhng**	氣床
8	airbed pump	**hei bām**	氣泵
9	mat	**deih din**	地墊
10	saucepan	**pìhng dái wohk**	平底鑊
11	handle (pan)	**wohk beng**	鑊柄
12	backpack	**bui bāau**	背包
13	rope	**séng**	繩
14	storm lantern	**fohng fūng dāng**	防風燈
15	tent	**jeung pùhng**	帳篷
16	tent peg	**jeung pùhng gwaa ngāu**	帳篷掛鉤
17	tent pole	**jeung pùhng chyúh**	帳篷柱
18	water bottle	**séui jēun**	水樽
19	flashlight	**dihn túng**	電筒

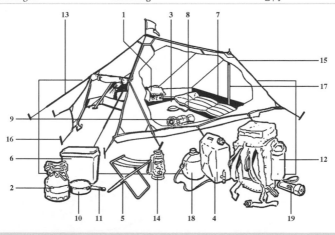

8. Money Matters

8.1 ATMs/Moneychangers
8.2 Settling the bill

In general, banks are open Monday to Friday from 9:00 a.m. to 5:00 p.m., Saturday from 9:00 a.m. to 1:00 p.m. Change money in hotels or moneychangers at the Hong Kong International Airport (HKIA), or at key tourist areas like Mongkok or Tsim Sha Tsui. Your passport is usually required for verification. ATMs are everywhere, and they provide 24-hour cash withdrawal facilities.

8.1 ATMs/Moneychangers

Where is the nearest ATM?	**Jeui káhn ge jih duhng gwaih yùhn gēi hái bīn douh a?** 最近嘅自動櫃員機喺邊度呀？
What are the charges for withdrawing money from this ATM?	**Hái jih duhng gwaih yùhn gēi ló chín, yiu béi māt yéh fai yuhng a?** 喺自動櫃員機攞錢，要俾乜嘢費用呀？
Can I withdraw money on my credit card here?	**Nī douh hó m̀h hó yíh yuhng seun yuhng kāat ló chín a?** 呢度可唔可以用信用卡攞錢呀？
What's the maximum amount?	**Yāt chi jeui dō hó yíh ló géi dō chín a?** 一次最多可以攞幾多錢呀？
What's the minimum amount?	**Yāt chi jeui síu yiu ló géi dō chín a?** 一次最少要攞幾多錢呀？
Can I get less than that?	**Hó m̀h hó yíh ló síu dī a?** 可唔可以攞少啲呀？
Can I get more than that?	**Hó m̀h hó yíh ló dō dī a?** 可唔可以攞多啲呀？
I'd like to change 100 pounds into Hong Kong dollars.	**Ngóh séung wuhn yāt baak Yīng bohng ge Góng baih.** 我想換一百英鎊嘅港幣。

I'd like to change 100 dollars into Hong Kong dollars.	**Ngóh séung wuhn yāt baak Méih gām ge Góng baih.** 我想換一百美金嘅港幣。
Could you write it down for me?	**Néih hó m̀h hó yíh sé dāi béi ngóh a?** 你可唔可以寫低俾我呀？
What's the exchange rate?	**Deui wuhn léut haih géi dō a?** 兌換率係幾多呀？
Could you give me some small bills?	**Néih hó m̀h hó yíh béi dī sáan jí ngóh a?** 你可唔可以俾啲散紙我呀？
This is not right.	**Nī douh m̀h ngāam sou.** 呢度唔啱數。

唔該喺呢度簽名。 **M̀h gōi hái nī douh chīm méng.**	Sign here, please.
唔該你填呢張表格。 **M̀h gōi néih tìhn nī jēung bíu gaak.**	Fill this out, please.
唔該俾我睇吓你嘅護照。 **M̀h gōi béi ngóh tái háh néih ge wuh jiu.**	Could I see your passport, please?
唔該俾我睇吓你嘅身分證。 **M̀h gōi béi ngóh tái háh néih ge sān fán jing.**	Could I see your identity card, please?
唔該俾我睇吓你嘅銀行卡／信用卡。 **M̀h gōi béi ngóh tái háh néih ge ngàhn hòhng kāat/seun yuhng kāat.**	Could I see your bank card/credit card, please?

8.2 Settling the bill

Could you put it on my bill?	**M̀h gōi yahp màaih ngóh jēung dāan gó douh.** 唔該入埋我張單嗰度。
Is everything included?	**Haih m̀h haih só yáuh yéh dōu bāau kut jó a?** 係唔係所有嘢都包括咗呀？
Is the tip included?	**Haih m̀h haih yíh gīng bāau kut jó tīp sí a?** 係唔係已經包括咗貼士呀？
Can I pay by credit card?	**Ngóh hó yíh yuhng seun yuhng kāat béi chín ma?** 我可以用信用卡俾錢嗎？

Can I pay with foreign currency?	**Ngóh hó yíh yuhng ngoih baih béi chín ma?** 我可以用外幣俾錢嗎？
You've given me too little change.	**Néih jáau síu jó chín béi ngóh la.** 你找少咗錢俾我喇。
You've given me too much change.	**Néih jáau dō jó chín béi ngóh la.** 你找多咗錢俾我喇。
Could you check this again, please?	**M̀h gōi néih joi sóu yāt háh.** 唔該你再數一下。
Could I have a receipt, please?	**M̀h gōi béi jēung sāu geui ngóh.** 唔該俾張收據我。
I don't have enough money on me.	**Ngóh daaih m̀h gau chín.** 我帶唔夠錢。
This tip is for you.	**Nī dī haih béi néih ge tīp sí.** 呢啲係俾你嘅貼士。
Keep the change.	**M̀h sái jáau.** 唔駛找。
Do you accept cash?	**Néih sāu m̀h sāu yihn gām a?** 你收唔收現金呀？
Do you accept autopay?	**Néih sāu m̀h sāu jih duhng jyún jeung a?** 你收唔收自動轉帳呀？
Do you accept Electronic Payment Services (EPS)?	**Néih sāu m̀h sāu Yih Baahn Sih a?** 你收唔收易辦事呀？
Do you accept Alipay?	**Néih sāu m̀h sāu Zī Fuh Bóu a?** 你收唔收支付寶呀？

對唔住，我哋唔收外幣。 **Deui m̀h jyuh, ngóh deih m̀h sāu ngoih baih.**	Sorry, we don't accept foreign currency.
對唔住，我哋唔收信用卡。 **Deui m̀h jyuh, ngóh deih m̀h sāu seun yuhng kāat.**	Sorry, we don't accept credit cards.

9. Mail, Phone and Internet

9.1 **Mail**
9.2 **Telephone**
9.3 **Internet/email**

Mail

Post offices are open Monday to Friday from 9:30 a.m. to 5:00 p.m. and half day on Saturday from 9:00 a.m. to 1:00 p.m. The cost of sending a letter for both surface and air mail depends on its weight. Postage stamps are also available in convenience stores all over Hong Kong.

post office **yàuh gúk** 郵局	envelope **seun fūng** 信封	money orders **dihn wuih/(yàuh jing gúk/ngàhn hòhng)/wuih piu** 電匯／(郵政局／銀行)／匯票
stamps **yàuh piu** 郵票	receiver **sāu gín yàhn** 收件人	registered item/packet **gwa houh yàuh gín/yàu bāau** 掛號郵件／郵包
parcels **bāau gwó** 包裹	sender **gei gín yàhn** 寄件人	EMS **yàuh jing chūk dàih fuhk mouh** 郵政速遞服務
address **deih jí** 地址	destination **muhk dīk deih** 目的地	

Where is the nearest post office?	**Jeui káhn ge yàuh gúk hái bīn douh a?** 最近嘅郵局喺邊度呀？
Where is the main post office?	**Yàuh jing júng gúk hái bīn douh a?** 郵政總局喺邊度呀？
Where is the nearest mail box?	**Jeui káhn ge seun sēung hái bīn douh a?** 最近嘅信箱喺邊度呀？
Which counter should I go to for general delivery?	**Ló yàuh gín heui bīn go gwaih tói a?** 攞郵件去邊個櫃檯呀？

| Is there any mail for me? | **Yáuh móuh ngóh ge seun a?**
有冇我嘅信呀？ |
| My name is… | **Ngóh giu…** 我叫… |

Stamps

What's the postage for a letter to the US?	**Gei bāau gwó dou Méih Gwok ge yàuh fai haih géi dō chín a?** 寄包裹到美國嘅郵費係幾多錢呀？
What's the postage for a postcard to the US?	**Gei mìhng seun pín dou Méih Gwok ge yàuh fai haih géi dō chín a?** 寄明信片到美國嘅郵費係幾多錢呀？
Are there enough stamps on it?	**Yàuh piu gau m̀h gau a?** 郵票夠唔夠呀？
I'd like [quantity] [value] stamps.	**Ngóh yiu…jēung…ge yàuh piu.** 我要…張…嘅郵票。
I'd like to send this by express mail.	**Ngóh séung gei faai yàuh.** 我想寄快郵。
I'd like to send this by air mail.	**Ngóh séung gei hūng yàuh.** 我想寄空郵。
I'd like to send this by registered mail.	**Ngóh séung gei gwa houh.** 我想寄掛號。
I'd like to send this by surface mail.	**Ngóh séung gei pìhng yàuh.** 我想寄平郵。
How many days will it take to send to the US?	**Gei heui Méih Gwok yiu géi dō yaht a?** 寄去美國要幾多日呀？
I'd like to EMS.	**Ngóh séung yiu yàuh jing chūk dàih fuhk mouh.** 我想要郵政速遞服務。
How much is it?	**Géi dō chín a?** 幾多錢呀？
This is what I want to EMS.	**Ngóh séung chūk dàih nī yéung yéh.** 我想速遞呢樣嘢。

Shall I fill out the form myself?	**Ngóh haih m̀h haih yiu jih géi tìhn bíu a?** 我係唔係要自己填表呀？
Can I make photocopies here?	**Nī douh yáuh móuh yíng yan a?** 呢度有冇影印呀？
How much is it per page?	**Yāt jēung géi dō chín a?** 一張幾多錢呀？

9.2 Telephone

Public telephones are still around in Hong Kong even though most people have their own smartphones. You can either dial overseas using Skype or Google Voice from your own smartphone (be sure to do this only when you have a high-speed Wi-Fi connection lest you rack up data costs) or from public telephones using either coins or phone cards, which can be purchased from convenience stores like 7-Eleven and have a value of HK$100. Follow the instructions on the payphone and dial either 001/007/0060/1666 depending on which company your phone card is from, followed by the relevant country code (USA 1), city code and number. To find a telephone number in Hong Kong, ring 1081. All operators speak English for English enquiries.

Is there a phone booth around here?	**Fuh gahn yáuh móuh gūng jung dihn wá a?** 附近有冇公眾電話呀？
May I use your phone, please?	**Ngóh hó yíh je yuhng néih ge dihn wá ma?** 我可以借用你嘅電話嗎？
Do you have a (city/region) phone directory?	**Yáuh móuh dihn wá bóu a?** 有冇電話簿呀？
Where can I get a phone card?	**Bīn douh hó yíh máaih dóu dihn wá kāat a?** 邊度可以買到電話卡呀？
Could you give me the international access code?	**M̀h gōi bōng ngóh chàh háh gwok jai dihn wá fuhk mouh ge houh máh?** 唔該幫我查吓國際電話服務嘅號碼？

Could you give me the country code?	**M̀h gōi bōng ngóh chàh háh gwok gā doih houh ā?** 唔該幫我查吓國家代號吖？
Could you give me the area code for Shenzhen?	**M̀h gōi bōng ngóh chàh háh Sām Zan ge kēui houh ā?** 唔該幫我查吓深圳嘅區號吖？
Could you check if this number is correct?	**M̀h gōi chàh háh nī go houh máh ngāam m̀h ngāam ā?** 唔該查吓呢個號碼啱唔啱吖？
Can I dial international (long distance) direct?	**Ngóh hó yíh jihk jip dá gwok jai chèuhng tòuh dihn wá ma?** 我可以直接打國際長途電話嗎？
Do I need to dial "0" first (before dialing out from the hotel)?	**Dá chéut heui yiu buht "lìhng" ma?** 打出去要撥"零"嗎？
Could you dial this number for me, please?	**M̀h gōi bōng ngóh dá nī go dihn wá.** 唔該幫我打呢個電話。
Could you put me through to extension…, please?	**M̀h gōi bōng ngóh jyún…houh fān gēi.** 唔該幫我轉…號分機。
I'd like to place a collect call.	**Ngóh séung dá yāt go chèuhng tòuh dihn wá, haih deui fōng béi chín ge.** 我想打一個長途電話，係對方俾錢嘅。
What's the charge per minute?	**Yāt fān jūng ge sāu fai haih géi dō chín a?** 一分鐘嘅收費係幾多錢呀？
Have there been any calls for me?	**Yáuh móuh yàhn dá gwo dihn wá béi ngóh a?** 有冇人打過電話俾我呀？

The conversation

Hello, this is…	**Wái, ngóh haih…** 喂，我係…
Who is this, please?	**Chíng mahn bīn wái?** 請問邊位？
Is this…?	**Néih haih m̀h haih…a?** 你係唔係…呀？
I'm sorry, I've dialed the wrong number.	**Deui m̀h jyuh, ngóh dá cho jó.** 對唔住，我打錯咗。

I can't hear you.	**Ngóh dēng m̀h chīng chó.** 我聽唔清楚。
I'd like to speak to…	**…hái m̀h hái douh a?** …喺唔喺度呀？

有人打電話俾你。 **Yáuh yàhn dá dihn wá béi néih.**	There's a phone call for you.
你要先撥"零"。 **Néih yiu sīn buht "lìhng".**	You have to dial "0" first.
唔該等一等。 **M̀h gōi dáng yāt dáng.**	One moment, please
冇人接電話。 **Móuh yàhn jip dihn wá.**	There's no answer.
有人講緊。 **Yáuh yàhn góng gán.**	The line's busy.
你想等吓嗎？ **Néih séung dáng háh ma?**	Do you want to hold?
唔好收線呀。 **M̀h hóu sāu sin a.**	Don't hang up.
我而家幫你接線。 **Ngóh yìh gā bōng néih jip sin.**	Connecting you.
你打錯喇。 **Néih dá cho la.**	You've got a wrong number.
佢唔喺(呢)度。 **Kéuih m̀h hái (nī)douh.**	He's/she's not here right now.
佢…點返嚟。 **Kéuih…dím fāan làih.**	He'll/she'll be back at…
呢個係…嘅留言信箱。 **Nī go haih…ge làuh yìhn seun sēung.**	This is the answering machine of…

Is there anybody who speaks English?	**Nī douh yáuh móuh yàhn sīk góng Yīng Mán a?** 呢度有冇人識講英文呀？
Extension…, please.	**M̀h gōi bōng ngóh jip…fān gēi.** 唔該幫我接…分機。
Could you ask him/her to call me back?	**Màh fàahn néih giu kéuih fūk ngóh dihn wá.** 麻煩你叫佢覆我電話。
My number's…	**Ngóh ge dihn wá houh máh haih…** 我嘅電話號碼係…
Could you tell him/her I called?	**M̀h gōi wah béi kéuih jī ngóh dá gwo dihn wá làih.** 唔該話俾佢知我打過電話嚟。
I'll call him/her back tomorrow.	**Ngóh tīng yaht joi dá dihn wá béi kéuih.** 我聽日再打電話俾佢。

Please send me a text message.	**Chíng néih béi go dyún seun ngóh.** 請你俾個短訊我。
I will send you a text message.	**Ngóh wúih béi go dyún seun néih.** 我會俾個短訊你。
Let's take a selfie!	**Ngóh deih wáan jih paak ā!** 我哋玩自拍吖!
The (phone) connection is not good; it keeps being cut off.	**Tìu dihn wá sin yáuh mahn tàih, yāt jihk tyúhn sin.** 條電話線有問題, 一直斷線。
What is your mobile number?	**Néih ge sáu gēi géi dō houh a?** 你嘅手機幾多號呀?
Do you have this app?	**Néih yáuh móuh nī go ying yuhng chìhng sīk a?** 你有冇呢个應用程式呀?
Do you have the Taobao app?	**Néih yáuh móuh Tòuh Bóu chìhng sīk a?** 你有冇淘寶程式呀?
Do you have the OpenRice app?	**Néih yáuh móuh Hōi Faahn Lāai chìhng sīk a?** 你有冇開飯啦程式呀?
Do you have the MTR app?	**Néih yáuh móuh góng tit chìhng sīk a?** 你有冇港鐵程式呀?
Do you have the translation app?	**Néih yáuh móuh fāan yihk ying yuhng chìhng sīk a?** 你有冇翻譯應用程式呀?
Do you have the group buy discounts/deals app?	**Néih yáuh móuh tyùhn kau ying yuhng chìhng sīk a?** 你有冇團購應用程式呀?
Do you have the fashion app?	**Néih yáuh móuh sìh zōng ying yuhng chìhng sīk a?** 你有冇時裝應用程式呀?

9.3 Internet/email

Hong Kong is one of the world's most 'connected' cities. Free Wi-Fi services are available at the Hong Kong International Airport as well as in many Wi-Fi hotspots. The prepaid Discover Hong Kong Tourist SIM Card offers free local calls, free Wi-Fi, mobile data, cheap international calls and SMS messages. There are many phone and Internet service providers in Hong Kong. Many mobile-phone and Internet packages are available, and it is worth shopping around for a package that suits your needs. A passport and proof of residence are necessary for all subscriptions, but not for a prepaid SIM card. Another alternative is to rent a portable Wi-Fi router, either from your home country or from Hong Kong.

Do you have a mobile phone?	**Néih yáuh móuh sáu gēi a?** 你有冇手機呀？
Do you have a portable Wi-Fi router (Wi-Fi egg)?	**Néih yáuh móuh làuh duhn séuhng móhng gēi (Wi Fi dáan) a?** 你有冇流動上網機(Wi-Fi 蛋) 呀？
Do you have a portable charger?	**Néih yáuh móuh chūng dihn hei a?** 你有冇充電器呀？
Do you have a charging cable?	**Néih yáuh móuh chūng dihn sin a?** 你有冇充電線呀？
Do you have a data SIM card?	**Néih yáuh móuh sou geui kāat a?** 你有冇數據卡呀？
Do you have Bluetooth?	**Néih yáuh móuh làahm ngàh a?** 你有冇藍牙呀？
Can I add you on Facebook?	**Hó yíh gā néih yahp Mihn Syū ma?** 可以加你入面書嗎？
Can I add you on WeChat?	**Hó yíh gā néih yahp Mèih Seun ma?** 可以加你入微信嗎？
Can I add you on Twitter?	**Hó yíh gā néih yahp Tēui Dahk ma?** 可以加你入推特嗎？
Any free Wi-Fi here?	**Nī douh yáuh móuh míhn fai mòuh sin séuhng móhng a?** 呢度有冇免費無線上網呀？
Where is the nearest free Wi-Fi hotspot?	**Jeui káhn ge míhn fai mòuh sin séuhng móhng dím hái bīn douh a?** 最近嘅免費無線上網點喺邊度呀？

I'd like to buy a Discover Hong Kong Tourist SIM card.

Ngóh yiu yāt jēung Hēung Góng Yahm Jūng Wàahng chyúh jihk kāat.
我要一張香港任縱橫儲值卡。

For five or eight days?

Ngh yaht dihng haih baat yaht a?
五日定係八日呀？

How much are they?

Haih géi dō chín a? 係幾多錢呀？

$88 for five days and $118 for eight days.

Ngh yaht haih baat sahp baat māan, baat yaht haih yāt baak yāt sahp baat māan.
五日係88蚊，八日係118蚊。

What does a five-day card include?

Ngh yaht chyúh jihk kāat bāau māt yéh a?
五日儲值卡包乜嘢呀？

It includes 1.5GB local data, unlimited local calls and unlimited Wi-Fi for five days.

Bāau yāt dím ngh gīk bún deih sou geui, ngh yaht mòuh haahn bún deih tūng wah tùhng mòuh haahn séuhng móhng.
包1.5激本地數據，五日無限本地通話同無限上網。

You can also use it for international calls, local and overseas SMS.

Néih juhng hó yíh dá chèuhng tòuh dihn wá, faat bún deih tùhng ngoih deih dyún seun. 你仲可以打長途電話，發本地同外地短訊。

You can check the rates online.

Néih hó yíh séuhng móhng tài sāu fai.
你可以上網睇收費。

How do I top up?

Dím yéung jāng jihk a? 點樣增值呀？

You can buy a recharge voucher at a convenience store.

Néih hó yíh hái bihn leih dim máaih jēung jāng jihk gyun.
你可以喺便利店買張增值券。

Or use a credit card to top up online.

Waahk jé yuhng seun yuhng kāat hái móhng seuhng jāng jihk.
或者用信用卡喺網上增值。

If you go outside Hong Kong, remember to turn off the data roaming It's very expensive.	**Néih chēut Hēung Góng, gei dāk sāan sou geui maahn yàuh gūng nahng. Hóu gwai ga.** 你出香港，記得閂數據漫遊功能。好貴㗎。
I cannot get on the Internet.	**Ngóh séuhng m̀h dóu móhng.** 我上唔到網。
You can find it on Google.com.	**Néih hó yíh heui Gūk Gō wáhn.** 你可以去谷歌搵。
Do you have a wireless connection here?	**Nī douh yáuh móuh mòuh sin séuhng móhng a?** 呢度有冇無線上網呀？
Do I need a password to connect to the Internet?	**Ngóh sái m̀h sái yuhng maht máh lìhn sin a?** 我使唔使用密碼連線呀？
The Internet is very fast.	**Go móhng hóu faai.** 個網好快。
The Internet is very slow.	**Go móhng hóu maahn.** 個網好慢。
Do you use Facebook?	**Néih yáuh móuh yuhng Mihn Syū a?** 你有冇用面書呀？
What is your blog address?	**Néih ge móhng ji deih jí haih māt yéh a?** 你嘅網誌地址係乜嘢呀？
I saved my (digital) photos in my computer.	**Ngóh jēung ngóh dī (sou máh) séung chóuh hái dihn nóuh yahp mihn.** 我將我啲(數碼)相儲喺電腦入面。
I will email you these photos.	**Ngóh wúih jēung nī dī séung dihn yàuh béi néih.** 我會將呢啲相電郵俾你。

10. Shopping

All shops in Hong Kong are open seven days a week. Corner shops are open from 7:00 a.m. till 10:00 p.m. Most supermarkets are open from 8:00 a.m. till 10:00 p.m., and some even open for 24 hours. Most department stores are open from 11:00 a.m. till 10:00 p.m. Convenience stores like 7-11 and Circle K open 24 hours a day all year round.

grocery shop **jaahp fo póu** 雜貨舖	stationery shop **màhn geuih dim** 文具店	fruit shop **sāang gwó póu** 生果舖
supermarket **chīu kāp síh chèuhng/chīu síh** 超級市場／超市	watches and clocks **jūng bīu dim** 鐘錶店	barber's **fēi faat póu** 飛髮舖
department store **baak fo gūng sī** 百貨公司	optical shop **ngáahn géng dim** 眼鏡店	hairdresser **léih faat sī** 理髮師
convenience store **bihn leih dim** 便利店	camera shop **sip yíng hei chòih dim** 攝影器材店	book shop **syū dim** 書店
laundry **sái yī dim** 洗衣店	clothing shop **fuhk jōng dim** 服裝店	toy shop **wuhn geuih dim** 玩具店
dry cleaner **gōn sái dim** 乾洗店	bread/cake shop **béng póu** 餅舖	costume jewelry **fuhk sīk dim** 服飾店
sporting goods **wahn duhng yuhng bán (dim)** 運動用品(店)	herbalist's shop **yeuhk chòih póu** 藥材舖	footwear **hàaih póu** 鞋舖

household goods	pharmacy	wet market
gā tìhng yuhng bán (dim)	**yeuhk fòhng**	**gāai síh**
家庭用品(店)	藥房	街市

household appliances	greengrocer	goldsmith
gā yuhng dihn hei dim	**sō choi séui gwó dim**	**gām póu**
家用電器店	蔬菜水果店	金舖

music shop (CDs, tapes, etc)	perfumery	newsstand
yām héuhng dim	**hēung séui dim**	**bou jí tāan**
音響店	香水店	報紙攤

leather goods	ice cream shop	beauty salon
pèih gaak yuhng bán (dim)	**syut gōu dim**	**méih yùhng Yún**
皮革用品(店)	雪糕店	美容院

household linen shop	confectioner's	florist
chòhng dāan tói bou dim	**tòhng gwó dim**	**fā dim**
床單檯布店	糖果店	花店

jeweler	delicatessen	fishmonger
jyū bóu sēung	**ngāu sīk jaahp fo póu**	**yùh póu**
珠寶商	歐式雜貨舖	魚舖

cosmetics shop	butcher's shop	
fa jōng bán dim	**yuhk póu**	
化妝品店	肉舖	

10.1 Shopping conversations

Where can I get…?	**Bīn douh hó yíh máaih dóu…a?**
	邊度可以買到…呀？

When is this shop open?	**Nī gāan pou táu géi dím hōi mùhn a?**
	呢間舖頭幾點開門呀？

Could you tell me where the…department is?	**Chíng mahn…bouh mùhn hái bīn douh a?**
	請問…部門喺邊度呀？

Could you help me, please?	**Màh fàahn néih bōng háh ngóh…?**
	麻煩你幫吓我…？

| I'm looking for… | **Ngóh wán…** 我搵… |

| Do you sell English language newspapers? | **Néih deih maaih m̀h maaih Yīng Màhn bou jí a?** 你哋賣唔賣英文報紙呀？ |

買啲乜嘢呢？ **Máaih dī māt yéh nē?** What do you want to buy?

仲要啲乜嘢呢？ **Juhng yiu dī māt yéh nē?** Would you like anything else?

I want to buy…	**Ngóh séung máaih…** 我想買…
I'm just looking.	**Ngóh tái háh jēk.** 我睇吓唧。
Yes, I'd also like…	**Ngóh juhng yiu…** 我仲要…
No, thank you. That's all.	**Jauh haih gam dō, m̀h gōi.** 就係咁多,唔該。
Could you show me…?	**M̀h gōi ló…béi ngóh tái háh.** 唔該攞…俾我睇吓。
I'd prefer…	**Ngóh jūng yi…** 我鐘意…
This is not what I'm looking for.	**Nī dī m̀h haih ngóh yiu ge.** 呢啲唔係我要嘅。
It's too expensive.	**Taai gwai la.** 太貴喇。
It's okay, I'll keep looking.	**Móuh só waih, ngóh gai juhk wán.** 冇所謂, 我繼續搵。
Do you have something less expensive?	**Yáuh móuh pèhng dī ge?** 有冇平啲嘅？
Do you have something smaller?	**Yáuh móuh sai dī ge?** 有冇細啲嘅？
Do you have something larger?	**Yáuh móuh daaih dī ge?** 有冇大啲嘅？
I'll take this one.	**Ngóh jauh yiu nī go.** 我就要呢個。
Does it come with instructions?	**Yáuh móuh syut mìhng syū a?** 有冇說明書呀？
I'll give you…	**Ngóh béi néih…mān.** 我俾你…蚊。
Could you keep this for me?	**Hó m̀h hó yíh bōng ngóh bóu chyùhn yat háh?** 可唔可以幫我保存一吓？

I'll come back for it later.	**Ngóh yāt jahn gāan fāan làih ló.** 我一陣間返嚟攞。
Do you have a bag for me, please?	**M̀h gōi béi go dói ngóh.** 唔該俾個袋我。
Could you gift wrap it, please?	**M̀h gōi bōng ngóh bāau hóu kéuih.** 唔該幫我包好佢。

對唔住, 我哋冇呢種。 **Deui m̀h jyuh, ngóh deih móuh nī júng.**	I'm sorry, we don't have that.
對唔住, 賣哂喇。 **Deui m̀h jyuh, maaih saai la.**	I'm sorry, we're sold out.
對唔住, 要等到…先至有貨。 **Deui m̀h jyuh, yiu dáng dou…sīn ji yáuh fo.**	I'm sorry, it won't come back in until…
唔該去收銀處俾錢。 **M̀h gōi heui sāu ngán chyu béi chín.**	Please pay at the cash register.
我哋唔接受信用卡。 **Ngóh deih m̀h jip sauh seun yuhng kāat.**	We don't accept credit cards.
我哋唔接受外幣。 **Ngóh deih m̀h jip sauh ngoih baih .**	We don't accept foreign currency.

10.2 Food

I'd like a pound of spare ribs.	**Ngóh yiu yāt bohng pàaih gwāt.** 我要一磅排骨。
I'd like a kilo of pork chops.	**Ngóh yiu yāt gūng gān jyū páa.** 我要一公斤豬扒。
I'd like a catty of chicken wings.	**Ngóh yiu yāt gān gāi yihk.** 我要一斤雞翼。
I'd like a catty of barbecued pork.	**Ngóh yiu yāt gān chā sīu.** 我要一斤叉燒。
I'd like half a chicken.	**Ngóh yiu bun jek gāi.** 我要半隻雞。

I'd like one roast goose.　　**Ngóh yiu yāt jek sīu ngòh.**
我要一隻燒鵝。

I'd like half a pound.　　**Ngóh yiu bun bohng.** 我要半磅。

Could you cut it up　　**M̀h gōi bōng ngóh chit hōi.**
for me, please?　　唔該幫我切開。

Can I order it?　　**Hó m̀h hó yíh dehng kau a?**
可唔可以訂購呀？

I'll pick it up tomorrow.　　**Ngóh tīng yaht làih ló.** 我聽日嚟攞。

Can you eat this?　　**Sihk m̀h sihk dāk ga?** 食唔食得㗎？

Can you drink this?　　**Yám m̀h yám dāk ga?** 飲唔飲得㗎？

What's in it?　　**Yahp bihn yáuh dī māt yéh a?**
入邊有啲乜嘢呀？

10.3　Clothing and shoes

I saw a dress in the　　**Ngóh hái chyùh chēung gó douh**
display window.　　**tái dóu yāt gihn sāam.**
我喺櫥窗嗰度睇到一件衫。

Shall I point it out?　　**Ngóh jí béi néih tái, hóu m̀h hóu a?**
我指俾你睇，好唔好呀？

I'd like something to go　　**Ngóh séung wán go pui nī go ge.**
with this.　　我想搵個配呢個嘅。

Do you have shoes to　　**Yáuh móuh pui nī gihn sāam ge hàaih?**
match this dress?　　有冇配呢件衫嘅鞋？

I'm a size 10 in the U.S.　　**Ngóh jeuk Méih Gwok sahp houh ge.**
我著美國十號嘅。

I'd like a large size.　　**Ngóh séung yiu daaih máh.**
我想要大碼。

I'd like an extra large size.　　**Ngóh séung yiu gā daaih máh.**
我想要加大碼。

I'd like a medium size.　　**Ngóh séung yiu jūng máh.** 我想要中碼。

I'd like a small size.	**Ngóh séung yiu sai máh.** 我想要細碼。
I'd like an extra small size.	**Ngóh séung yiu gā sai máh.** 我想要加細碼。
Can I try this on?	**Ngóh hó yíh jeuk háh ma?** 我可以著吓嗎？
Where's the fitting room?	**Si sān sāt hái bīn douh a?** 試身室喺邊度呀？
It doesn't suit me.	**Nī gihn sāam m̀h ngāam ngóh.** 呢件衫唔啱我。
It is too loose.	**Nī gihn taai sūng.** 呢件太鬆。
It is too tight.	**Nī gihn taai gán.** 呢件太緊。
It is too long.	**Nī gihn taai chèuhng.** 呢件太長。
It is too short.	**Nī gihn taai dyún.** 呢件太短。
This is the right size.	**Nī go sāai sí ngāam ngāam hóu.** 呢個晒士啱啱好。
It doesn't look good on me.	**Ngóh jeuk héi làih m̀h hóu tái.** 我著起嚟唔好睇。
Do you have these in any other colors?	**Nī dī yáuh móuh kèih tāa ngàan sīk ga?** 呢啲有冇其他顏色㗎？
The heel's too high.	**Hàaih jāang taai gōu la.** 鞋踭太高啦。
The heel's too low.	**Hàaih jāang taai ngái la.** 鞋踭太矮啦。
Is this real leather?	**Haih m̀h haih jān péi làih ga?** 係唔係真皮嚟㗎？
Is this genuine hide?	**Haih m̀h haih jān ge sau pèih làih ga?** 係唔係真嘅獸皮嚟㗎？
I'm looking for a shirt for a four-year-old child.	**Ngóh séung wán gihn sēut sāam sung béi yāt go sei seui ge sai mān jái.** 我想搵件恤衫送俾一個四歲嘅細蚊仔。
I'd like a silk blouse.	**Ngóh yiu yāt gihn jān sī ge néuih jōng sēut sāam**. 我要一件真絲嘅女裝恤衫。

I'd like a cotton shirt.	**Ngóh yiu yāt gihn mìhn ge sēut sāam.** 我要一件綿嘅恤衫。
I'd like a woolen jacket.	**Ngóh yiu yāt gihn yèuhng mòuh ge ngoih tou.** 我要一件羊毛嘅外套。
I'd like a pair of linen pants.	**Ngóh yiu yāt tìuh màh bou ge fu.** 我要一條麻布嘅褲。
At what temperature should I wash it?	**Yīng gōi yuhng géi nyúhn ge séui làih sái a?** 應該用幾暖嘅水嚟洗呀？
Will it shrink in the wash?	**Wúih m̀h wúih sūk séui ga?** 會唔會縮水㗎？

手洗 **Sáu sái** Hand wash	勿用熨斗熨 **Maht yuhng tong dáu tong** Do not iron	勿用乾衣機 **Maht yuhng gōn yī gēi** Do not spin dry
乾洗 **Gōn sái** Dry clean	可用洗衣機洗 **Hóh yuhng sái yī gēi sái.** Machine washable	平放 **Pìhng fong** Lay flat

At the cobbler

Could you mend these shoes?	**Nī deui hàaih hó m̀h hó yíh bóu a?** 呢對鞋可唔可以補呀？
Could you resole these shoes?	**Nī deui hàaih hó m̀h hó yíh dá jéung a?** 呢對鞋可唔可以打掌呀？
Could you reheel these shoes?	**Nī deui hàaih hó m̀h hó yíh wuhn jāang a?** 呢對鞋可唔可以換踭呀？
When will they be ready?	**Géi sìh hó yíh làih ló a?** 幾時可以嚟攞呀？
I'd like a can of shoe polish, please.	**Ngóh séung yiu yāt hahp hàaih yáu.** 我想要一盒鞋油。
I'd like a pair of shoe-laces, please.	**Ngóh séung yiu yāt deui hàaih dái.** 我想要一對鞋帶。
I'd like an insole, please.	**Ngóh séung yiu yāt go hàaih din.** 我想要一個鞋墊。

| I'd like a pair of gel cushions, please. | **Ngóh séung yiu yāt deui yìhng gāau din.**
我想要一對凝膠墊。 |

10.4 Photographs and videos

I'd like to look at the digital cameras.	**Ngóh séung tái háh dī sou máh séung gēi.** 我想睇吓啲數碼相機。
I'd like to look at the video cameras.	**Ngóh séung tái háh dī luhk yíng gēi.** 我想睇吓啲錄影機。
Do you sell selfie sticks?	**Yáuh móuh maaih jih paak gwan a?** 有冇賣自拍棍呀？
I'd like batteries for this (digital) camera.	**Ngóh séung pui nī fún (sou máh) séung gēi ge dihn chìh.** 我想配呢款(數碼)相機嘅電池。
I'd like a 64GB memory card please.	**Ngóh séung yiu yāt jēung luhk sahp sei gīk ge gei yīk kāat, m̀h gōi.** 我想要一張64激嘅記憶卡, 唔該。
Two AA batteries, please.	**Léuhng lāp yih A dihn chìh, m̀h gōi.** 兩粒2A電池, 唔該。
May I have a USB flash drive?	**Ngóh séung yiu yāt go USB gei yīk pùn.** 我想要一個USB記憶盤。
Please scan the document and email it to me.	**M̀h gōi sou miù fahn màhn gín yìhn hauh dihn yàuh béi ngóh.** 唔該掃描份文件然後電郵俾我。

Problems

Because the size of the photo is too big, I have to compress it.	**Yān waih jēung séung taai daaih, só jíh yāt dihng yiu ngaat sūk.** 因為張相太大, 所以一定要壓縮。
Please delete the photo.	**M̀h gōi sāan chèuih jēung séung.** 唔該刪除張相。
Please copy the photo.	**M̀h gōi fūk yan jēung séung.** 唔該複印張相。

Can you put in the batteries for me, please?	**Hó m̀h hó yíh bōng ngóh yahp dihn chìh, m̀h gōi?** 可唔可以幫我入電池, 唔該?
Should I replace the batteries?	**Sái m̀h sái wuhn dihn chìh a?** 駛唔駛換電池呀？
Could you have a look at my camera, please?	**M̀h gōi bōng ngóh tái háh séung gēi yáuh móuh waaih.** 唔該幫我睇吓相機有冇壞。
It's not working	**Waaih jó** 壞咗
The...is broken	**...waaih jó** …壞咗
The camera memory is full.	**Séung gēi ge gei yīk kāat múhn saai.** 相機嘅記憶咭滿晒。
I need to change the memory card.	**Ngóh yiu wuhn gwo yāt jēung gei yīk kāat.** 我要換過一張記憶咭。
The flash isn't working.	**Sím gwōng dāng waaih jó.** 閃光燈壞咗。
My computer ran out of battery.	**Ngóh ge dihn nóuh móuh dihn chìh la.** 我嘅電腦冇電池啦。
The computer has a hardware problem.	**Nī bouh dihn nóuh ge ngaahng gín yáuh mahn tàih.** 呢部電腦嘅硬件有問題。
The computer has a software problem.	**Nī bouh dihn nóuh ge yúhn gín yáuh mahn tàih.** 呢部電腦嘅軟件有問題。

Processing and prints

I'd like to print these pictures, please.	**Ngóh séung saai séung.** 我想晒相。
I'd like two glossy prints for each of these pictures.	**Ngóh séung múih jēung séung saai léuhng jēung gwōng mín ge.** 我想每張相晒兩張光面嘅。
I'd like two matte prints for each of these pictures.	**Ngóh séung múih jēung séung saai léuhng jēung yúng mín ge.** 我想每張相晒兩張絨面嘅。

I'd like two 6 x 9 prints for each of these pictures.	**Ngóh séung múih jēung séung saai léuhng jēung luhk chyun sìhng gáu chyun ge.** 我想每張相晒兩張六寸乘九寸嘅。
I'd like 4R/5R prints.	**Ngóh séung saai sei R/ngh R séung.** 我想晒4R／5R相。
I'd like to order reprints of these photos.	**Ngóh séung joi saai nī dī séung.** 我想再晒呢啲相。
I'd like to have this photo enlarged.	**Ngóh séung fong daaih nī jēung séung.** 我想放大呢張相。
How much is processing?	**Chūng saai yiu géi dō chín a?** 沖晒要幾多錢呀？
How much is printing?	**Saai séung yiu géi dō chín a?** 晒相要幾多錢呀？
How much are the reprints?	**Joi saai yiu géi dō chín a?** 再晒要幾多錢呀？
How much is it for enlargement?	**Fong daaih yiu géi dō chín a?** 放大要幾多錢呀？
When will they be ready?	**Géi sìh hó yíh ló séung a?** 幾時可以攞相呀？

10.5 At the hairdresser

Do I have to make an appointment?	**Sái m̀h sái yuh yeuk a?** 駛唔駛預約呀？
Can I come in right now?	**Yìh gā làih dāk m̀h dāk a?** 而家嚟得唔得呀？
How long is the wait?	**Yiu dáng géi noih a?** 要等幾耐呀？
I'd like a shampoo.	**Ngóh séung sái tàuh.** 我想洗頭。
I'd like a haircut.	**Ngóh séung jín faat.** 我想剪髮。
I'd like a scalp treatment.	**M̀h gōi ngóh séuhng ngon mō tàuh pèih.** 唔該我想按摩頭皮。

I'd like a perm.	**Ngóh séung dihn faat.** 我想電髮。
I'd like a shampoo for oily hair, please.	**Ngóh séung sái tàuh. Ngóh dī tàuh faat hóu yàuh.** 我想洗頭。我啲頭髮好油。
I'd like a shampoo for dry hair, please.	**Ngóh séung sái tàuh. Ngóh dī tàuh faat hóu gōn.** 我想洗頭。我啲頭髮好乾。
I'd like an anti-dandruff shampoo.	**Ngóh séung sái tauh, m̀h gōi yuhng heui tàuh pèih ge sái faat séui.** 我想洗頭，唔該用去頭皮嘅洗髮水。
I'd like a color-rinse shampoo, please.	**Ngóh séung sái tauh, m̀h gōi yuhng bóu sīk ge sái faat séui.** 我想洗頭，唔該用保色嘅洗髮水。
I'd like a 2 in 1 shampoo with conditioner, please.	**Ngóh séung sái tauh, m̀h gōi yuhng yih hahp yāt ge sái faat séui.** 我想洗頭，唔該用二合一嘅洗髮水。
I'd like highlights, please.	**M̀h gōi gā dī hín ngáahn ge ngàahn sīk.** 唔該加啲顯眼嘅顏色。
I'd like to dye my hair.	**Ngóh séung yìhm tauh faat.** 我想染頭髮。
Do you have a color chart, please?	**Néih deih yáuh móuh sīk póu a?** 你哋有冇色譜呀？
I'd like to keep the same color.	**Ngóh séung bóu chìh yāt yéung ge ngàahn sīk.** 我想保持一樣嘅顏色。
I'd like it darker.	**Ngóh séung sām sīk yāt dī.** 我想深色一啲。
I'd like it lighter.	**Ngóh séung chín sīk yāt dī.** 我想淺色一啲。
I'd like hairspray.	**Ngóh séung pan dihng yìhng gāau.** 我想噴定型膠。
I don't want hairspray.	**Ngóh m̀h séung pan dihng yìhng gāau.** 我唔想噴定型膠。
I'd like gel.	**Ngóh yiu faat laahp.** 我要髮蠟。
I'd like shampoo.	**Ngóh yiu sái faat séui.** 我要洗髮水。

I'd like conditioner. **Ngóh yiu wuh faat louh.** 我要護髮露。

I'd like short bangs. **Ngóh yiu dyún ge làuh hói.**
我要短嘅劉海。

Not too short at the back. **M̀h gōi hauh mihn dī tàuh faat m̀h hóu
jín dāk taai dyún.**
唔該後面啲頭髮唔好剪得太短。

Not too long. **M̀h hóu jín dāk taai chèuhng.**
唔好剪得太長。

I'd like it curly. **M̀h gōi bōng ngóh dihn lyūn dī.**
唔該幫我電攣啲。

I'd like it not too curly. **M̀h gōi bōng ngóh dihn lyūn síu síu.**
唔該幫我電攣少少。

It needs a little taken off. **M̀h gōi bōng ngóh jín síu síu.**
唔該幫我剪少少。

It needs a lot taken off. **M̀h gōi bōng ngóh jín dō dī.**
唔該幫我剪多啲。

I'd like a completely
different style. **M̀h gōi bōng ngóh jín daih yih go
faat yìhng.** 唔該幫我剪第二個髮型。

I'd like it the same as in
this photo. **M̀h gōi bōng ngóh jín nī jēung séung yāt
yeuhng ge faat yìhng.**
唔該幫我剪呢張相一樣嘅髮型。

I'd like it the same
as that woman's. **M̀h gōi bōng ngóh jín nī wái néuih sih
yāt yeuhng ge faat yìhng.**
唔該幫我剪呢位女士一樣嘅髮型。

Could you turn the
drier up a bit? **M̀h gōi jēung go fūng túhng hōi
daaih dī.** 唔該將個風筒開大啲。

Could you turn the
drier down a bit? **M̀h gōi jēung go fūng túhng hōi sai dī.**
唔該將個風筒開細啲。

How do you want it cut? **Néih séung dím yéung jín a?**
你想點樣剪呀？

你想剪乜嘢髮型呀?
Néih séung jín māt yéh faat yìhng a?

What style did you have in mind?

你想染乜嘢顏色呀?
Néih séung yíhm māt yéh ngàahn sīk a?

What color did you want it?

溫度啱唔啱呀?
Wān douh ngāam m̀h ngāam a?

Is the temperature all right for you?

你想睇啲乜嘢雜誌呀?
Néih séung tái dī māt yéh jaahp ji a?

Would you like something to read?

你想飲啲乜嘢呀?
Néih séung yám dī māt yéh a?

Would you like a drink?

I'd like a facial.	**Ngóh séung jouh go mihn mók.** 我想做個面膜。
I'd like a manicure.	**Ngóh séung sāu jí gaap.** 我想修指甲。
I'd like a pedicure.	**Ngóh séung sāu geuk gaap.** 我想修腳甲。
I'd like a massage.	**Ngóh séung jouh go ngon mō.** 我想做個按摩。
Could you trim my bangs, please?	**M̀h gōi bōng ngóh sāu háh làuh hói.** 唔該幫我修吓劉海。
Could you trim my beard, please?	**M̀h gōi bōng ngóh sāu háh wùh sōu.** 唔該幫我修吓鬍鬚。
Could you trim my moustache, please?	**M̀h gōi bōng ngóh sāu háh yih pit gāi.** 唔該幫我修吓二撇雞。
I'd like a shave, please.	**M̀h gōi bōng ngóh tai sōu.** 唔該幫我剃鬚。
I'd like a wet shave, please.	**M̀h gōi bōng ngóh yuhng séui tai sōu.** 唔該幫我用水剃鬚。

11. Tourist Activities

11.1   Places of interest
11.2   Going out
11.3   Booking tickets

You can find a fair bit of travel information about Hong Kong on the Internet. One useful site is http://discoverhongkong.com. The Hong Kong Tourism Board (HKTB) offers a Visitor Hotline: +852 2508 1234 which is available from 9am to 6pm daily. HKTB also operates a few visitor centres which provide information about all the sights, sounds and happenings in Hong Kong. The **Hong Kong International Airport Visitor Centre** is located at Buffer Halls A and B, Arrivals Level, Terminal 1. The Hong Kong Island Visitor Centre is at The Peak Piazza, and the Kowloon Visitor Centre is at the Star Ferry Concourse, Tsim Sha Tsui. You can go to the above centers and ask for information about tourist spots and day trips. Your hotel information desk can also introduce you to a range of tourist agencies to help plan your holiday.

11.1 Places of interest

老襯亭
Lóuh Chan Tìhng
Peak Pavilion (Victoria Peak)

山頂
Sāan Déng
Victoria Peak

快活谷
Faai Wuht Gūk
Happy Valley (Hong Kong
  Jockey Club)

淺水灣
Chín Séui Wāan
Repulse Bay

香港文化中心
Hēung Góng Màhn Fa Jūng Sām
Hong Kong Cultural Center

海洋公園
Hói Yèuhng Gūng Yún
Ocean Park

迪士尼樂園
Dihk Sī Nèih Lohk Yùhn
Disneyland

赤柱街市
Chek Chyúh Gāai Síh
Stanley Market

香港會展中心
Hēung Góng Wuih Jín Jūng Sām
Hong Kong Conference and
  Exhibition Center

香港仔海鮮坊
Hēung Góng Jái Hói Sīn Fóng
Floating Seafood Restaurant
  (Aberdeen)

香港藝術館
Hēung Góng Ngaih Seuht Gwún
Hong Kong Museum of Art

三棟屋
Sāam Duhng Ngūk
Hakka Museum

香港太空館
Hēung Góng Taai Hūng Gwún
Hong Kong Space Museum

志蓮淨苑
Ji Lìhn Jihng Yún
Chilin Nunnery

寶蓮寺
Bóu Lìhn Jí
Po Lin Buddhist Temple

蘭桂坊
Làahn Gwai Fōng
Lan Kwai Fong

Where's the Tourist Information Centre, please?	**Chíng mahn léuih haak jī sēun jūng sām hái bīn douh a?** 請問旅客諮詢中心喺邊度呀？
What are the places of interest in Hong Kong?	**Hēung Góng yáuh māt yéh deih fōng hóu wáan ā?** 香港有乜嘢地方好玩呀？
I'd like to visit the countryside.	**Ngóh séung heui gāau ngoih tái háh.** 我想去郊外睇吓。
I'd like to visit Wong Tai Sin Temple.	**Ngóh séung heui Wòhng Daaih Sin Míu tái háh.** 我想去黃大仙廟睇吓。
I'd like to visit Apliu Street.	**Ngóh séung heui Aap Lìuh Gāai tái háh.** 我想去鴨寮街睇吓。
I'd like to visit Temple Street.	**Ngóh séung heui Míu Gāai tái háh.** 我想去廟街睇吓。
I'd like to visit Women Street.	**Ngóh séung heui Néuih Yán Gāai tái háh.** 我想去女人街睇吓。
I'd like to visit Lamma Island.	**Ngóh séung heui Làahm ā Dóu tái háh.** 我想去南丫島睇吓。
I'd like to visit Tai O.	**Ngóh séung heui Daaih Ou tái háh.** 我想去大澳睇吓。

Do you have a city map?	**Yáuh móuh bún síh deih tòuh a?** 有冇本市地圖呀？
Where is the museum?	**Bok maht gwún hái bīn douh a?** 博物館喺邊度呀？
Where can I find a church?	**Bīn douh yáuh gaau tòhng a?** 邊度有教堂呀？
Could you give me some information about…?	**Hó m̀h hó yíh béi ngóh yáuh gwāan…ge jī líu a?** 可唔可以俾我有關…嘅資料呀？
How much is this?	**Nī go géi dō chín a?** 呢個幾多錢呀？
Could you point them out on the map?	**M̀h gōi hái deih tòuh seuhng mihn jí béi ngóh tái háh.** 唔該喺地圖上面指俾我睇吓。
Which places do you recommend seeing?	**Néih tēui jin bīn géi go gíng dím a?** 你推薦邊幾個景點呀？
We'll be here for a few hours.	**Ngóh deih wúih hái (nī) douh géi go jūng tàuh.** 我哋會喺(呢)度幾個鐘頭。
We'll be here for a day.	**Ngóh deih wúih hái (nī) douh (jyuh) yāt yaht.** 我哋會喺(呢)度(住)一日。
We're interested in…	**Ngóh deih deui…gám hing cheui.** 我哋對…感興趣。
Is there a scenic walk around the city?	**Yáuh móuh yāt tìuh yàuh láahm síh yùhng ge louh sin a?** 有冇一條遊覽市容嘅路線呀？
How long does it take?	**Nī tìuh louh yiu hàahng géi noih a?** 呢條路要行幾耐呀？
Where does it start/end?	**Hái bīn douh hōi chí/yùhn a?** 喺邊度開始／完呀？
Are there any boat trips?	**Yáuh móuh chóh syùhn léuih yàuh ge louh sin a?** 有冇坐船旅遊嘅路線呀？
Where can we board?	**Hái bīn douh séuhng syùhn a?** 喺邊度上船呀？

Are there any bus tours?	**Yáuh móuh chóh léuih yàuh chē ge louh sin a?** 有冇坐旅遊車嘅路線呀？
Where do we get on?	**Hái bīn douh séuhng chē a?** 喺邊度上車呀？
Is there a guide who speaks English?	**Yáuh móuh wúih góng Yīng Mán ge douh yàuh a?** 有冇會講英文嘅導遊呀？
What trips can we take around the area?	**Fuh gahn yáuh móuh gíng dím hó yíh heui ga?** 附近有冇景點可以去㗎？
Are there any excursions?	**Yáuh móuh dyún tòuh ge léuih yàuh louh sin a?** 有冇短途嘅旅遊路線呀？
Where do these excursions go?	**Nī dī dyún tòuh louh sin heui bīn douh a?** 呢啲短途路線去邊度呀？
We'd like to go to…	**Ngóh deih séung heui…** 我哋想去…
How long is the excursion?	**Nī tìuh dyún tòuh louh sin yáuh géi yúhn a?** 呢條短途路線有幾遠呀？
How long do we stay in…?	**Ngóh deih hái…géi noih a?** 我哋喺…幾耐呀？
Are there any guided tours?	**Yáuh móuh dī léuih hàhng tyùhn bāau màaih douh yàuh ga?** 有冇啲旅行團包埋導遊㗎？
How much free time will we have there?	**Heui dou gó douh (ngóh deih) yáuh géi dō jih yàuh wuht duhng ge sìh gaan a?** 去到嗰度(我哋)有幾多自由活動嘅時間呀？
We want to have a walk around.	**Ngóh deih séung hái fuh gahn hàahng háh.** 我哋想喺附近行吓。
Can we hire a guide?	**Ngóh deih hó m̀h hó yíh chéng go douh yàuh a?** 我哋可唔可以請個導遊呀？
What time does…open?	**…géi dím hōi mùhn a?** …幾點開門呀？
What days is…closed?	**…bīn yaht sāan mùhn a?** …邊日閂門呀？

What's the admission price?	**Yahp chèuhng fai géi dō chín a?** 入場費幾多錢呀？
Is there a group discount?	**Tyùhn tái yáuh móuh yāu waih a?** 團體有冇優惠呀？
Is there a child discount?	**Sai mān jái yáuh móuh yāu waih a?** 細蚊仔有冇優惠呀？
Is there a student discount?	**Hohk sāang yáuh móuh yāu waih a?** 學生有冇優惠呀？
Is there a discount for senior citizens?	**Jéung jé yáuh móuh yāu waih a?** 長者有冇優惠呀？
Can I take (flash) photos here?	**Nī douh hó m̀h hó yíh yuhng sím gwōng dāng a?** 呢度可唔可以用閃光燈呀？
Can I film here?	**Nī douh hó m̀h hó yíh luhk yíng a?** 呢度可唔可以錄影呀？
Do you have any postcards of…?	**Yáuh móuh…ge mìhng seun pín a?** 有冇…嘅明信片呀？
Do you have an English catalog?	**Yáuh móuh Yīng Mán ge muhk luhk a?** 有冇英文嘅目錄呀？
Do you have an English program?	**Yáuh móuh Yīng Mán ge jit muhk bíu a?** 有冇英文嘅節目表呀？
Do you have an English brochure?	**Yáuh móuh Yīng Mán ge léuih yàuh sáu chaak a?** 有冇英文嘅旅遊手冊呀？

Going out

There are many bars, discos, late-night restaurants and coffee shops In Hong Kong. Tourists like to go to Lan Kwai Fong (**Làahn Gwai Fōng** 蘭桂坊) at Central, Wan Chai (**Wāan Jái** 灣仔), Tsim Sha Tsui (**Jīm Sā Jéui** 尖沙咀), and Causeway Bay (**Tùhng Lòh Wāan** 銅鑼灣). Try to watch a concert at the Hong Kong Stadium (**Hēung Góng Tái Yuhk Gwún** 香港體育館), City Hall (**Daaih Wuih Tòhng** 大會堂) on Hong Kong Island or the Cultural Center (**Hēung Góng Màhn Fa Jūng Sām** 香港文化中心) in Tsim Sha Tsui.

What's on tonight?	**Gām máahn yáuh māt yéh hóu jit muhk a?** 今晚有乜嘢好節目呀？
We want to go to…	**Ngóh deih séung heui…** 我哋想去…
What's showing at the cinema?	**Hei yún jouh māt yéh hei a?** 戲院做乜嘢戲呀？
What sort of film is it?	**Haih māt yéh pín a?** 係乜嘢片呀？
It's suitable for everyone.	**Daaih yàhn yìh tùhng dōu sīk yìh gwūn hon.** 大人兒童都適宜觀看。
It's not suitable for people under 16.	**Sahp luhk seui yíh hah ge yìh tùhng bāt yìh gwūn hon.** 十六歲以下嘅兒童不宜觀看。
– original version	**jing báan** 正版
– 2D/3D version	**yih dī/sāam dī báan** 2D/3D版
– subtitled	**yáuh jih mohk** 有字幕
– dubbed	**pui yām** 配音
Where can I find an iMax cinema around here?	**Fuh gahn bīn douh yáuh iMax hei yún a?** 附近邊度有iMax戲院呀？
What's on at the theater?	**Kehk yún jouh māt yéh jit muhk a?** 劇院做乜嘢節目呀？
What's on at the opera?	**Gō kehk yún jouh māt yéh gō kehk a?** 歌劇院做乜嘢歌劇呀？
I'd like to see Peking opera.	**Ngóh séung tái Gīng kehk.** 我想睇京劇。
I'd like to see Cantonese opera.	**Ngóh séung tái Yuht kehk.** 我想睇粵劇。
I'd like to see an acrobatic performance.	**Ngóh séung tái jaahp geih bíu yín.** 我想睇雜技表演。
I'd like to see a martial arts performance.	**Ngóh séung tái móuh seuht bíu yín.** 我想睇武術表演。
I'd like to see folk dances.	**Ngóh séung tái màhn gāan móuh douh.** 我想睇民間舞蹈。

I'd like to see a ballet.	**Ngóh séung tái bā lèuih móuh.** 我想睇芭蕾舞。
I'd like to see a Chinese classical music concert.	**Ngóh séung tái gwok ngohk yín jau.** 我想睇國樂演奏。
I'd like to see a kung fu movie.	**Ngóh séung tái móuh hahp pín.** 我想睇武俠片。
I'd like to see an action movie.	**Ngóh séung tái duhng jok pín.** 我想睇動作片。
I'd like to go to a concert.	**Ngóh séung heui tēng yām ngohk wúi.** 我想去聽音樂會。
I'd like to go to a singing recital.	**Ngóh séung heui tēng yín cheung wúi.** 我想去聽演唱會。
Are there English subtitles?	**Yáuh móuh Yīng Màn jih mohk ga?** 有冇英文字幕㗎？
What's happening at the concert hall?	**Yām ngohk tēng yáuh māt yéh bíu yín a?** 音樂廳有乜嘢表演呀？
Where can I find a good disco around here?	**Fuh gahn bīn douh yáuh hóu ge *disco* a?** 附近邊度有好嘅 disco呀？
Is it members only?	**Haih m̀h haih wúi yùhn sīn ji yahp dāk a?** 係唔係會員先至入得呀？
Where can I find a good nightclub around here?	**Fuh gahn bīn douh yáuh hóu ge yeh júng wúi a?** 附近邊度有好嘅夜總會呀？
Is it evening wear only?	**Yiu jeuk máahn láih fuhk ma?** 要著晚禮服嗎？
Should we dress up?	**Ngóh deih haih m̀h haih yiu jeuk dāk hóu jíng chàih a?** 我哋係唔係要著得好整齊呀？
What time does the show start?	**Bíu yín géi sìh hōi chí a?** 表演幾時開始呀？
When's the next soccer match?	**Hah yāt chèuhng jūk kàuh choi haih géi sìh a?** 下一場足球賽係幾時呀？

Who's playing?	**Bīn deuih deui bīn deuih a?** 邊隊對邊隊呀？
Is there a cover charge?	**Yáuh móuh jeui dāi sīu fai a?** 有冇最低消費呀？
Is it Ladies' Night?	**Haih m̀h haih néuih sih jī yeh a?** 係唔係女士之夜呀？
What is your signature drink?	**Yáuh móuh dahk sīk yám bán a?** 有冇特色飲品呀？
When is the next race day?	**Hah chi choi máh yaht haih géi sìh a?** 下次賽馬日係幾時呀？
Who is the best jockey in Hong Kong?	**Bīn go haih Hēung Góng jeui hóu ge kèh sī a?** 邊個係香港最好嘅騎師呀？
Do you have any drinks with rum?	**Yáuh móuh gā lām jáu ge yám bán a?** 有冇加冧酒嘅飲品呀？
Do you have any drinks with tequila?	**Yáuh móuh gā lùhng sit làahn jáu ge yám bán a?** 有冇加龍舌蘭酒嘅飲品呀？
Do you have any drinks with vodka?	**Yáuh móuh gā fukh dahk gā ge yám bán a?** 有冇加伏特加嘅飲品呀？
I don't drink alcohol. I'll have a Coke.	**Ngóh m̀h yám dāk jáu a, ngóh yám hó lohk.** 我唔飲得酒呀，我飲可樂。
What cocktail would you recommend?	**Yáuh móuh gāi méih jáu gaai siuh a?** 有冇雞尾酒介紹呀？
I like sweet drinks.	**Ngóh jūng yi tìhm jáu.** 我鍾意甜酒。
I like champagne.	**Ngóh jūng yi hēung bān.** 我鍾意香檳。
Where's Lan Kwai Fong?	**Làahn Gwai Fōng hái bīn douh a?** 蘭桂坊喺邊度呀？
Where's the bar?	**Jáu bā hái bīn douh a?** 酒吧喺邊度呀？
Please bring me a beer.	**Béi būi bē jáu ngóh, m̀h gōi.** 俾杯啤酒我，唔該。

I'd like a glass of whisky neat (without ice).	**Ngóh séung yiu būi wāi sih géi m̀h gā bīng.** 我想要杯威士忌唔加冰。
I'd like a glass of whisky up (with ice).	**Ngóh séung yiu būi wāi sih géi gā bīng.** 我想要杯威士忌加冰。
What musical/opera/ theatre show would you recommend?	**Néih yáuh māt yéh yām ngohk/gō kehk/hei kehk bíu yín gaai siuh a?** 你有乜嘢音樂／歌劇／戲劇表演介紹呀？
Are the songs in Cantonese or English?	**Haih Gwóng Dūng Wá dihng haih Yīng Mán gō a?** 係廣東話定係英文歌呀？
What's there to do in the evening?	**Máahn hāk yáuh dī māt yéh yùh lohk jit muhk a?** 晚黑有啲乜嘢娛樂節目呀？
Go to the Peak to see the night view.	**Séuhng Sāan Déng tái yeh gíng lā.** 上山頂睇夜景啦。
Go to Temple Street to see the night market.	**Heui Míu Gāai hàahng yeh síh lā.** 去廟街行夜市啦。
Is there a massage parlor here?	**Nī douh yáuh móuh ngon mō dim a?** 呢度有冇按摩店呀？
I'd like to have a full body massage.	**Ngóh séung jouh chyùhn sān ngon mō.** 我想做全身按摩。
I'd like to have a foot massage.	**Ngóh séung jouh geuk dái ngon mō.** 我想做腳底按摩。
I'd like to have a head massage.	**Ngóh séung jouh tàuh bouh ngon mō.** 我想做頭部按摩。
I'd like to have a shoulder massage.	**Ngóh séung jouh gīn bouh ngon mō.** 我想做肩部按摩。

11.3 Booking tickets

Could you reserve some tickets for us?	**M̀h gōi bōng ngóh deih dehng géi jēung fēi.** 唔該幫我哋訂幾張飛。
We'd like to book two seats.	**Ngóh séung dehng léuhng go wái.** 我想訂兩個位。

We'd like to book a table for two. | **Ngóh séung dehng jēung léuhng go yàhn ge tói.** 我想訂張兩個人嘅檯。

We'd like two front row seats. | **Ngóh séung dehng léuhng go chìhn pàaih ge wái.** 我想訂兩個前排嘅位。

We'd like a table for two at the front. | **Ngóh séung dehng jēung hái chìhn mihng ge yih yàhn tói.** 我想訂張喺前面嘅二人檯。

We'd like two seats in the middle. | **Ngóh séung dehng léuhng go jūng gāan ge wái.** 我想訂兩個中間嘅位。

We'd like a table for two in the middle. | **Ngóh séung dehng jēung hái jūng gāan ge yih yàhn tói.** 我想訂張喺中間嘅二人檯。

We'd like two seats at the back. | **Ngóh séung dehng léuhng go hauh mihn ge wái.** 我想訂兩個後面嘅位。

We'd like a table for two at the back. | **Ngóh séung dehng hái hauh mihn léuhng go yàhn ge tói.** 我想訂喺後面兩個人嘅檯。

I'd like to reserve three tickets for the 8 p.m. show. | **Ngóh séung dehng sāam jēung baat dím ge fēi.** 我想訂三張八點嘅飛。

Are there any tickets left for tonight? | **Juhng yáuh móuh gām máahn ge fēi a?** 仲有冇今晚嘅飛呀？

How much is a ticket? | **Géi dō chín yāt jēung fēi a?** 幾多錢一張飛呀？

Must tickets be purchased in advance? | **Haih m̀h haih yāt dihng yiu tàih chìhn máaih fēi a?** 係唔係一定要提前買飛呀？

How much are the least expensive tickets? | **Jeui pèhng ge fēi géi dō chín a?** 最平嘅飛幾多錢呀？

How much are front row seats? | **Chìhn pàaih ge joh wái géi dō chín a?** 前排嘅座位幾多錢呀？

When can I pick up the tickets?	**Géi sìh sīn jī hó yíh ló fēi a?** 幾時先至可以攞飛呀？
I've got a reservation.	**Ngóh dehng jó fēi la.** 我訂咗飛喇。
My name's...	**Ngóh go méng giu...** 我個名叫…

你想訂邊一場嘅飛呀？ **Néih séung dehng bīn yāt chèuhng ge fēi a?**	Which performance do you want to reserve for?
你想坐喺邊度呀？ **Néih séung chóh hái bīn douh a?**	Where would you like to sit?
飛都賣晒喇。 **Fēi dōu maaih saai la.**	Everything's sold out.
淨係有企位。 **Jihng haih yáuh kéih wái.**	It's standing room only.
我哋只係剩番樓廳嘅飛喇。 **Ngóh deih jí haih jihng fāan làuh tēng ge fēi la.**	We've only got circle seats left.
我哋只係剩番上層樓廳嘅飛喇。 **Ngóh deih jí haih jihng fāan seuhng chàhng làuh tēng ge fēi la.**	We've only got upper circle seats left.
我哋只係剩番樂隊席嘅飛喇。 **Ngóh deih jí haih jihng fāan ngohk déui jihk ge fēi la.**	We've only got orchestra seats left.
我哋只係剩番前排嘅飛喇。 **Ngóh deih jí haih jihng fāan chìhn pàaih ge fēi la.**	We've only got front row seats left.
我哋只係剩番後排嘅飛喇。 **Ngóh deih jí haih jihng fāan hauh pàaih ge fēi la.**	We've only got seats left at the back.
你要幾多張飛呀？ **Néih yiu géi dō jēung fēi a?**	How many seats would you like?
你要喺…點之前嚟攞飛。 **Néih yiu hái...dím jī chìhn làih ló fēi.**	You'll have to pick up the tickets before...o'clock.
唔該俾我睇吓你張飛。 **Mh gōi béi ngóh tái háh néih jēung fēi.**	Tickets, please.
呢個係你嘅位。 **Nī go haih néih ge wái.**	This is your seat.
唔好意思，你坐錯位喇。 **Mh hóu yi si, néih chóh cho wái la.**	Excuse me, you are in the wrong seat.

12. Sports Activities

12.1 Sporting questions
12.2 By the waterfront
12.3 Summer sports

12.1 Sporting questions

Watersports **Séui seuhng wahn duhng** 水上運動	Diving **Chìhm séui** 潛水	Soccer **Jūk kàuh** 足球
Kayaking **Pèi wāa teng wahn duhng** 皮划艇運動	Windsurfing **Fūng fàahn** 風帆	Golf **Gōu yíh fū kàuh** 高爾夫球

Where can we kayak around here?	**Nī douh bīn douh hó yíh wáan pèi wāa teng a?** 呢度邊度可以玩皮划艇呀?
Can we hire a yacht?	**Ngóh deih hó m̀h hó yíh jōu yàuh teng a?** 我哋可唔可以租遊艇呀?
Can we take windsurfing lessons?	**Ngóh deih hó m̀h hó yíh séuhng fūng fàahn tòhng a?** 我哋可唔可以上風帆堂呀?
How much is that per hour?	**Géi dō chín yāt go jūng a?** 幾多錢一個鐘呀?
How much is that per day?	**Géi dō chín yāt yaht a?** 幾多錢一日呀?
How much is each one?	**Géi dō chín yāt go a?** 幾多錢一個呀?
Do you need to get a permit first?	**Néih yiu m̀h yiu ló héui hó jing sīn a?** 你要唔要攞許可證先呀?
Where can I get the permit?	**Ngóh hái bīn douh ló héui hó jing a?** 我喺邊度攞許可證呀?
Where's the stadium/ gymnasium?	**Tái yuhk gwún hái bīn douh a?** 體育館喺邊度呀?

I'd like to see a ball game.	**Ngóh séung heui tái dá bō.** 我想去睇打波。
Can we go to see a basketball game?	**Ngóh deih hó m̀h hó yíh heui tái làahm kàuh béi chōi a?** 我哋可唔可以去睇籃球比賽呀？
I'd like to see a badminton match.	**Ngóh séung heui tái yúh mòuh kàuh béi choi.** 我想去睇羽毛球比賽。
I'd like to see a volleyball game.	**Ngóh séung heui tái pàaih kàuh béi choi.** 我想去睇排球比賽。
I'd like to see a table tennis match.	**Ngóh séung heui tái bīng bām bō béi choi.** 我想去睇乒乓波比賽。
I'd like to see a tennis match.	**Ngóh séung heui tái móhng kàuh béi choi.** 我想去睇網球比賽。
I'd like to see a baseball game.	**Ngóh séung heui tái páahng kàuh béi choi.** 我想去睇棒球比賽。
I'd like to see a softball game.	**Ngóh séung heui tái lèuih kàuh béi choi.** 我想去睇壘球比賽。
When does the game begin?	**Béi choi géi sìh hōi chí a?** 比賽幾時開始呀？
Which teams are going to play?	**Bīn deuih tùhng bīn deuih dá a?** 邊隊同邊隊打呀？
What's the score?	**Béi sou haih géi dō a?** 比數係幾多呀？
I've won.	**Ngóh yèhng jó.** 我贏咗。
I've lost.	**Ngóh syū jó.** 我輸咗。
We're even.	**Ngóh deih dá wòh.** 我哋打和。

By the waterfront

| Is it far to walk to the sea? | **Nī douh heui hói bīn yúhn m̀h yúhn a?**
呢度去海邊遠唔遠呀？ |

Is there a swimming pool around here?	**Nī douh yáuh móuh yàuh wihng chìh a?** 呢度有冇游泳池呀？
Is there a sandy beach around here?	**Nī douh yáuh móuh sā tāan a?** 呢度有冇沙灘呀？
Are there any rocks here?	**Nī douh yáuh móuh sehk tàuh a?** 呢度有冇石頭呀？
When's high/low tide?	**Géi sìh chìuh jeung/chìuh teui a?** 幾時潮漲／潮退呀？
What's the water temperature?	**Séui ge wān douh haih géi dō douh a?** 水嘅溫度係幾多度呀？
Is it deep here?	**Nī douh dī séui sām m̀h sām a?** 呢度啲水深唔深呀？
Is it safe (for children) to swim here?	**(Sai mān jái) hái nī douh yàuh séui ngōn m̀h ngōn chyùhn ga?** (細蚊仔)喺呢度游水安唔安全㗎？
Are there any currents?	**Nī douh yáuh móuh gāp làuh a?** 呢度有冇急流呀？
Are there any sharks?	**Nī douh yáuh móuh sā yùh a?** 呢度有冇鯊魚呀？
Are there any jellyfish?	**Nī douh yáuh móuh baahk ja a?** 呢度有冇白蚱呀？
What does that flag mean?	**Gó jī kèih haih māt yéh yi sī a?** 嗰枝旗係乜嘢意思呀？
What does that buoy mean?	**Gó go fàuh bīu haih māt yéh yi sī a?** 嗰個浮標係乜嘢意思呀？
Is there a lifeguard on duty?	**Nī douh yáuh móuh gau sāang yùhn jihk bāan a?** 呢度有冇救生員值班呀？
Are dogs allowed here?	**Nī douh hó m̀h hó yíh daai gáu a?** 呢度可唔可以帶狗呀？

釣魚區 **Diu yú kēui** Fishing waters	唔准滑水 **M̀h jéun waaht séui** No surfing	唔准游水 **M̀h jéun yàuh séui** No swimming
只限有許可證者 **Jí haahn yáuh héui hó jing jé** Permits only	危險 **Ngàih hím** Danger	唔准釣魚 **M̀h jéun diu yú** No fishing

Is camping on the beach allowed?	**Hói tāan jéun m̀h jéun louh yìhng a?** 海灘准唔准露營呀？
Can we light a fire?	**Ngóh deih hó yíh dím fó ma?** 我哋可以點火嗎？

12.3 Summer sports

Where can I find a good golf course around here?	**Nī douh fuh gahn bīn douh yáuh hóu ge gōu yíh fū kàuh chèuhng a?** 呢度附近邊度有好嘅高爾夫球場呀？
What are the green fees?	**Gwó léhng fai géi dō chin a?** 果嶺費幾多錢呀？
Do I have to be a member?	**Yiu m̀h yiu haih wúi yùhn a?** 要唔要係會員呀？
We'd like to rent a tennis court.	**Ngóh deih séung jōu móhng kàuh chèuhng.** 我哋想租網球場。
We'd like to rent a soccer field.	**Ngóh deih séung jōu jūk kàuh chèuhng.** 我哋想租足球場。
We'd like to rent diving equipment.	**Ngóh deih séung jōu chìhm séui yuhng bán.** 我哋想租潛水用品。
We'd like to rent a wakeboard.	**Ngóh deih séung jōu fā sīk waaht séui báan.** 我哋想租花式滑水板。
We'd like to rent a surfboard.	**Ngóh deih séung jōu waaht séui báan.** 我哋想租滑水板。
We'd like to rent a canoe.	**Ngóh deih séung jōu duhk muhk jāu.** 我哋想租獨木舟。

We'd like to rent a kayak.	**Ngóh deih séung jōu pèi wāa teng.** 我哋想租皮划艇。
We'd like to rent a badminton court.	**Ngóh deih séung jōu yúh mòuh kàuh chèuhng.** 我哋想租羽毛球場。
We'd like to rent a wetsuit.	**Ngóh deih séung jōu chìhm séui yī.** 我哋想租潛水衣。
Where can I get sunscreen lotion?	**Ngóh hó yíh haih bīn douh wáhn taai yèuhng yàuh a?** 我可以喺邊度搵太陽油呀？
Where can I get a bathing suit?	**Ngóh hó yíh haih bīn douh wáhn wihng yī a?** 我可以喺邊度搵泳衣呀？
Where can I get a chair?	**Ngóh hó yíh haih bīn douh wáhn dang a?** 我可以喺邊度搵凳呀？
Where can I get a beach umbrella?	**Ngóh hó yíh haih bīn douh wáhn taai yèuhng jē a?** 我可以喺邊度搵太陽遮呀？
Where can I get a towel?	**Ngóh hó yíh haih bīn douh wáhn mòuh gān a?** 我可以喺邊度搵毛巾呀？
Where can I get a hat?	**Ngóh hó yíh haih bīn douh wáhn yāt déng móu a?** 我可以喺邊度搵一頂帽呀？
Where can I get a pair of sunglasses?	**Ngóh hó yíh haih bīn douh wáhn yāt deui taai yèuhng ngáahn géng a?** 我可以喺邊度搵一對太陽眼鏡呀？
Where can I have a shower?	**Bīn douh hó yíh chūng lèuhng a?** 邊度可以沖涼呀？

13. Health Matters

Hong Kong provides excellent health care, and both private and public systems are available. The public hospitals provide good services, though the waiting time is usually long. Non-residents requiring accident and emergency services are charged a higher fee than the locals, but will always be treated, even if they cannot pay immediately. Medical centers and private medical practices are found in all shopping centers to provide treatments for minor illnesses.

English is spoken by most public and private sector medical professionals. For emergency services, dial 999.

13.1 Calling a doctor

Could you call (get) a doctor quickly, please?	**M̀h gōi faai dī bōng ngóh wán go yī sāng.** 唔該快啲幫我搵個醫生。
When does the doctor start seeing patients?	**Yī sāng géi dím hōi chí tái behng a?** 醫生幾點開始睇病呀？
When can the doctor come?	**Yī sāng géi sìh hó yíh làih a?** 醫生幾時可以嚟呀？
Could I make an appointment to see the doctor?	**Ngóh séung yuh yeuk tái behng.** 我想預約睇病。
I've got an appointment to see the doctor at...o'clock.	**Ngóh yuh yeuk jó...dím tái behng.** 我預約咗…點睇病。
Which doctor is on night duty?	**Yeh máahn bīn wái yī sāng dōng jihk a?** 夜晚邊位醫生當值呀？

Which pharmacy is open on weekends?	**Jāu muht bīn gāan yeuhk fòhng hōi a?** 周末邊間藥房開呀？

13.2 What's wrong?

I don't feel well.	**Ngóh gok dāk yáuh dī m̀h syū fuhk.** 我覺得有啲唔舒服。
I'm dizzy.	**Ngóh gok dāk tàuh wàhn.** 我覺得頭暈。
I'm ill.	**Ngóh m̀h syū fuhk.** 我唔舒服。
I feel sick (nauseous).	**Ngóh yáuh dī jok ngáu.** 我有啲作嘔。
I've got a cold.	**Ngóh sēung fūng.** 我傷風。
I've got diarrhea.	**Ngóh tóu ngō.** 我肚痾。
I have trouble breathing.	**Ngóh fū kāp yáuh dī kwan nàahn.** 我呼吸有啲困難。
I feel tired all over.	**Ngóh chyùhn sān syūn yúhn móuh lihk.** 我全身酸軟冇力。
I've burnt myself.	**Ngóh sīu sēung jó jih géi.** 我燒傷咗自己。
It hurts here.	**Nī douh tung.** 呢度痛。
I've been sick (vomited).	**Ngóh ngáu gwo.** 我嘔過。
I'm running a temperature of...degrees.	**Ngóh faat sīu...douh.** 我發燒⋯度。
I've been stung by a wasp.	**Ngóh béi wòhng fūng gāt chān.** 我俾黃蜂刮親。
I've been stung by an insect.	**Ngóh béi chùhng ngáauh chān.** 我俾蟲咬親。
I've been stung by a jellyfish.	**Ngóh béi baahk ja jíng chān.** 我俾白蚱整親。
I've been bitten by a dog.	**Ngóh béi gáu ngáauh chān.** 我俾狗咬親。

I've been bitten by a snake. **Ngóh béi sèh ngáauh chān.**
我俾蛇咬親。

I've cut myself. **Ngóh got chān jih géi.** 我割親自己。

I've grazed/scratched myself. **Ngóh gwaat sēung jó jih géi.**
我刮傷咗自己。

I've had a fall. **Ngóh dit jó yāt gāau.** 我跌咗一跤。

I've sprained my ankle. **Ngóh náau chān geuk jāang.**
我扭親腳踭。

Could I have a female doctor, please? **Hó m̀h hó yíh bōng ngóh wán go néuih yī sāng a?** 可唔可以幫我搵個女醫生呀？

I'd like the morning-after pill. **Ngóh séung máaih sih hauh yún.**
我想買事後丸。

13.3 The consultation

你邊度唔舒服呀？
Néih bīn douh m̀h syū fuhk a?

What seems to be the problem?

你唔舒服咗幾耐喇？
Néih m̀h syū fuhk jó géi noih la?

How long have you been unwell?

你呢個病情有咗幾耐喇？
Néih nī go behng chìhng yáuh jó géi noih la?

How long have you had these complaints?

你食緊乜嘢藥呀？
Néih sihk gán māt yéh yeuhk a?

What medicines are you taking?

食咗幾耐喇？
Sihk jó géi noih la?

How long have you been taking them?

你以前有過咁嘅病嗎？
Néih yíh chìhn yáuh gwo gám ge behng ma?

Have you had this trouble before?

有冇發燒呀？幾多度呀？
Yáuh móuh faat sīu a? Géi dō douh a?

Do you have a temperature? What is it?

唔該你噏高件衫。 **M̀h gōi néih ná gō gihn sāam.**

Lift your shirt, please.

唔該你除咗上面件衫。
M̀h gōi néih chèuih jó seuhng mihn gihn sāam.

Strip to the waist, please.

你可以喺呢度除衫。
Néih hó yíh hái nī douh chèuih sāam.
You can undress there.

捲起左邊／右邊衫袖啦。
Gyún héi jó bihn/yàuh bihn sāam jauh lā.
Roll up your left/right sleeve, please.

唔該你瞓低。 **Ṁh gōi néih fan dāi.**
Lie down here, please.

咁樣痛唔痛呀？ **Gám yéung tung m̀h tung a?**
Does this hurt?

深呼吸。 **Sām fū kāp.**
Breathe deeply.

擘大個口。 **Maak daaih go háu.**
Open your mouth.

Patients' medical history

I'm a diabetic.
Ngóh yáuh tòhng niuh behng.
我有糖尿病。

I have a heart condition.
Ngóh yáuh sām johng behng.
我有心臟病。

I'm asthmatic.
Ngóh yáuh hāau chyún.
我有哮喘。

I'm allergic to…
Ngóh deui…gwo máhn. 我對…過敏。

I'm…months pregnant.
Ngóh yáuh jó…go yuht sān géi.
我有咗…個月身紀。

I'm on a diet.
Ngóh jit gán sihk. 我節緊食。

I'm on medication.
Ngóh sihk gán yeuhk. 我食緊藥。

I'm on the pill.
Ngóh sihk gán beih yahn yún.
我食緊避孕丸。

I've had a heart attack once before.
Ngóh yíh chìhn si gwo yāt chi sām johng behng faat jok.
我以前試過一次心臟病發作。

I've had a(n)…operation.
Ngóh yíh chìhn jouh gwo…sáu seuht.
我以前做個…手術。

I've been ill recently.
Ngóh jeui gahn behng gwo yāt chi.
我最近病過一次。

I've got a stomach ulcer.	**Ngóh yáuh waih kwúi yèuhng.** 我有胃潰瘍。
I've got my period.	**Ngóh ngāam ngāam làih yuht gīng.** 我啱啱嚟月經。

你對乜嘢過敏呀？ **Néih deui māt yéh gwo máhn a?**	Do you have any allergies?
你而家食緊乜嘢藥呀？ **Néih yìh gā sihk gán māt yéh yeuhk a?**	Are you on any medication?
你係唔係節緊食呀？ **Néih haih m̀h haih jit gán sihk a?**	Are you on a diet?
你係唔係有咗身紀呀？ **Néih haih m̀h haih yáuh jó sān géi a?**	Are you pregnant?
你有冇打破傷風針呀？ **Néih yáuh móuh dá po sēung fūng jām a?**	Have you had a tetanus injection?

I've had a previous injury on my wrist.	**Ngóh sáu wún yíh chìhn sauh gwo sēung.** 我手腕以前受過傷。
I've had a previous injury on my ankle.	**Ngóh geuk jāang yíh chìhn sauh gwo sēung.** 我腳踭以前受過傷。
I've had a previous injury on my knee.	**Ngóh sāt tàuh gō yíh chìhn sauh gwo sēung.** 我膝頭哥以前受過傷。
I've had a previous injury on my shoulder.	**Ngóh bok tàuh yíh chìhn sauh gwo sēung.** 我膊頭以前受過傷。

The diagnosis

冇乜事，唔駛擔心。 **Móuh māt sih, m̀h sái dāam sām.**	It's nothing serious.
你嘅…斷咗。 **Néih ge…tyúhn jó.**	Your…is broken.
你扭傷咗… **Néih náu sēung jó…**	You've got a sprained…
你嘅…扯傷咗。 **Néih ge…ché sēung jó.**	You've got a torn…
你感染到… **Néih gám yíhm dóu…**	You've got an infection.

你嘅⋯發炎。
Néih ge…faat yìhm.

You…is inflamed.

你有盲腸炎。 **Néih yáuh màahng chéung yìhm.**

You've got appendicitis.

你感染到支氣管炎。
Néih gám yíhm dóu jī hei gwún yìhm.

You've got bronchitis.

你有性病。
Néih yáuh sing behng.

You've got a venereal disease.

你感冒嘞。 **Néih gám mouh laak.**

You've got the flu.

你有過輕微嘅心臟病發作。 **Néih yáuh gwo hīng mèih ge sām johng behng faat jok.**

You've had a mild heart attack.

你有肺炎。 **Néih yáuh fai yìhm.**

You've got pneumonia.

你有胃炎。 **Néih yáuh waih yìhm.**

You've got gastritis.

你有胃潰瘍。 **Néih yáuh waih kwúi yèuhng.**

You've got an ulcer.

你扯傷咗肌肉。 **Néih ché sēung jó gēi yuhk.**

You've pulled a muscle.

你嘅陰道發炎。
Néih ge yām douh faat yìhm.

You've got a vaginal infection.

你食物中毒。
Néih sihk maht jung duhk.

You've got food poisoning.

你中暑。 **Néih jung syú.**

You've got sunstroke.

你對⋯過敏。 **Néih deui…gwo máhn.**

You're allergic to…

你懷孕喇。 **Néih wàaih yahn la.**

You're pregnant.

我幫你驗血／尿／大便。
Ngóh bōng néi yihm hyut/niuh/daaih bihn.

I'd like to have your blood/urine/stools tested.

要聯傷口。 **Yiu lyùhn sēung háu.**

It needs stitches.

我要轉介你俾專科醫生。
Ngóh yiu jyún gaai néih béi jyūn fō yī sāng.

I'm referring you to a specialist.

我而家送你入醫院。
Ngóh yìh gā sung néih yahp yī yún.

I'm sending you to the hospital.

你想去公立定係私立醫院呀？ **Néih séung heui gūng lahp ding haih sī lahp yī yún a?**

Do you want to go to a public or private hospital?

你要照X光。
Néih yiu jiu X gwōng.

You'll need some x-rays taken.

唔該你喺候診室等。
Mh gōi néih hái hauh chén sāt dáng.

Could you wait in the waiting room, please?

你需要做手術。 **Néih sēui yiu jouh sáu seuht.**

You'll need an operation.

I need something for diarrhea.	**Ngóh yiu dī yī tóuh ngō ge yeuhk.** 我要啲醫肚痾嘅藥。
I need something for flu.	**Ngóh yiu dī yī gám mouh ge yeuhk.** 我要啲醫感冒嘅藥。
Is it contagious?	**Wúih m̀h wúih chyùhn yím béi yàhn ga?** 會唔會傳染俾人㗎？
How long do I have to rest?	**Ngóh yiu yāu sīk géi noih a?** 我要休息幾耐呀？
How long do I have to stay in bed?	**Ngóh yiu fan chòhng géi noih a?** 我要瞓床幾耐呀？
How long do I have to stay in the hospital?	**Ngóh yiu hái yī yún jyuh géi noih a?** 我要喺醫院住幾耐呀？
Do I have to go on a special diet?	**Sái m̀h sái sihk dahk biht ge yìhng yéuhng chāan a?** 駛唔駛食特別嘅營養餐呀？
Am I allowed to travel?	**Ngóh hó yíh heui léuih hàhng ma?** 我可以去旅行嗎？
Can I make another appointment?	**Ngóh hó yíh joi yuh yeuk go sìh gaan ma?** 我可以再預約個時間嗎？

你聽日／…日再返嚟覆診 **Néih tīng yaht/...yaht joi fāan làih fūk chán.**	Come back tomorrow/ in...days' time.

When do I have to come back for another consultation?	**Ngóh géi sìh joi fāan làih fūk chán a?** 我幾時再返嚟覆診呀？
I'll come back tomorrow.	**Ngóh tīng yaht fāan làih.** 我聽日返嚟。
How do I take this medicine?	**Nī júng yeuhk dím yéung sihk a?** 呢種藥點樣食呀？

13.4 Medications and prescriptions

How many pills each time?	**Múih chi sihk géi dō lāp a?** 每次食幾多粒呀？
How many drops each time?	**Múih chi géi dō dihk a?** 每次幾多滴呀？
How many spoonfuls each time?	**Múih chi sihk géi dō gāng a?** 每次食幾多羹呀？
How many injections each time?	**Múih chi dá géi jām a?** 每次打幾針呀？
How many times a day?	**Yāt yaht sihk géi dō chi a?** 一日食幾多次呀？
I've forgotten my medication.	**Ngóh m̀h gei dāk jó sihk yeuhk.** 我唔記得咗食藥。
At home I take...	**Hái ngūk kéi ngóh sihk...** 喺屋企我食…
Could you write a prescription for me, please?	**M̀h gōi bōng ngóh hōi jēung yeuhk dāan.** 唔該幫我開張藥單。

我幫你開抗生素。 **Ngóh bōng néih hōi kong sāng sou.**	I'm prescribing antibiotics.
我幫你開咳藥水。 **Ngóh bōng néih hōi kāat yeuhk séui.**	I'm prescribing a cough syrup.
我幫你開鎮靜劑。 **Ngóh bōng néih hōi jang jihng jāi.**	I'm prescribing a tranquilizer.
我幫你開止痛藥。 **Ngóh bōng néih hōi jí tung yeuhk.**	I'm prescribing painkillers.
休息多啲。 **Yāu sīk dō dī.**	Have lots of rest.
唔好出街。 **M̀h hóu chēut gāai.**	Stay indoors.
瞓床。 **Fan chòhng.**	Stay in bed.

唔可以食嘢。	Ṁh hó yíh sihk yéh.	No food is allowed.
可以飲水。	Hó yíh yám séui.	You can drink water.
飲多啲水。	Yám dō dī séui.	Drink plenty of water.

pills **yeuhk yún** 藥丸	dissolve in water **yùhng hái séui douh** 溶喺水度	rub on **chàh** 搽
before meals **faahn chìhn** 飯前	This medication impairs your driving. **Nī júng yeuhk wúih yíng héung** **néih jā chē.** 呢種藥會影響你揸車。	injection **dá jām** 打針
after meals **faahn hauh** 飯後	Finish the prescription. **Nī júng yeuhk yiu chyùhn bouh** **sihk yùhn.** 呢種藥要全部食完。	ointment **yeuhk gōu** 藥膏
swallow (whole) **sèhng lāp tān** 成粒吞	take **sihk (yeuhk)/yám (yeuhk séui)** 食(藥)／飲(藥水)	…times a day **múih yaht sihk…chi** 每日食…次
tablets **yeuhk béng** 藥餅	spoonful/teaspoonful **gēng/chàh gēng** 羹／茶羹	for…days **sihk…yaht** 食…日
drops **dihk jāi** 滴劑		external use only **ngoih yuhng** 外用
every…hours **múih…jūng tàuh/síu sìh** 每…鐘頭／小時		

13.5 At the dentist

Do you know a good dentist?	**Néih sīk m̀h sīk dāk hóu ge ngàh yī a?** 你識唔識得好嘅牙醫呀？
Could you make a dentist's appointment for me?	**M̀h gōi bōng ngóh yuh yeuk go ngàh yī.** 唔該幫我預約個牙醫。
It's urgent.	**Hóu gán gāp ga.** 好緊急㗎。
Can I come in today, please?	**Hó m̀h hó yíh gām yaht làih a?** 可唔可以今日嚟呀？

I have a (terrible) toothache.	**Ngóh jek ngàh tung dāk hóu leih hoih.** 我隻牙痛得好厲害。
Could you prescribe/ give me a painkiller?	**Hó m̀h hó yíh hōi dī jí tung yeuhk béi ngóh sihk a?** 可唔可以開啲止痛藥俾我食呀？
I've got a broken tooth.	**Ngóh jek ngàh johng bāng jó.** 我隻牙撞崩咗。
My filling's come out.	**Ngóh dī bóu ngàh líu lāt jó chēut làih.** 我啲補牙料甩咗出嚟。
I've got a broken crown.	**Ngóh ge ngàh tok johng laahn jó.** 我嘅牙托撞爛咗。
I'd like a local anesthetic.	**M̀h gōi bōng ngóh dá màh jeui jām.** 唔該幫我打麻醉針。
I don't want a local anesthetic.	**Ngóh m̀h séung dá màh jeui jām.** 我唔想打麻醉針。
I'm giving you a local anesthetic.	**Ngóh yìh gā bōng néih dá màh jeui jām.** 我而家幫你打麻醉針。
Could you do a temporary repair?	**Hó m̀h hó yíh bōng ngóh làhm sìh bóu yāt bóu ngàh a?** 可唔可以幫我臨時補一補牙呀？
I don't want this tooth pulled.	**Ngóh m̀h séung māng nī jek ngàh a.** 我唔想擝呢隻牙呀。
My denture is broken.	**Ngóh fu gá ngàh johng làahn jó.** 我副假牙撞爛咗。
Can you fix it?	**Hó m̀h hó yíh jíng fāan a?** 可唔可以整番呀？
Do I have to come back to remove the stitches?	**Ngóh sái m̀h sái fāan làih chaak sin a?** 我駛唔駛返嚟拆線呀？
When should I come back to remove the stitches?	**Ngóh géi sìh fāan làih chaak sin a?** 我幾時返嚟拆線呀？

It hurts a lot/it's very painful!	**Nī douh hóu tung a!** 呢度好痛呀!

你邊隻牙痛呀? **Néih bīn jek ngàh tung a?**	Which tooth hurts?
你嘅牙肉腫脹。 **Néih ge ngàh yuhk júng jeung.**	Your gum is swollen.
我要幫你擝咗呢隻牙。 **Ngóh yiu bōng néih māng jó nī jek ngàh.**	I'll have to pull this tooth.
我要幫你補呢隻牙。 **Ngóh yiu bōng néih bóu nī jek ngàh.**	I'll have to fill this tooth.
我要幫你銼平呢隻牙。 **Ngóh yiu bōng néih cho pìhng nī jek ngàh.**	I'll have to file this tooth.
我要鑽呢隻牙。 **Ngóh yiu jyun nī jek ngàh.**	I'll have to drill it.
唔該擘大個口。 **Ṁh gōi maak daaih go háu.**	Open wide, please.
唔該擘大啲個口。 **Ṁh gōi maak daaih di go háu.**	Open wider, please.
唔該合埋口。 **Ṁh gōi hahp maaih háu.**	Close your mouth, please.
唔該咬緊你啲牙。 **Ṁh gōi ngáau gán néih dī ngàh.**	Bite together, please.
唔該嗽口。 **Ṁh gōi lóng háu.**	Rinse, please.
仲痛唔痛呀? **Juhng tung ṁh tung a?**	Does it hurt still?

14. Emergencies

14.1 Asking for help

Help!	**Gau mehng a!** 救命呀！
Get help quickly!	**Faai dī wán yàhn làih bōng sáu!** 快啲搵人嚟幫手！
Fire!	**Fó jūk a!** 火燭呀！
Police!	**Giu gíng chaat!** 叫警察！
Get a doctor!	**Wán yī sāng!** 搵醫生！
Quick!/Hurry!	**Faai dī!** 快啲！
Danger!	**Ngàih hím!** 危險！
Watch out!/Be careful!	**Síu sām a!** 小心啲！
Stop!	**M̀h hóu yūk!** 唔好郁！
Get your hands off me!	**Ló hōi néih jek sáu!** 攞開你隻手！
Let go!	**Fong hōi ngóh!** 放開我！
Stop thief!	**Jūk chaak a!** 捉賊呀！
Could you help me, please?	**M̀h gōi bōng háh ngóh ā.** 唔該幫吓我吖。
Where's the police station?	**Gíng chaat gúk hái bīn douh a?** 警察局喺邊度呀？
Where's the fire department?	**Sīu fòhng gúk hái bīn douh a?** 消防局喺邊度呀？

Where's the fire escape?	**Taai pìhng tāi hái bīn douh a?** 太平梯喺邊度呀？
Where's the nearest fire extinguisher?	**Jeui káhn ge miht fó hei hái bīn douh a?** 最近嘅滅火器喺邊度呀？
Get a fire engine!	**Giu fó jūk chē!** 叫火燭車！
Call an ambulance!	**Giu gau sēung chē!** 叫救傷車！
Could I use your phone?	**Hó m̀h hó yíh je néih ge dihn wá yuhng háh a?** 可唔可以借你嘅電話用吓呀？
What's the emergency number?	**Gán gāp houh máh haih géi dō houh a?** 緊急號碼係幾多號呀？
What's the number for the police?	**Gíng chaat gúk ge dihn wá haih géi dō houh a?** 警察局嘅電話係幾多號呀？

14.2 Lost items

I've lost my wallet/purse.	**Ngóh m̀h gin jó ngàhn bāau.** 我唔見咗銀包。
I lost my tablet here yesterday.	**Ngóh kàhm yaht hái nī douh m̀h gin jó pìhng bán dihn nóuh.** 我琴日喺呢度唔見咗平板電腦。
I lost my mobile phone here yesterday.	**Ngóh kàhm yaht hái nī douh m̀h gin jó sáu gēi.** 我琴日喺呢度唔見咗手機。
I lost my laptop here.	**Ngóh hái nī douh m̀h gin jó ngóh ge sáu tàih dihn nóuh.** 我喺呢度唔見咗我嘅手提電腦。
It's very valuable.	**Hóu jihk chín ga.** 好值錢㗎。
Did you find my passport?	**Néih wán m̀h wán dóu ngóh ge wuh jiu a?** 你搵唔搵到我嘅護照呀？
It was right here.	**Ngóh gei dāk haih fong hái nī douh ga.** 我記得係放喺呢度㗎。
Where's the lost and found office?	**Sāt maht doih líhng chyu hái bīn douh a?** 失物待領處喺邊度呀？

14.3 Accidents

There's been an accident.	**(Nī douh) faat sāng jó yi ngoih.** (呢度)發生咗意外。
Someone's fallen into the water.	**Yáuh yàhn dit jó lohk séui!** 有人跌咗落水！
Is anyone hurt?	**Yáuh móuh yàhn sauh sēung a?** 有冇人受傷呀？
Nobody has been injured.	**Móuh yàhn sauh sēung.** 冇人受傷。
Someone's still trapped inside the car.	**Yáuh yàhn juhng hái chē yahp bihn.** 有人仲喺車入邊。
It's not too bad.	**M̀h haih taai chā.** 唔係太差。
Don't worry.	**M̀h sái dāam sām.** 唔駛擔心。
Leave everything the way it is, please.	**M̀h hóu yūk yahm hòh ge yéh.** 唔好郁任何嘅嘢。
I want to talk to the police first.	**Ngóh yiu sīn tùhng gíng chaat góng.** 我要先同警察講。
I want to take a photo first.	**Ngóh yiu sīn yíng jēung séung.** 我要先影張相。
Here's my name and address.	**Nī go haih ngóh ge méng tùhng deih jí.** 呢個係我嘅名同地址。
May I have your name and address?	**M̀h gōi béi néih go méng tùhng deih jí ngóh.** 唔該俾你個名同地址我。
Could I see your identity card?	**M̀h gōi béi ngóh tái háh néih ge sān fán jing.** 唔該俾我睇吓你嘅身分證。
Could I see your insurance papers?	**M̀h gōi béi ngóh tái háh néih ge bóu hím dāan.** 唔該俾我睇吓你嘅保險單。
Could I see your passport?	**M̀h gōi béi ngóh tái háh néih ge wuh jiu.** 唔該俾我睇吓你嘅護照。
Will you act as a witness?	**Néih yuhn yi jouh jing yàhn ma?** 你願意做證人嗎？
I need this information for insurance purposes.	**Ngóh ge bóu hím gūng sī sēui yiu nī dī jī líu.** 我嘅保險公司需要呢啲資料。

Are you insured?	**Néih yáuh móuh máaih bóu hím a?** 你有冇買保險呀？
Third party (insurance) or all inclusive?	**Néih máaih ge haih daih sām jé bóu hím dihng haih chyùhn bóu a?** 你買嘅係第三者保險定係全保呀？
Could you sign here, please?	**M̀h gōi néih hái nī douh chīm go méng.** 唔該你喺呢度簽個名。

14.4 Theft

喺邊度發生㗎？ **Hái bīn douh faat sāng ga?**		Where did it happen?
幾時發生㗎？ **Géi sìh faat sāng ga?**		What time did it happen?
你唔見咗乜嘢呀？ **Néih m̀h gin jó māt yéh a?**		What's missing?
俾人偷咗啲乜嘢呀？ **Béi yàhn tāu jó dī māt yéh a?**		What's been taken?
有冇証人呀？ **Yáuh móuh jing yàhn a?**		Are there any witnesses?
你需唔需要個翻譯員呀？ **Néih sēui m̀h sēui yiu go fāan yihk yùhn a?**		Do you want an interpreter?

I've been robbed.	**Ngóh béi yàhn chéung gip.** 我俾人搶劫。
My credit card has been stolen.	**Ngóh seun yuhng kāat béi yàhn tāu jó.** 我信用卡俾人偷咗。
My handbag has been snatched.	**Ngóh sáu dói béi yàhn chéung jó.** 我手袋俾人搶咗。
My briefcase has been snatched.	**Ngóh gūng sih bāau béi yàhn chéung jó.** 我公事包俾人搶咗。
My car's been broken into.	**Ngóh gā chē béi yàhn giuh hōi jó.** 我架車俾人撬開咗。

14.5 Missing persons

| I've lost my child. | **Ngóh go jái/néui jáu sāt jó.**
我個仔／女走失咗。 |
| Could you help me find him/her? | **Néih hó m̀h hó yíh bōng ngóh wán háh kéuih a?** 你可唔可以幫我搵吓佢呀？ |

Have you seen a lost child?	**Néih yáuh móuh gin gwo yāt go dohng sāt louh ge sai mān jái a?** 你有冇見過一個蕩失路嘅細蚊仔呀？
He's/she's…years old.	**Kéuih…seui.** 佢…歲。
She's got long hair.	**Kéuih ge tàuh faat haih chèuhng ge.** 佢嘅頭髮係長嘅。
He's got short hair.	**Kéuih ge tàuh faat haih dyún ge.** 佢嘅頭髮係短嘅。
She's got blond hair.	**Kéuih ge tàuh faat haih gām sīk ge.** 佢嘅頭髮係金色嘅。
He's got black hair.	**Kéuih ge tàuh faat haih hāk sīk ge.** 佢嘅頭髮係黑色嘅。
His/her hair is curly/ straight/frizzy.	**Kéuih ge tàuh faat haih lyūn/jihk/sai hyūn ge.** 佢嘅頭髮係攣／直／細圈嘅。
Her hair is in a ponytail.	**Kéuih ge tàuh faat haih sō máh méih ge.** 佢嘅頭髮係梳馬尾嘅。
Her hair is in braids.	**Kéuih ge tàuh faat haih sō bīn ge.** 佢嘅頭髮係梳辮嘅。
Her hair is in a bun.	**Kéuih ge tàuh faat haih sō gai ge.** 佢嘅頭髮係梳髻嘅。
He's/she's got blue/ brown/green eyes.	**Kéuih deui ngáahn haih làahm sīk/gā fē sīk/luhk sīk ge.** 佢對眼係藍色／咖啡色／綠色嘅。
He/she's wearing sports shoes.	**Kéuih jeuk jyuh bō hàaih.** 佢著住波鞋。
He/she's wearing glasses.	**Kéuih daai ngáahn géng.** 佢戴眼鏡。
He/she's not wearing glasses.	**Kéuih móuh daai ngáahn géng.** 佢冇戴眼鏡。
He/she's carrying a bag.	**Kéuih līng jyuh go dói.** 佢拎住個袋。
He is tall.	**Kéuih sāang dāk gòu.** 佢生得高。
She is short.	**Kéuih sāang dāk ngái.** 佢生得矮。

This is a photo of him/her. **Nī jēung haih kéuih ge séung.**
呢張係佢嘅相。

14.6 The police

An arrest

唔該俾我睇吓你嘅駕駛執照。 **M̀h gōi béi ngóh tái háh néih ge ga sái jāp jiu.**	Your driver's licence, please.
唔該俾我睇吓你嘅身份證。 **M̀h gōi béi ngóh tái háh néih ge sān fán jing.**	Your identity card, please.
你開快車。 **Néih hōi faai chē.**	You were speeding.
呢度唔准泊車。 **Nī douh m̀h jéun paak chē.**	You're not allowed to park here.
你冇放錢喺角子機入面。 **Néih móuh fong chín hái gok jí gēi yahp mihn.**	You haven't put money in the parking meter.
你嘅車頭燈／車尾燈唔著。 **Néih ge chē tàuh dāng/chē méih dāng m̀h jeuhk.**	Your lights aren't working.
呢個係…罰款。 **Nī go haih…faht fún.**	That's a…fine.

I have a passport.	**Ngóh yáuh wuh jiu.** 我有護照。
I have an international driver's licence.	**Ngóh yáuh gwok jai ga sái jāp jiu.** 我有國際駕駛執照。
I don't speak Cantonese.	**Ngóh m̀h sīk góng Gwóng Dūng Wá.** 我唔識講廣東話。
I didn't see the sign.	**Ngóh tái m̀h dóu louh páai.** 我睇唔到路牌。
I don't understand what it says.	**Ngóh tái m̀h mìhng seuhng mihn góng māt yéh.** 我睇唔明上面講乜嘢。
I was only doing… kilometers an hour.	**Ngóh hàahng ge sìh chūk jí haih… gūng léih.** 我行嘅時速只係…公里。
I'll have my car checked.	**Ngóh jīk hāk heui gím chàh ngóh ga chē.** 我即刻去檢查我架車。
I was blinded by oncoming lights.	**Yìhng mihn ge chē tàuh dāng chàahng jyuh ngóh deui ngáahn.** 迎面嘅車頭燈燦住我對眼。

At the police station

I want to report a collision.	**Ngóh yiu bou ngon, haih johng chē.** 我要報案，係撞車。
I want to report a missing person.	**Ngóh yiu bou ngon, haih sāt jūng.** 我要報案，係失蹤。
I want to report a rape.	**Ngóh yiu bou ngon, haih kèuhng gāan.** 我要報案，係強姦。
Could you make a statement, please?	**Néih hó m̀h hó yíh béi háu gūng a?** 你可唔可以俾口供呀？
Could I have a copy?	**Ngóh hó m̀h hó yíh yiu yāt fahn fu bún a?** 我可唔可以要一份副本呀？
I've lost everything.	**Ngóh só yáuh ge yéh dōu m̀h gin jó la.** 我所有嘅嘢都唔見咗喇。
I've no money left, I'm desperate.	**Ngóh ge chín dōu yuhng yùhn la, ngóh jáu tàuh mòuh louh la.** 我嘅錢都用完喇，我走頭無路喇。
Could you lend me some money?	**Néih hó m̀h hó yíh je dī chín béi ngóh a?** 你可唔可以借啲錢俾我呀？
I'd like an interpreter.	**Ngóh sēui yiu go fāan yihk yùhn.** 我需要個翻譯員。
I'm innocent.	**Ngóh haih mòuh gū ga.** 我係無辜㗎。
I don't know anything about it.	**Ngóh māt yéh dōu m̀h jī dou.** 我乜嘢都唔知道。
I want to speak to someone from the American embassy.	**Ngóh yiu tùhng Méih Gwok daaih síh gwún ge yàhn góng yéh.** 我要同美國大使館嘅人講嘢。
– Australian	**Ngou Jāu** 澳洲
– British	**Yīng Gwok** 英國
– Canadian	**Gā Nàh Daaih** 加拿大
I want a lawyer who speaks English.	**Ngóh yiu wán go wúih góng yīng mán ge leuht sī.** 我要搵個會講英文嘅律師。

15. English-Cantonese Dictionary

The following dictionary is meant to supplement the chapters in this book. Some of the words not on this list can be found elsewhere in this book. Food items can be found in sections 4.7 and 4.8, and the parts of a car on page 75 and the parts of a bicycle on page 78.

A

abacus **syun pùhn** 算盤

about (approximately) **daaih yeuk** 大約

about (regarding) **yáuh gwāan** 有關

above **seuhng mihn** 上面

abroad **gwok ngoih** 國外

accident **yi ngoih** 意外

accommodation **jyuh sūk** 住宿

activity **wuht duhng** 活動

address **deih jí** 地址

adult **sìhng yàhn** 成人

advice **yi gin** 意見

aeroplane **fēi gēi** 飛機

afraid **pa** 怕

after **jī hauh** 之後

afternoon (midday) **jūng ngh** 中午

afternoon (3 pm to dusk) **hah ngh** 下午

again **joi** 再

ago **yíh chìhn** 以前

agree, to **tùhng yi** 同意

air **hūng hei** 空氣

air-conditioning **láahng hei/hūng tiuh** 冷氣／空調

airmail **hūng yàauh** 空郵

airplane **fēi gēi** 飛機

airport **fēi gēi chèuhng** 飛機場

alcohol, liquor **jáu** 酒

allergy **gwo máhn** 過敏

allocate **fān pui** 分配

alike **sēung tùhng** 相同

a lot **hóu dō** 好多

almost **gēi fùh** 幾乎

alone **dāan duhk** 單獨

alphabet **jih móuh** 字母

already **yíh gīng** 已經

also **dōu** 都

altogether, in total **yāt guhng** 一共

always **gīng sèuhng** 經常

ambassador **daaih síh** 大使

America **Méih Gwok** 美國

American (in general) **Méih Gwok ge** 美國嘅

American (people) **Méih Gwok yàhn** 美國人

American dollars **Méih gām** 美金

amount **sou muhk** 數目

ancestor **jóu sīn** 祖先

ancient **gú doih** 古代

and **tùhng màaih** 同埋

angry **faat nāu/lāu** 發嬲

animal **duhng maht** 動物

ankle **geuk jāang** 腳踭

another (different) **daih yih go** 第二個

another (same) **joi làih yāt go** 再嚟一個

answer the phone **jip dihn wá** 接電話

antibiotics **kong sāng sou** 抗生素

anybody, anyone **yahm hòh yàhn** 任何人

apartment **gūng yuh** 公寓

apologize, to **douh hip** 道歉

apple **pìhng gwó** 蘋果

appointment **yeuk wuih/yuh yeuk** 約會／預約

April **Sei yuht** 四月

architecture **gin jūk** 建築

area **deih kēui** 地區

area code **kēui houh** 區號

around (nearby) **fuh gahn** 附近

arrive, to **dou** 到

Asia **Nga Jāu** 亞洲

ask about, to **mahn** 問

ask for, to **yiu** 要

asleep **fan jeuhk** 瞓着

assist, to **bōng joh/bōng mòhng** 幫助／幫忙

as well **dōu haih** 都係

at **hái** 喺

at home **hái ngūk kéi** 喺屋企

at least **héi máh/ji síu** 起碼／至少

at night **yeh máahn** 夜晚

at once **jīk hāk** 即刻

at the latest **jeui chìh** 最遲

attempt, to **si** 試

attend, to **chāam gā** 參加

attitude **taai douh** 態度

August **Baat yuht** 八月

Australia **Ngou Jāu** 澳洲

Australian (people) **Ngou Jāu yàhn** 澳洲人

Australian (in general) **Ngou Jāu ge** 澳洲嘅

Australian dollars **Ngou baih** 澳幣

Automated Teller Machine (ATM) **Jih Duhng Gwaih Yùhn Gēi** 自動櫃員機

automobile, car **chē** 車

autopay **jih duhng jyún jeung** 自動轉帳

autumn **chāu tīn** 秋天

available (to buy) **máaih dāk dóu** 買得到

available (to make) **jéun beih hóu** 準備好

average (numbers) **pìhng gwān** 平均

average (so-so, just okay) **yāt būn/màh má déi** 一般／麻麻地

awake **séng** 醒

awake, wake up **séng jó** 醒咗

awaken, wake someone up **giu séng** 叫醒

aware **jī dou** 知道

B

baby **bìh bī** BB

back, rear **hauh mihn** 後面

back, to go **fāan heui** 返去

backpack **bui bāau** 背包

backward **lohk hauh** 落後

bad **waaih** 壞

bad luck **m̀h hóu wahn/dóu mùih** 唔好運／倒霉

bag **dói** 袋

ball **bō** 波

ballpoint pen **yùhn jí bāt** 原子筆

banana **hēung jiu** 香蕉

bandage **bāng dáai** 繃帶

bank (finance) **ngàhn hòhng** 銀行

banquet **yin wuih** 宴會

bar (serving drinks) **jáu bā** 酒巴

barbecue **sīu hāau** 燒烤

barbecued goose **sīu ngó** 燒鵝

barbecued pork **chā sīu** 叉燒

barber **faat yìhng sī** 髮型師

bargain, to **góng ga** 講價

basket **láam** 籃

basketball **làahm kàuh** 籃球

bathtub **yuhk gōng** 浴缸

bathe **chūng lèuhng** 沖涼

bathe, swim **yàuh séui** 游水

bathrobe **yuhk yī** 浴衣

bathroom **chūng lèuhng fóng** 沖涼房

battery **dihn chìh** 電池

be, exist **yáuh** 有

beach **hói tāan** 海灘

beancurd **dauh fuh** 豆腐

beautiful (of things and places) **leng/jeng** 靚／正

because **yān waih** 因為

bed **chòhng** 床

bedroom **seuih fóng** 睡房

bedsheet **chòhng dāan** 床單

beef **ngàuh yuhk** 牛肉

beer **bē jáu** 啤酒

before (in time) **yíh chìhn** 以前

before (in front of) **hái...chìhn mihn** 喺⋯前面

beforehand, earlier **jī chìhn** 之前

begin, to **hōi chí** 開始

behave **bíu yihn** 表現

behind **hái...hauh mihn** 喺⋯後面

Beijing **Bāk Gīng** 北京

belief, faith **seun yéuhng** 信仰

believe, to **sēung seun** 相信

below **hah mihn** 下面

belt **pèih dáai** 皮帶

beside **hái...pòhng bīn** 喺⋯旁邊

besides **chèuih jó...jī ngoih** 除咗之外

best **jeui hóu** 最好

Best wishes **Jūk néih hóu wahn** 祝你好運

better **gang hóu/hóu dī** 更好／好啲

between **hái...jī gāan** 喺⋯之間

bicycle **dāan chē** 單車

big **daaih** 大

bill **dāan** 單

bill, to pay **màaih dāan** 埋單

bird **jéuk** 雀

birth, to give **sāang** 生

birthday **sāang yaht** 生日

biscuit **béng gōn** 餅乾

bit (slightly) **yāt dī** 一啲

bite, to **ngáauh** 咬

bitter **fú** 苦

black **hāk sīk** 黑色

bland **dāan diuh** 單調

blanket **jīn** 氈

bleed, to **làuh hyut** 流血

blog **móhng ji** 網誌

blood **hyut** 血

blouse **néuih jōng sēut sāam** 女裝恤衫

blue **làahm sīk** 藍色

Bluetooth **Làahm ngàh** 藍牙

board, to (bus, train) **séuhng chē** 上車

board, to (boat) **séuhng syùhn** 上船

boat **syùhn** 船

body **sān tái** 身體

body massage **chyùhn sān ngon mō**
全身按摩

boil, to **jyú** 煮

boiled **jyú gwo ge** 煮過嘅

Bon voyage! **Yāt fàahn fūng seuhn!**
一帆風順!

book **syū** 書

book shop **syū dim** 書店

bored **muhn/mòuh lìuh** 悶／無聊

boring **móuh yi sī** 冇意思

born, to be **chēut sai** 出世

borrow, to **je** 借

botanic gardens **jihk maht yùhn**
植物園

both **léuhng (go)** 兩(個)

bother, disturb **dá gáau** 打擾

bottle **jēun** 樽

bottom (buttocks) **lō yáu/pei gú**
攞柚／屁股

bowl **wún** 碗

box **sēung** 箱

box (cardboard) **jí háp** 紙盒

boy **nàahm/làahm jái** 男仔

boyfriend **nàahm pàhng yáuh**
男朋友

bra **hūng wàih** 胸圍

bracelet **sáu ngáak** 手鈪

brain **nóuh** 腦

brake, to brake **saat jai** 刹掣

branch (company) **fān hóng** 分行

branded **mìhng pàaih** 名牌

brandy **baahk lāan déi** 白蘭地

bread **mihn bāau** 麵包

break, shatter **dá laahn** 打爛

break down, to (car, machine)
waaih jó 壞咗

breakfast, morning meal **jóu
chāan** 早餐

breakfast, to eat **sihk jóu chāan**
食早餐

bridge **kìuh** 橋

briefcase **gūng sih bāau** 公事包

bring, to **ló** 攞

Britain **Yīng Gwok** 英國

British (in general) **Yīng Gwok ge**
英國嘅

British (people) **Yīng Gwok yàhn**
英國人

broccoli **sāi làahn fā** 西蘭花

broken **waaih jó** 壞咗

bronze **tùhng/chīng tùhng**
銅／青銅

brother (older) **gòh gō/daaih lóu**
哥哥／大佬

brother (younger) **dàih dái/sai lóu**
弟弟／細佬

brown (coffee color) **jyū gū līk sīk**
朱古力色

bruise **yú hāk** 瘀黑

brush **cháat** 刷

bubble tea **jān jyū náaih chàh** 珍珠
奶茶

Buddhism **Faht Gaau** 佛教

Buddhist (in general) **Faht Gaau
ge** 佛教嘅

Buddhist (people) **Faht Gaau tòuh**
佛教徒

building **daaih hah** 大廈

burn (injury) **sīu sēung** 燒傷

Burma, Myanmar **Míhn Dihn**
緬甸

Burmese (in general) **Míhn Dihn
ge** 緬甸嘅

Burmese (people) **Míhn Dihn yàhn**
緬甸人

bus **bā sí** 巴士

bus stop **bā sí jaahm** 巴士站

business **sēung yihp** 商業

business person **sēung yàhn** 商人

business trip **gūng gon** 公幹

busy (with something) **mòhng** 忙

but **daahn haih** 但係

butter **ngàuh yàuh** 牛油

buy, to **máaih** 買

by the means of **yuhng** 用

C

cabbage **yèh choi** 椰菜

cabbage, Chinese **baak choi** 白菜

cake, pastry **daahn gōu** 蛋糕

calculator **gais sou gēi** 計數機

call on the telephone **dá dihn wá** 打電話

called, named **giu** 叫

Cambodia **Gáan Pòuh Jaaih** 柬埔寨

Cambodian (in general) **Gáan Pòuh Jaaih ge** 柬埔寨嘅

Cambodian (people) **Gáan Pòuh Jaaih yàhn** 柬埔寨人

camera **yíng séung gēi** 影相機

can, be able to **wúih** 會

can, may **hó yíh** 可以

can, tin **gwun táu** 罐頭

Canada **Gā Nàh Daaih** 加拿大

Canada (in general) **Gā Nàh Daaih ge** 加拿大嘅

Canadian (people) **Gā Nàh Daaih yàhn** 加拿大人

Canadian dollars **Gā baih** 加幣

cancel **chéui sīu** 取消

candle **laahp jūk** 蠟燭

candy, sweets **tóng** 糖

canoe **duhk muhk jāu** 獨木舟

can't see **tái m̀h gin** 睇唔見

can't see clearly **tái m̀h chīng chó** 睇唔清楚

Cantonese (in general) **Gwóng Dūng ge** 廣東嘅

Cantonese (language) **Gwóng Dūng wá** 廣東話

Cantonese (people) **Gwóng Dūng yàhn** 廣東人

Cantonese-style congee **sāang gwán zūk** 生滾粥

capture, to **jūk dóu** 捉到

car, automobile **chē** 車

car park **tìhng chē chèuhng** 停車場

car space **chē wái** 車位

card **kāat** 咭

care of, to take **jiu gu** 照顧

careful **síu sām** 小心

carrot **hùhng lòh baahk** 紅蘿蔔

carry, to **daai/ló** 帶／攞

carton, a **yāt tìuh** 一條

cash, money **yihn gām** 現金

cash a check, to **deui yihn** 兌現

cashier **sāu ngán chyu** 收銀處

casino **dóu chèuhng** 賭場

casualty (hospital) **gāp jing sāt** 急症室

cat **māau** 貓

catamaran **sēung tái syùhn** 雙體船

catch, to **jūk** 捉

Catholic (in general) **Tīn Jyú Gaau ge** 天主教嘅

Catholic (people) **Tīn Jyú Gaau tòuh** 天主教徒

catty (measure) **gān** 斤

cauliflower **yèh choi fā** 椰菜花

cautious **síu sām** 小心

cave **ngàahm duhng** 岩洞

CD (compact disc) **Gwōng díp** 光碟

celebrate, to **hing jūk** 慶祝

center, middle **jūng gāan** 中間

certain, sure **yāt dihng** 一定

chair **dang** 凳

champagne **hēung bān** 香檳

chance, opportunity **gēi wuih** 機會

change, small **sáan ngán** 散銀

change, to (conditions, situations) **gói bin** 改變

change (clothes) **wuhn** 換

charging cable **chūng dihn sin** 充電線

cheap **pèhng** 平

cheat, to **ngāk/āk(yàhn)** 呃(人)

check, verify **gím chàh** 檢查

Cheers! **Yám sing!** 飲勝!

cheese **jī sí** 芝士

chess **gwok jai jeuhng kéi** 國際象棋

chest (breast) **hūng** 胸

chicken **gāi** 雞

child (young person) **sai mān jái** 細蚊仔

child (offspring) **jái néui** 仔女

children **yìh tùhng** 兒童

chilli pepper **laaht jīu** 辣椒

chilli sauce **laaht jīu jeung** 辣椒醬

China **Jūng Gwok** 中國

Chinese (in general) **Jūng Gwok ge** 中國嘅

Chinese (language) **Jūng mán/ Jūng màhn** 中文

Chinese (people) **Jūng Gwok yàhn** 中國人

Chinese chess **jeuhng kéi** 象棋

Chinese Renminbi **Yàhn màhn baih** 人民幣

chocolate **jyū gū līk** 朱古力

choice, to choose **syún jaahk** 選擇

chopsticks **faai jí** 筷子

Christian **Gēi Dūk tòuh** 基督徒

Christianity **Gēi Dūk gaau** 基督教

church **gaau tòhng/tóng** 教堂

cigarette **yīn jái** 煙仔

cinema **hei yún** 戲院

circle **yùhn hyūn** 圓圈

citizen **síh màhn/gūng màhn** 市民／公民

city **sìhng síh** 城市

claypot rice **bōu jái faahn** 煲仔飯

clean **gōn jehng** 乾淨

clean, to **jíng gón jehng** 整乾淨

clear (of weather) **hóu tīn** 好天

clever **chūng mìhng** 聰明

climate **hei hauh** 氣候

clock **jūng** 鐘

close to, nearby **káhn/kaau gahn** 近／靠近

close, to cover **kám màaih** 哚埋

closed (door/shop) **sāan mùhn** 閂門

closed (road) **fūng só jó** 封鎖咗

clothes, clothing **yī fuhk** 衣服

cloudy, overcast **dō wàhn** 多雲

coat, jacket **ngoih yī** 外衣

coat, overcoat **daaih lāu** 大褸

Coca-Cola **Hó háu hó lohk** 可口可樂

cockroaches **gaaht jáat** 甲曱

cocktail **gāi méih jáu** 雞尾酒

coffee **ga fē** 咖啡

coin **ngaahng baih/sáan ngán** 硬幣／散銀

cold **dung** 凍

cold, flu **sēung fūng** 傷風

colleague **tùhng sih** 同事

collect payment, to **sāu chín** 收錢

collision, to collide **johng** 撞

colour **ngàahn sīk** 顏色

comb **sō** 梳

come, to **làih** 嚟

come back **fāan làih** 返嚟

come in **yahp làih** 入嚟

comfortable **syū fuhk** 舒服

comics **lihn wàahn tòuh** 連環圖

company, firm **gūng sī** 公司

compared with, to compare **béi gaau** 比較

compass **jí nàahm jām** 指南針

compensated **pùih** 賠

complain, to **póuh yun** 抱怨

complaint **tàuh sou** 投訴

complete (whole) **chyùhn bouh** 全部

complete, to **yùhn sìhng** 完成

complicated **fūk jaahp** 複雜

compress **ngaat sūk** 壓縮

computer **dihn nóuh** 電腦

concert **yām ngohk wúi** 音樂會

concert hall **yām ngohk tēng** 音樂廳

conditioner (hair) **wuh faat louh** 護髮露

condom **beih yahn tou** 避孕套

confirm **kok yihng** 確認

Confucianism **Yùh Gā sī séung** 儒家思想

Congratulations! **Gūng héi néih!** 恭喜你!

connect **lìhn sin** 連線

consider **háau leuih** 考慮

consulate **líhng sih gún** 領事館

consultation (by doctor) **tái behng** 睇病

contact, connection **lyùhn lok** 聯絡

contact lens **yán yìhng ngáahn géng** 隱型眼鏡

contagious **chyùhn yíhm** 傳染

continue, to **gai juhk** 繼續

contraceptive **beih yahn** 避孕

contraceptive pill **beih yahn yún** 避孕丸

convenience store **bihn leih dim** 便利店

convenient **fōng bihn** 方便

cook (person) **chyùh sī** 廚師

cookie **kūk kèih** 曲奇

cool (temperature) **lèuhng sóng** 涼爽

copper **tùhng/jí tùhng** 銅／紫銅

copy **fu bún/fūk yan** 副本／複印

corn, grain **sūk máih** 粟米

corner **gok lōk táu** 角落頭

correct **ngāam/jing kok** 啱／正確

correspond (write letters) **tūng seun** 通信

corrupt **fuh baaih** 腐敗

cosmetics **fa jōng bán** 化妝品

cost **sìhng bún** 成本

cost (price) **ga chìhn** 價錢

costly **gwai** 貴

cotton **mìhn bou** 棉布

cotton wool **mìhn fā** 棉花

couch, sofa **sō fá** 梳化

cough, to **kāt** 咳

cough drop/lolly **yeuhn hàuh tóng** 潤喉糖

cough syrup **kāt yeuhk séui** 咳藥水

could, might **hó nàhng** 可能

count **sóu** 數

country (nation) **gwok gā** 國家

country code **gwok gā doih houh** 國家代號

countryside **gāau ngoih** 郊外

courtesy **láih maauh** 禮貌

cover, to **jē** 遮

crab **háaih** 蟹

cracker, salty biscuit **hàahm béng gōn** 鹹餅乾

crafts **sáu gūng ngaih** 手工藝

crashed (car) **johng chē** 撞車

credit card **seun yuhng kāat** 信用卡

cross, go over **gwo** 過

crossroads **sahp jih louh háu** 十字路口

crowded **bīk** 逼

cucumber **wòhng gwā** 黃瓜

culture **màhn fa** 文化

cup, glass **būi** 杯

curly **lyūn** 攣

curler, eyelash **jit mòuh gyún** 睫毛捲

curler, hair **faat gyún** 髮捲

custom, tradition **jaahp juhk** 習俗

cut, to **chit/got** 切／割

cute, appealing **hó ngoi** 可愛

D

daily **yaht sèuhng** 日常

dairy **náih leuih sihk bán** 奶類食品

damage, to **jíng waaih** 整壞

damp **chìuh sāp** 潮濕

dance, to **tiu móuh** 跳舞

danger **ngàih hím** 危險

dark **ngam** 暗

date (of the month) **yaht kèih** 日期

date (to) **yeuk wuih** 約會

date of birth **chēut sāng yaht kèih** 出生日期

daughter **néui** 女

daughter-in-law **sīk fúh** 媳婦

day **yaht** 日

day after tomorrow **hauh yaht** 後日

day before yesterday **chìhn yaht** 前日

data SIM card **sou geui kāat** 數據卡

dead **séi jó** 死咗

December **Sahp yih yuht** 十二月

decision, to decide **kyu dihng** 決定

declare, to **bou gwāan** 報關

deep **sām** 深

defecate, to **daaih bihn** 大便

degrees (temperature) **douh** 度

delay, to **dāam ngh** 耽誤

delete, to **sāan chèuih** 刪除

delicious **hóu sihk** 好食

delivery **sung wahn** 送運

depart, to **lèih hōi** 離開

department store **baak fo gūng sī** 百貨公司

departure **chēut faat** 出發

deposit **ngon gām** 按金

desk **syū tói** 書檯

dessert **tìhm bán** 甜品

destination **muhk dīk deih** 目的地

detergent **sái git jīng** 洗潔精

dial, to (telephone) **dá dihn wá** 打電話

diamond **jyun sehk** 鑽石

diary **yaht gei** 日記

dictionary **chìh dín/jih dín** 詞典／字典

die, to **séi** 死

different, other **m̀h tùhng** 唔同

difficult **kwan nàahn** 困難

digital camera **sou máh séung gēi** 數碼相機

dim sum **dím sām** 點心

dinner, evening meal **máahn faahn** 晚飯

dinner, to eat **sihk máahn faahn** 食晚飯

direction **fōng heung** 方向

dirty **wū jōu** 污糟

disappointed **sāt mohng** 失望

discount **gáam ga** 減價

dish, platter **dihp** 碟

dish (particular food) **sung** 餸

dish towel **sái wún gān** 洗碗巾

distance **kéuih lèih** 距離

disturb, to **dá gáau** 打擾

divorce, to **lèih fān** 離婚

diving **chìhm séui** 潛水

divorced **lèih jó fān** 離咗婚

do, perform an action **jouh** 做

document **màhn gín** 文件

Don't mention it! **M̀h hóu haak hei!** 唔好客氣!

do one's best **jeuhn só nàhng** 盡所能

doctor **yī sāng** 醫生

dog **gáu** 狗

door **mùhn** 門

double **sēung púih** 雙倍

down, downward **heung hah** 向下

downstairs **làuh hah** 樓下

downtown **síh jūng sām** 市中心

dozen **yāt dā** 一打

draw, to **waahk** 畫

drawer **gwaih túng** 櫃桶

dream **muhng** 夢

dream, to **faat muhng** 發夢

dressed, to get **wuhn sāam** 換衫

dressing gown **sàhn lāu** 晨褸

drink, refreshment **yám yéh** 飲嘢

drink, to **yám** 飲

drive, to (a car) **hōi chē** 開車

drug (medicine) **yeuhk** 藥

drugstore, pharmacy **yeuhk fòhng** 藥房

drunk **yám jeui** 飲醉

dry **gōn** 乾

dry (weather) **gōn chou** 乾燥

dry, to **chēui gōn** 吹乾

dry cleaners **gōn sái dim** 乾洗店

duck **ngaap/aap** 鴨

during **hái...kèih gāan** 喺⋯期間

E

ear **yíh jái** 耳仔

earrings **yíh wáan** 耳環

early **jóu** 早

early in the morning **jīu jóu** 朝早

east **dūng bīn/bihn** 東邊

easy **yùhng yih** 容易

eat, to **sihk** 食

eat breakfast **sihk jóu chāan** 食早餐

eat dinner **sihk máahn faahn** 食晚餐

eat lunch **sihk ngaan jau** 食晏晝

egg **gāi dáan** 雞蛋

eggplant, aubergine **ngái gwā** 矮瓜

eight **baat** 八

eighteen **sahp baat** 十八

eighty **baat sahp** 八十

either **yāt haih...yāt haih** 一係⋯一係

Electronic Payment Services (EPS) **Yih Baahn Sih** 易辦事

elegant **gōu ngáh** 高雅

elevator **dihn tāi** 電梯

eleven **sahp yāt** 十一

email **dihn yàuh** 電郵

email address **dihn yàuh deih jí** 電郵地址

embassy **daaih síh gwún** 大使館

embroidered **sau fā ge** 繡花嘅

embroidery **chi sau** 刺繡

emergency **gāp chán** 急診

empty **hūng ge** 空嘅

engaged (telephone) **yáuh yàhn góng gán** 有人講緊

engaged (to be married) **dihng fān** 訂婚

engine **gēi hei** 機器

engineer **gūng chìhng sī** 工程師

England **Yīng Gwok** 英國

English (in general) **Yīng Gwok ge** 英國嘅

English (language) **Yīng Mán/ Yīng Màhn/Yīng Yúh** 英文／英語

English (person) **Yīng Gwok yàhn** 英國人

enlarge, to **fong daaih** 放大

enough **jūk gau** 足夠

enquire, to **mahn** 問

enquiry **chàh sēun** 查詢

enter, to **yahp làih** 入嚟

entrance, way in **yahp háu** 入口

envelope **seun fūng** 信封

envious, envy **sihn mouh** 羨慕

environment, the **wàahn gíng** 環境

escalator **dihn tāi** 電梯

Europe **Ngāu Jāu** 歐洲

Euro **Ngāu yùhn** 歐元

evening **yeh máahn** 夜晚

everybody, everyone **múih go yàhn** 每個人

every kind of **gok sīk gok yeuhng** 各式各樣

everything **yat chai** 一切

every time **múih chi** 每次

everywhere **dou chyu** 到處

exact, exactly **kok saht** 確實

exam, test **háau síh** 考試

examine, to **gím chàh** 檢查

exchange, to (money, opinion) **deui wuhn** 兌換

exchange rate **deui wuhn léut** 兌換率

excited **hīng fáhn** 興奮

exciting **lihng yàhn hīng fáhn** 令人興奮

Excuse me (attracting attention) **Chéng/Chíng mahn** 請問

Excuse me (getting past) **Ṁh gōi je je** 唔該借借

Excuse me (apology) **Deui ṁh jyuh** 對唔住

exit, way out **chēut háu** 出口

expenses **fai yuhng** 費用

expensive **gwai** 貴

explain, to **gáai sīk** 解釋

export, to export **chēu tháu** 出口

eye **ngáahn** 眼

eyeglasses, spectacles **ngáahn géng** 眼鏡

F

fabric, textile **bou liú** 布料

face **mihn** 臉

face (respect) **mihn jí** 面子

Facebook **Mihn Syū** 面書

fall (season) **chāu tīn** 秋天

fall, to **dit** 跌

fall over **dit dóu** 跌倒

false (imitation) **mouh pàaih fo/gá mouh ge** 冒牌貨／假冒嘅

family **gā tìhng** 家庭

famous **yáuh méng/chēut méng** 有名／出名

far **yúhn** 遠

fast, rapid **faai** 快

fatty, greasy **fèih neih/yàuh neih** 肥膩／油膩

father **bàh bā** 爸爸

father-in-law **ngoih fú** 外父

fashion **sìh zōng** 時裝

favourite **jeui jūng yi ge** 最鍾意嘅

fax, to fax **chyùhn jān** 傳真

fear **pa** 怕

February **Yih yuht** 二月

fee **sāu fai** 收費

feel, to **gok dāk** 覺得

female **néuih sing** 女性

festival **jit yaht** 節日

fetch, to **ló** 攞

fever **faat sīu** 發燒

few **géi go** 幾個

fiancé **meih fān fū** 未婚夫

fiancée **meih fān chāi** 未婚妻

fifteen **sahp ngh** 十五

fifty **ngh sahp** 五十

Filipino (Tagalog) **Fēi Leuht Bān wá** 菲律賓話(塔加拉族語)

Filipino (general) **Fēi Leuht Bān ge** 菲律賓嘅

Filipino (person) **Fēi Leuht Bān yàhn** 菲律賓人

fill out (form) **tìhn bíu** 填表

film, movie **dihn yíng** 電影

find, to **wán** 搵

finger **sáu jí** 手指

fire **fó** 火

fireworks **yīn fā** 煙花

first, earlier, beforehand **sīn** 先

fish **yú** 魚

fish, to **diu yú** 釣魚

fitting room **si sān sāt** 試身室

five **ngh** 五

flash (camera) **sím gwōng dāng** 閃光燈

flashlight, torch **dihn túng** 電筒

flavour **meih douh** 味道

flight **bāan gēi** 班機

flight attendant (female) **hūng jūng síu jé** 空中小姐

flight attendant (male) **hūng jūng siu yèh** 空中少爺

flight number **bāan gēi houh máh** 班機號碼

floor **láu** 樓

florist **fā dim** 花店

flower **fā** 花

fly (insect) **wū yīng** 烏蠅

flu **gám mouh** 感冒

fog **mouh** 霧

folding chair **jip dang** 摺凳

follow along, to **seuhn jyuh** 順住

follow behind, to **gān jyuh** 跟住

fond of, to be **jūng yi/héi fūn** 鍾意／喜歡

food **sihk maht** 食物

food poisoning **sihk maht jung duhk** 食物中毒

foot **geuk** 腳

foot massage **geuk dái ngon mō** 腳底按摩

forbid, to **gam jí** 禁止

foreign **ngoih gwok ge** 外國嘅

foreign currency **ngoih baih** 外幣

foreigner **ngoih gwok yàhn** 外國人

forget, to **mòhng gei** 忘記

fork **chā** 叉

fortunately **hóu chói** 好彩

forty **sei sahp** 四十

forward **heung chìhn** 向前

four **sei** 四

fourteen **sahp sei** 十四

France **Faat Gwok** 法國

French (in general) **Faat Gwok ge** 法國嘅

French (language) **Faat Mán/Faat Màhn** 法文

French (people) **Faat Gwok yàhn** 法國人

free, independent **jih yàuh** 自由

free of charge **míhn fai** 免費

frequent **gīng sèuhng** 經常

fresh **sān sīn** 新鮮

Friday **Sīng kèih ngh** 星期五

friend **pàhng yáuh** 朋友

friend, boy **nàahm pàhng yáuh** 男朋友

friend, girl **néuih pàhng yáuh** 女朋友

friendly, outgoing **yáuh sihn** 友善

front **chìhn mihn** 前面

fruit **sāang gwó** 生果

fry, to **jīn** 煎

full, eaten one's fill **báau** 飽

fun, to have **wáan** 玩

funny **hóu siu** 好笑

future; in future **jēung lòih** 將來

G

gamble **dóu bok** 賭博

game **yàuh hei** 遊戲

garage (for repairs) **chē fòhng** 車房

garbage **laahp saap** 垃圾

gardens, park **gūng yún** 公園

garlic **syun tàuh** 蒜頭

garment **yī fuhk** 衣服

gas cooker **sehk yàuh hei lòuh** 石油氣爐

gasoline **dihn yàuh** 電油

gasoline station **yàuh jaahm** 油站

gel **faat laahp** 髮蠟

Germany **Dāk Gwok** 德國

German (in general) **Dāk Gwok ge** 德國嘅

German (language) **Dāk Mán/Dāk Màhn** 德文

German (people) **Dāk Gwok yàhn** 德國人

get off (bus/train) **lohk chē** 落車

get off (boat) **lohk syùhn** 落船

get on (bus/train) **séuhng chē** 上車

get on (boat) **séuhng syùhn** 上船

get ready (to go out) **jéun beih chēut gāai** 準備出街

get ready (to prepare) **jéun beih** 準備

get up (from bed) **héi sān** 起身

gift **láih maht** 禮物

gigabyte **gīk** 激

give, to **béi** 俾

given name **méng** 名

glad **gōu hing** 高興

glass (for water) **séui būi** 水杯

glass (of wine) **jáu būi** 酒杯

glasses, spectacles **ngáahn géng** 眼鏡

go, to **heui** 去

go around, visit **fóng mahn** 訪問

go home **fāan ngūk kéi** 返屋企

go out, exit **chēut heui** 出去

go to bed **fan gaau** 瞓覺

gold **gām** 金

golf **gōu yíh fū kàuh** 高爾夫球

golf course **gōu yíh fū kàuh chèuhng** 高爾夫球場

good **hóu** 好

good afternoon **hah nǵh hóu** 下午好

good morning **jóu sàhn** 早晨

good night **jóu táu** 早抖

goodbye **joi gin** 再見

Good luck! **Jūk néih hóu wahn!** 祝你好運!

grapes **(pòuh) tàih jí** (葡)提子

green **luhk sīk** 綠色

group buy **tyùhn kau** 團購

grow, cultivate **jung** 種

Guangzhou (Canton) **Gwóng Jāu** 廣州

guesthouse **bān gwún** 賓館

guide, lead **douh yàuh** 導遊

guidebook **léuih yàuh jí nàahm** 旅遊指南

gymnasium **tái chōu chèuhng** 體操場

gymnastics **tái chōu** 體操

H

hair **tàuh faat** 頭髮

haircut **jín faat** 剪髮

half **yāt bun** 一半

hammock **diu chòhng** 吊床

hand **sáu** 手

handbag **sáu dói** 手袋

handicraft **sáu gūng ngaih** 手工藝

hand-made **sáu jouh** 手做

handsome **yīng jeun** 英俊

happen, occur **faat sāng** 發生

happy **hōi sām/gōu hing** 開心／高興

Happy Birthday! **Sāang yaht faai lohk!** 生日快樂!

Happy Chinese New Year! **Gūng Héi Faat Chòih!** 恭喜發財!

harbour **hói góng** 海港

hardware **ngaahng gín** 硬件

hardworking, industrious **kàhn lihk** 勤力

harmonious **yùhng hāp** 融洽

have, own **yáuh** 有

have to, must **yāt dihng yiu** 一定要

he, him **kéuih** 佢

head **tàuh** 頭

headache **tàuh tung** 頭痛

healthy **gihn hōng** 健康

hear, to **tēng** 聽

heart **sām johng** 心臟

heatwave **yiht lohng** 熱浪

heavy **chúhng** 重

hello, hi **néih hóu** 你好

Hello (on phone) **Wái** 喂

Help! **Gau mehng a!** 救命啊！

help, to **bōng/bōng mòhng** 幫／幫忙

her, hers **kéuih ge** 佢嘅

here **nī douh/nī syu** 呢度／呢處

high **gōu** 高

hiking **hàahng sāan** 行山

hill **sāan** 山

hire, to **jōu** 租

his **kéuih ge** 佢嘅

history **lihk sí** 歷史

hit, strike **dá** 打

hobby **ngoi hou/si hou** 愛好／嗜好

holiday (festival) **jit yaht** 節日

holiday (vacation) **ga kèih** 假期

home, house **ngūk kéi** 屋企

honest **sìhng saht** 誠實

honey **maht tòhng** 蜜糖

Hong Kong **Hēung Góng** 香港

Hong Kong dollars **Góng baih** 港幣

Hong Kong people **Hēung Góng yàhn** 香港人

Hong Kong style **Góng sīk** 港式

hope, to **hēi mohng** 希望

horse **máh** 馬

hospital **yī yún** 醫院

hospital, public **gūng lahp yī yún** 公立醫院

hospital, private **sī lahp yī yún** 私立醫院

hostel **léuih gwún** 旅館

hot (spicy) **laaht** 辣

hot (temperature) **yiht** 熱

hotel **jáu dim** 酒店

hotpot **fó wō** 火鍋

hot spring **wān chyùhn** 溫泉

hour **jūng tàuh** 鐘頭

housewife **gā tìhng jyú fúh** 家庭主婦

how **dím/yùh hòh** 點／如何

how are you **néih hóu ma** 你好嗎

however **daahn haih** 但係

how far **géi yúhn** 幾遠

how long **géi chèuhng** 幾長

how many **géi go** 幾個

how much **géi dō chín** 幾多錢

how old **géi daaih nìhn géi** 幾大年紀

humid **chìuh sāp** 潮濕

humor **yāu mahk** 幽默

hundred **baak** 百

hundred thousand **sahp maahn** 十萬

hundred million **yīk** 億

hungry **ngoh** 餓

hurry, in a **gón sìh gaan** 趕時間

hurry up! **faai dī** 快啲

hurt (injured) **sauh sēung** 受傷

husband **jeuhng fū** 丈夫

hydrofoil **séui yihk syùhn** 水翼船

I

I, me **ngóh** 我

ice **bīng** 冰

ice cream **syut gōu** 雪糕

idea **jyú yi** 主意

identity card **sān fán jing** 身份證

if **yùh gwó** 如果

illegal **fēi faat** 非法

ill, sick **m̀h syū fuhk** 唔舒服

illness **behng** 病

immediately **laahp hāk** 立刻

impolite **móuh láih maauh** 冇禮貌

import duty **yahp háu seui** 入口稅

important **juhng yiu** 重要

impossible **móuh hó nàhng** 冇可能

in, at (space) **hái...yahp bihn** 喺…入邊

in (time, years) **hái...hauh** 喺…後

included **bāau kwut** 包括

increase, to increase **jāng gā** 增加

indigenous (in general) **tóu jyu ge** 土著嘅

indigenous (people) **tóu jyu** 土著

India **Yan Douh** 印度

Indian (general) **Yan Douh ge** 印度嘅

Indian (people) **Yan Douh yàhn** 印度人

Indonesia **Yan Nèih/Yan Douh Nèih Sāi a** 印尼／印度尼西亞

Indonesian (in general) **Yan Nèih ge** 印尼嘅

Indonesian (language) **Yan Nèih yúh** 印尼語

Indonesian (people) **Yan Nèih yàhn** 印尼人

inexpensive **pèhng** 平

influence, to **yíng héung** 影響

inform, to **tūng jī** 通知

information **seun sīk** 信息

information desk **sēun mahn chyu** 詢問處

injection **dá jām** 打針

innocent **mòuh gū** 無辜

insect **chùhng** 蟲

inside **léuih mihn/yahp bihn** 裡面／入邊

inside of **hái...yahp bihn** 喺…入邊

inspect, to **gím chàh** 檢查

insurance **bóu hím** 保險

intend, to **dá syun** 打算

interested in **gám hing cheui** 感興趣

international **gwok jai** 國際

international drivers license **gwok jai ga sái jāp jiu** 國際駕駛執照

Internet **Séuhng móhng** 上網

interpreter **fāan yihk yùhn** 翻譯員

intersection **sahp jih louh háu** 十字路口

introduce someone, to **gaai siuh** 介紹

invitation, to invite **yīu chíng** 邀請

Ireland **Ngoi Yíh Làahn** 愛爾蘭

Irish (in general) **Ngoi Yíh Làahn ge** 愛爾蘭嘅

Irish **Ngoi Yíh Làahn yàhn** 愛爾蘭人

iron (metal) **tit** 鐵

iron (for clothing) **tong dáu** 熨斗

iron, to **tong** 熨

Islam **Yī Sī Làahn Gaau/Wùih Gaau** 伊斯蘭教／回教

island **dóu** 島

Italian (in general) **Yi Daaih Leih ge** 意大利嘅

Italian (language) **Yi Daaih Leih Mán/Màhn** 意大利文

Italian (people) **Yi Daaih Leih yàhn** 意大利人

Italy **Yi Daaih Leih** 意大利

items **math bán** 物品

ivory **jeuhng ngàh** 象牙

J

jacket **ngoih tou** 外套

jam **gwó jeung** 果醬

January **Yāt yuht** 一月

Japan **Yaht Bún** 日本

Japanese (in general) **Yaht Bún ge** 日本嘅

Japanese (language) **Yaht Mán/Màhn** 日文

Japanese (people) **Yaht Bún Yàhn** 日本人

Japanese Yen **Yaht yùhn** 日元

jewelry **sáu sīk** 首飾

job **gūng jok** 工作

jockey **kèh sī** 騎師

join, go along **chāam gā** 參加

joke **siu wá** 笑話

joke, to **góng siu** 講笑

journey **louh chìhng** 路程

juice **gwó jāp** 果汁

July **Chāt yuht** 七月

jump, to **tiu** 跳

June **Luhk yuht** 六月

just, fair **gūng pìhng** 公平

just now **ngāam ngāam/āam āam**
嗌嗌

K

karaoke **kā lāai OK** 卡啦OK

kayak **pèi wāa teng** 皮划艇

keep, to **bóu làuh** 保留

key (to room) **só sìh** 鎖匙

kilogram **gūng gān** 公斤

kilometre **gūng léih** 公里

kind, good (of persons) **hóu sām** 好心

kind, type **júng leuih** 種類

kitchen **chyùh fóng** 廚房

knee **sāt tàuh gō** 膝頭哥

knife **dōu** 刀

know, be acquainted with **sīk** 識

know, be informed **jī dou** 知道

Korea, North **Bāk Hòhn/Chìuh Sīn** 北韓／朝鮮

Korea, South **Nàahm Hòhn/Hòhn Gwok** 南韓／韓國

Korean (North) **Chìuh Sīn yàhn** 朝鮮人

Korean (South) **Hòhn Gwok yàhn** 韓國人

Korean (language) **Hòhn Yúh/Chìuh Sīn Yúh** 韓語／朝鮮語; **Hòhn Màhn/Chìuh Sīn Màhn** 韓文／朝鮮文

L

lady **néuih sih** 女士

lake **wùh** 湖

lamb, mutton **yèuhng yuhk** 羊肉

lane (of a highway) **chē douh/chē sin** 車道／車線

language **yìhn yúh** 言語

Laos **Lìuh Gwok** 寮國

Laotian **Lìuh Gwok yàhn** 寮國人

laptop **sáu tàih dihn nóuh** 手提電腦

large **daaih** 大

last (final) **jeui hauh** 最後

laugh, to **siu** 笑

laundry **sái yī dim** 洗衣店

last (endure) **yìhn juhk** 延續

last night **kàhm/chàhm máahn** 琴／尋晚

last week **seuhng (go) sīng kèih** 上(個)星期

last year **gauh nín** 舊年

late (for an appointment) **chìh dou** 遲到

later **gwo yāt jahn gāan** 過一陣間

lawyer **leuht sī** 律師

lazy **láahn doh** 懶惰

lead (tour guide) **douh yàuh** 導遊

leaded petrol **hàhm yùhn dihn yàuh** 含鉛電油

learn, to **hohk** 學

least (smallest amount) **jeui síu** 最少

least; at least **ji síu** 至少

leather **péi** 皮

leave **jáu** 走

left-hand side **jó bīn/bihn** 左邊

leg **téui** 腿

legal **hahp faat** 合法

lend, to **je** 借

lessen, reduce **gáam síu** 減少

let someone know, to **wah béi...jī** 話俾…知

letter **seun** 信

level (height) **gōu douh** 高度

level (standard) **bīu jéun** 標準

library **tòuh syū gwún** 圖書館

license (for driving) **ga sái jāp jiu** 駕駛執照

lie, tell a falsehood **góng daaih wah** 講大話

lift, elevator **dihn tāi** 電梯

light (not heavy) **hēng** 輕

light (bright) **gwōng** 光

light (lamp) **dāng** 燈

lighter **dáh fóh gēi** 打火機

like **jūng yi** 鍾意

like, as **hóu chíh** 好似

line up, to **pàaih déui** 排隊

listen, to **tēng** 聽

litres **gūng sīng** 公升

little (not much) **yāt dī** 一啲

little (small) **sai** 細

live (stay in a place) **jyuh** 住

local **bún deih** 本地

lock, to **só** 鎖

long (time) **noih** 耐

long (size) **chèuhng** 長

look at, see **tái** 睇

look for **wáhn** 搵

Look out! **Tái jyuh!** 睇住!

look up (find in book) **chàh** 查

lose, be defeated **syū** 輸

lose something **wàih sāt/m̀h gin jó** 遺失／唔見咗

lose weight, to **gáam bóng/gáam fèih** 減磅／減肥

loud **daaih sēng** 大聲

love **ngoi/oi** 愛

love, to **ngoi/oi chìhng** 愛情

lovely **hó ngoi/oi** 可愛

lucky **hahng wahn/hóu chói** 幸運／好彩

luggage **hàhng léih** 行李

lunch, midday meal **ńgh chāan/ngaan jau** 午餐／晏晝

lychee **laih jī** 荔枝

M

Macau **Ngou mún** 澳門

madam (term of address) **taai táai** 太太

magazine **jaahp ji** 雜誌

mahjong **màh jeuk** 麻雀

mail, to **gei** 寄

major (important) **juhng yiu** 重要

make, to **jouh** 做

Malaysia **Máh Lòih Sāi Nga** 馬來西亞

Malaysian (in general) **Máh Lòih Sāi Nga ge** 馬來西亞嘅

Malaysian (people) **Máh Lòih Sāi Nga yàhn** 馬來西亞人

male **nàahm sing** 男性

man **nàahm yán** 男人

manager **gīng léih** 經理

Mandarin (language) **Póu tūng wá/Gwok yúh** 普通話／國語

manga **maahn wá** 漫畫

mango **mōng gwó** 芒果

manicure **sāu jí gaap** 修指甲

manicurist **sāu gaap sī** 修甲師

manners **láih maauh** 禮貌

manufacture, to **jai jouh** 製造

many, much **hóu dō** 好多

map **deih tòuh** 地圖

March **Sāam yuht** 三月

market **síh chèuhng** 市場

marry, get married **git fān** 結婚

Mass Transit Railway (MTR) **Góng Tit/deih tit** 港鐵／地鐵

massage **ngon mō** 按摩

match, game **béi choi** 比賽

mattress **chòhng din** 床墊

May **Ńgh yuht** 五月

maybe **waahk jé** 或者

meaning **yi sī** 意思

measure, to **lèuhng** 量

measurements **chek chyun/daaih síu** 尺寸／大細

meat **yuhk** 肉

medicine **yeuhk** 藥

meet, to **gin mihn** 見面

member **wúi yùhn** 會員

memory **gei jīk** 記憶

memory card **gei jīk kāat** 記憶咭

menstruate, to **làih yuht gīng** 嚟月經

menu **choi páai** 菜牌

mess, in a **lyuhn chāt baat jōu** 亂七八糟

message **làuh yìhn** 留言

meter **gūng chek** 公尺

midday **ngaan jau/jūng ngh** 晏晝／中午

middle, centre **jūng gāan** 中間

midnight **bun yeh** 半夜

mild (not spicy) **chīng daahm** 清淡

mild (not cold) **wòh nyúhn** 和暖

milk **ngàuh náaih** 牛奶

milk tea and coffee **yīn yēung** 鴛鴦

millimeter **hòuh máih** 毫米

million **baak maahn** 百萬

mind, brain **nóuh** 腦

mind, to be displeased **gaai yi** 介意

mineral water **kwong chyùhn séui** 礦泉水

mini **màih néih** 迷你

mini-bus **síu bā** 小巴

mini-bus stop **síu bā jaahm** 小巴站

minute **fān (jūng)** 分(鐘)

mirror **geng** 鏡

Miss **síu jé** 小姐

miss, to (bus, flight etc.) **jáu jó (bā sí, fēi gēi)** 走咗(巴士, 飛機)

miss, to (loved one) **gwa jyuh** 掛住

mistaken **gáau cho** 搞錯

misunderstanding **ngh wuih** 誤會

mobile phone **sáu tàih dihn wá/sáu gēi** 手提電話／手機

mobile phone charger **chùng dihn hei** 充電器

modern **yihn doih** 現代

moment (in a moment) **dáng yāt jahn** 等一陣

Monday **Sīng kèih yāt** 星期一

money **chín** 錢

month **yuht** 月

moon **yuht leuhng** 月亮

more (comparative) **dō dī** 多啲

more of (things) **gang dō** 更多

more or less **daaih koi** 大概

moreover **yìh ché** 而且

morning **jīu jóu** 朝早

mosque **Wùih Gaau míu** 回教廟

mosquito **mān** 蚊

most (superlative) **jeui** 最

most (the most of) **jeui dō** 最多

mostly **daaih bouh fahn** 大部分

mother **màh mā** 媽媽

mother-in-law **ngoih móu** 外母

motorcycle **dihn dāan chē** 電單車

motor vehicle **sī gā chē** 私家車

mountain **sāan** 山

mouse (animal) **lóuh syú** 老鼠

mouth **jéui/háu** 嘴／口

move (from one place to another) **būn** 搬

movement, motion **duhng jok** 動作

movie **dihn yíng** 電影

movie house **hei yún** 戲院

Mr **sīn sāang** 先生

Mrs **taai táai** 太太

MSG **Meih jīng** 味精

MTR **Góng Tit** 港鐵

much, many **hóu dō** 好多

muscle **gēi yuhk** 肌肉

music **yām ngohk** 音樂

musical instrument **ngohk hei** 樂器

museum **bok maht gún** 博物館

mushrooms **mòh gū/cóu gū** 蘑菇／草菇

Muslim (in general) **Wùih Gaau ge** 回教嘅

Muslim (people) **Wùih Gaau tòuh** 回教徒

must **yāt dihng** 一定

mutton **yèuhng yuhk** 羊肉

my, mine **ngóh ge** 我嘅

myself **ngóh jih géi** 我自己

N

nail (finger, toe) **jí gaap** 指甲

name **méng** 名

narrow **jaak** 窄

nation, country **gwok gā** 國家

national **chyùhn gwok sing** 全國性

nationality **gwok jihk** 國籍

natural **jih yìhn ge** 自然嘅

nature **daaih jih yìhn** 大自然

naughty **wàahn pèih** 頑皮

nearby **fuh gahn** 附近

nearly **gēi fùh** 幾乎

neat, orderly **jíng chàih** 整齊

necessary **bīt sēui** 必須

neck **géng** 頸

necklace **géng lín** 頸鏈

necktie **léhng tāai** 領呔

need, to need **sēui yiu** 需要

needle **jām** 針

neither **léuhng go dōu m̀h haih** 兩個都唔係

Never mind! **M̀h gán yiu!** 唔緊要!

nevertheless **bāt gwo** 不過

new **sān** 新

news **sān mán** 新聞

newspaper **bou jí** 報紙

New Zealand **Sān Sāi Làahn** 新西蘭

New Zealander **Sān Sāi Làahn yàhn** 新西蘭人

next to **pòhng bīn** 旁邊

next month **hah go yuht** 下個月

next week **hah (go) sīng kèih** 下(個)星期

next year **mìhng nín/chēut nín** 明年／出年

nice **hóu** 好

night **yeh máahn(hāk)** 夜晚(黑)

nightclothes, nightdress **seuih yī** 睡衣

nine **gáu** 九

nineteen **sahp gáu** 十九

ninety **gáu sahp** 九十

no, not have **móuh** 冇

no, not **m̀h haih** 唔係

nobody **móuh yàhn** 冇人

noise **sēng** 聲

noisy **chòuh** 嘈

noodles **mihn** 麵

noon **jūng ngh** 中午

normal **jing sèuhng** 正常

north **bāk bihn** 北邊

north-east **dūng bāk** 東北

north-west **sāi bāk** 西北

nose **beih gō** 鼻哥

not **m̀h/m̀h haih** 唔／唔係

not yet **juhng meih** 仲未

note (written) **jih tìuh** 字條

note down, to **gei dāi** 記低

nothing **móuh yéh** 冇嘢

notice **tūng jī** 通知

notice, to **jyu yi** 注意

novel **síu syut** 小說

November **Sahp yāt yuht** 十一月

now **yìh gā** 而家

nowadays **yihn sìh** 現時

nowhere **bīn douh dōu m̀h hái** 邊度都唔係

number **houh máh** 號碼

O

o'clock **dím(jūng)** 點(鐘)

obedient **tēng wah** 聽話

obey, to **fuhk chùhng** 服從

object, thing **yéh** 嘢

object, to protest **fáan deui** 反對

occasionally **ngáuh yìhn** 偶然

occupation **jīk yihp** 職業

ocean **hói yèuhng** 海洋

October **Sahp yuht** 十月

octopus **baat jáau yùh** 八爪魚

Octopus card **Baat Daaht Tūng** 八達通

odor, bad smell **chau hei** 臭氣

of, from **(suhk yū)...ge** (屬於)···嘅

of course **dōng yìhn** 當然

off (gone bad) **waaih jó** 壞咗

off (turned off) **sāan jó** 閂咗

offend **dāk jeuih** 得罪

offer, suggest **tàih yíh** 提議

offering **tàih gūng** 提供

office **sé jih làuh/baahn gūng sāt** 寫字樓／辦公室

officials (government) **gūng mouh yùhn** 公務員

often **gīng sèuhng** 經常

oil **yàuh** 油

okay **dāk** 得

old (of persons) **lóuh** 老

old (of things) **gauh** 舊

olden times, in **gauh sìh** 舊時

older **nìhn géi daaih dī** 年紀大啲

oldest **nìhn géi jeui daaih** 年紀最大

Olympics **Ngou wahn wúi** 奧運會

on, at **hái** 喺

on, turn something **hōi** 開

on fire **fó jūk** 火燭

on foot **hàahng louh heui** 行路去

on the way **làih gán** 嚟緊

on the whole **daaih ji seuhng** 大致上

on time **jéun sìh** 準時

once **yāt chi** 一次

one **yāt** 一

one-way street **dāan chìhng louh** 單程路

one-way ticket **dāan chìhng piu** 單程票

onion **yèuhng chūng** 洋蔥

only **jihng haih** 淨係

open **hōi** 開

open, to **dá hōi** 打開

opera, Cantonese **Yuht kehk** 粵劇

opera, Peking **Gīng kehk** 京劇

opinion **yi gin** 意見

opportunity **gēi wuih** 機會

oppose, to **fáan deui** 反對

opposite (facing) **deui mihn** 對面

opposite (contrary) **sēung fáan** 相反

optical shop **ngáahn géng dim** 眼鏡店

optician **ngáahn géng dim yùhn** 眼鏡店員

or **waahk jé** 或者

orange, citrus **cháang** 橙

orange (colour) **cháang sīk** 橙色

orange juice **cháang jāp** 橙汁

orange juice (freshly squeezed) **sīn jā cháang jāp** 鮮榨橙汁

order (placed for food) **dím choi** 點菜

order, sequence **chi jeuih** 次序

organize, arrange **ngōn pàaih** 安排

origin **héi yùhn** 起源

original **jeui chō** 最初

ornament **jōng sīk bán** 裝飾品

other **kèih tā** 其他

other (alternative) **lihng ngoih** 另外

ought to **yīng gōi** 應該

our **ngóh/óh deih ge** 我哋嘅

out **chēut jó gāai** 出咗街

outside **ngoih mihn** 外面

oval (shape) **tóh yùhn yìhng** 橢圓形

overcast, cloudy **yām tīn** 陰天

overseas **hói ngoih/ngoih deih** 海外／外地

over there **gó bīn/bihn** 嗰邊

owe, to **him** 欠

own, personal **jih géi ge** 自己嘅

oyster **hòuh** 蠔

P

pack, a pack of **yāt bāau** 一包

pack, to **bāau jōng** 包裝

paid **béi jó chín** 俾咗錢

pain, painful **tung** 痛

pain killers **jí tung yeuhk** 止痛藥

painting **wá** 畫

pair of, a **yāt deui** 一對

pajamas **seuih yī** 睡衣

palace **wòhng gūng** 王宮

pan **wohk** 鑊

panorama **chyùhn gíng** 全景

pants **fu** 褲

paper **jí** 紙

parcel **bāau gwó** 包裹

Pardon me? **Mē wá?** 咩話?

parents **fuh móuh** 父母

park **gūng yún** 公園

park, to (car) **paak chē** 泊車

parking meter **gok jí gēi** 角子機

part (not whole) **bouh fahn** 部分

participate, to **chāam gā** 參加

particularly, especially **yàuh kèih sih** 尤其是

partly **yāt bouh fahn** 一部分

partner (business) **paak dong** 拍擋

partner (relationship) **buhn léuih** 伴侶

pass, go past **gīng gwo** 經過

pass, to (exam) **hahp gaak** 合格

passenger **sìhng haak** 乘客

passport **wuh jiu** 護照

password **maht máh** 密碼

past, former **gwo heui** 過去

pastime **sīu hín** 消遣

patient, a **behng yàhn** 病人

patient (calm) **noih sām** 耐心

pay, to **béi chín** 俾錢

pay attention **làuh yi/juh yi** 留意／注意

peach **tóu** 桃

peak, summit **sāan déng** 山頂

peak tram **sāan déng laahm chē** 山頂纜車

peak tram station **sāan déng laahm chē jaahm** 山頂纜車站

peanut **fā sāng** 花生

pear **léi** 梨

pearl **jān jyū** 珍珠

pedicure **sāu geuk gaap** 修腳甲

pen **mahk séui bāt** 墨水筆

pencil **yùhn bāt** 鉛筆

penis **yām ging** 陰莖

pen knife **jip dōu** 摺刀

people **yàhn** 人

pepper (black) **hāk wùh jīu fán** 黑胡椒粉

pepper (chilli) **laaht jīu** 辣椒

percent **baak fahn jī** 百分之

percentage **baak fahn léut** 百分率

perform **yín chēut** 演出

performance, acrobatic **jaahp geih bíu yín** 雜技表演

performance, song and dance **gō móuh bíu yín** 歌舞表演

performance, martial arts **móuh seuht bíu yín** 武術表演

perfume **hēung séui** 香水

perhaps **waahk jé** 或者

perhaps, probably **hó nàhng** 可能

period (end of a sentence) **geui houh** 句號

period (of time) **sìh kèih** 時期

perm **dihn faat** 電髮

permit **héui hó jing** 許可證

permit, to allow **jéun héui** 准許

person **yàhn** 人

personality **sing gaak** 性格

perspire, to **chēut hohn** 出汗

pet animal **chúng maht** 寵物

petrol **dihn yàuh** 電油

petrol station **dihn yàuh jaahm** 電油站

pharmacy, drugstore **yeuhk fòhng** 藥房

Philippines **Fēi leuht bān** 菲律賓

photocopy, to photocopy **fūk yan** 複印

photograph **séung** 相

photograph, to **yíng séung** 影相

pick, choose **gáan** 揀

pick up, to (someone) **jip** 接

pick up, lift (something) **jāp** 執

pickpocket **pàh sáu** 扒手

picture **wá** 畫

piece, item **gihn** 件

pierce, penetrate **chyūn** 穿

pig **jyū** 豬

pills **yeuhk yún** 藥丸

pillow **jám tàuh** 枕頭

pineapple **bō ló** 菠蘿

pineapple bun with butter **bō ló yàuh** 菠蘿油

pink **fán hùhng sīk** 粉紅色

pity **hó lìhn** 可憐

pity, what a pity **hó sīk** 可惜

place **deih fōng** 地方

place, put **fong** 放

plan **gai waahk** 計劃

plan, to **dá syun** 打算

plane **fēi gēi** 飛機

plant **jihk maht** 植物

plant, to **jung** 種

plastic **sok gāau** 塑膠

plate **dihp** 碟

platform **yuht tòih** 月臺

play, to **wáan** 玩

play ball games **dá bō** 打波

play bridge **dá kìuh páai** 打橋牌

play computer games **dá gēi** 打機

play mahjong **dá màh jéuk** 打麻雀

playground **yàuh lohk chèuhng** 遊樂場

please go ahead, please **chíng** 請

pleased **gōu hing** 高興

plug (bath) **sāk** 塞

plug (electric) **chaap táu** 插頭

plum **bou lām** 布冧

pneumonia **fai yìhm** 肺炎

pocket **dói** 袋

point out **jí chēut** 指出

poisonous **yáuh duhk ge** 有毒嘅

police station **gíng chaat gúk** 警察局

police officer **gíng chaat** 警察

polite **yáuh láih maauh** 有禮貌

Poon choi **pùhn choi** 盆菜

poor (not rich) **kùhng** 窮

popular **làuh hàhng** 流行

population **yàhn háu** 入口

pork **jyū yuhk** 豬肉

port **hói góng** 海港

portable charger **chūng dih hei** 充電器

portable Wi-Fi router **làuh duhn séuhng móhng gēi** 流動上網機

portion, serve **yāt fahn** 一份

possess, to **yúng yáuh** 擁有

possessions **chòih maht** 財物

possible, possibly **hó nàhng** 可能

post/mail **gei** 寄

postcard **mìhng seun pín** 明信片

post office **yàuh gúk** 郵局

postal code **yàuh kēui houh máh** 郵區號碼

postpone, to **yìhn kèih** 延期

pound (weight) **bohng** 磅

pound sterling **Yīng bón** 英鎊

pour, to **dóu** 倒

power **lihk** 力

practice, to practice **lihn jaahp** 練習

praise, to **jaan** 讚

prawn **hā** 蝦

prayer, to pray **kèih tóu** 祈禱

prefer, to **jūng yi** 鐘意

pregnant **wàaih yahn** 懷孕

prepare **jéun beih** 準備

prepared, ready **jéun beih hóu** 準備好

prescription **yeuhk dāan** 藥單

present (now) **yìh gā** 而家

present (gift) **láih maht** 禮物

presently, nowadays **gahn lòih** 近來

present moment, at the **muhk chìhn** 目前

pressure **ngaak lihk** 壓力

pretend, to **ja dai** 詐帝

pretty **leng** 靚

prevent, to **jó jí** 阻止

price **ga chìhn** 價錢

pride **jih hòuh/jih jyūn sām** 自豪／自尊心

priest **sàhn fuh** 神父

prison **gāam yuhk** 監獄

private **sī yàhn** 私人

probably **daaih koi** 大嘅

problem **mahn tàih** 問題

profession **jīk yihp** 職業

program, schedule **jit muhk** 節目

promise, to **daap ying** 答應

pronounce, to **faat yām** 發音

proof **jing geui** 証據

prove, to **jing mìhng** 証明

public **gūng guhng** 公共

pull, to **lāai** 拉

pump **bām** 泵

punctual **jéun sìh** 準時

pupil **hohk sāang** 學生

pure **sèuhn** 純

purple **jí sīk** 紫色

purpose **muhk dīk** 目的

purse (money) **ngàhn bāau** 銀包

push, to **tēui** 推

put, place **fong** 放

put off, delay **yìhn chìh** 延遲

put on (clothes) **jeuk** 著

pyjamas **seuih yī** 睡衣

Q

qualification **jī gaak** 資格

quarter **sei fahn jī yāt** 四分之一

question **mahn tàih** 問題

queue, line **chèuhng lùhng** 長龍

queue, to line up **pàaih déui** 排隊

quick **faai** 快

quiet **ngōn jihng** 安靜

quite (fairly) **sēung dōng** 相當

R

race day **choi máh yaht** 賽馬日

radio **sāu yām gēi** 收音機

rail, by rail **chóh fó chē** 坐火車

railroad, railway **tit louh** 鐵路

rain **yúh** 雨

rain, to **lohk yúh** 落雨

raise, lift **tàih gōu** 提高

raise, to (children) **fú yéuhng** 撫養

rank, station in life **deih waih** 地位

rarely, seldom **nàahn dāk** 難得

rat **lóuh syú** 老鼠

rate, tariff **sāu fai** 收費

rate of exchange **deui wuhn léut** 兌換率

rather, fairly **béi gaau** 比較

rather than **nìhng hó** 寧可

raw, uncooked, rare **sāang ge** 生嘅

reach, get to **daaht dou** 達到

reaction, response **fáan ying** 反應

read, to **tái syū** 睇書

ready **yihn sìhng** 現成

ready, to get **jéun beih** 準備

really (very) **fēi sèuhng** 非常

Really? **Haih mē?** 係咩?

rear, tail **hauh mihn** 後面

reason **yùhn yān** 原因

reasonable (sensible) **hahp chìhng hahp léih** 合情合理

reasonable (price) **gūng douh** 公道

receipt **sāu geui** 收據

receive, to **sāu dóu** 收到

recharge voucher **jāng jihk gyun** 增值券

recipe **sihk póu** 食譜

recognize, to **yihng dāk** 認得

recommend, to **tēui jin** 推薦

recover (cured) **hōng fuhk** 康復

rectangle **chèuhng fōng yìhng** 長方形

red **hùhng sīk** 紅色

reduce, to **gáam ga** 減價

reduction **gáam síu** 減少

refrigerator **syut gwaih** 雪櫃

refusal, to refuse **kéuih jyuht** 拒絕

region **deih kēui** 地區

register, to **gwa houh** 掛號

registered post **gwa houh seun** 掛號信

relatives, family **chān chīk** 親戚

relax, to **fong sūng** 放鬆

religion **jūng gaau** 宗教

remainder, leftover **jihng lohk làih** 剩落嚟

remains (historical) **gú jīk** 古蹟

remember, to **gei dāk** 記得

remind, to **tàih séng** 提醒

rent, to **jōu** 租

repair, to **sāu léih** 修理

repeat, to **chùhng fūk** 重複

replace, to **doih tai** 代替

reply, response **daap fūk** 答覆

report **bou gou** 報告

reporter **gei jé** 記者

request, to **yīu kàuh** 要求

rescue, to **gau** 救

research, to **yìhn gau** 研究

resemble **chíh** 似

reserve, to **yuh dehng** 預訂

respect, to **jyūn ging** 尊敬

respond, react **fáan ying** 反應

response, reaction **daap fūk** 答覆

responsibility **jaak yahm** 責任

responsible, to be **fuh jaak** 負責

rest, to relax **yāu sīk** 休息

restaurant **chāan gún** 餐館

restroom **sái sáu gāan** 洗手間

result **sìhng jīk** 成績

retired **teui yāu** 退休

return, to give back **wàahn** 還

return, to go back **fāan jyun tàuh** 番轉頭

return ticket **lòih wùih piu** 來回票

reverse, to go back **diuh tàuh** 掉頭

rice (cooked) **baahk faahn** 白飯

rice (uncooked grains) **máih** 米

rich **fu yuh** 富裕

ride (in car) **chóh chē** 坐車

ride (horse) **kèh máh** 騎馬

ride (bicycle) **cháai dāan chē** 踩單車

ride (motorcycle) **jā dihn dāan chē** 揸電單車

right, correct **jing kok** 正確

right-hand side **yauh bihn** 右邊

right now **laahp hāk** 立刻

ring (jewelry) **gaai jí** 戒指

ring, to (bell) **gahm jūng** 撳鐘

rip open, to **sī hōi** 撕開

ripe **suhk ge** 熟嘅

rise, increase **jāng gā** 增加

river **hòh** 河

road **louh** 路

road signs **louh páai** 路牌

roaming service **maahn yàuh gūng nahng** 漫遊功能

roast goose **sīu ngó** 燒鵝

rock **sehk tàuh** 石頭

room **fóng** 房

rope **sìhng** 繩

rotten **fuh laahn** 腐爛

roughly, approximately **daaih yeuk** 大約

round (shape) **yùhn yìhng** 圓形

round, around **wàahn yíu** 環繞

rude **móuh láih maauh** 冇禮貌

rules **kwāi jāk** 規則

rum **lām jáu** 冧酒

run out **hou jeuhn** 耗盡

s

sad **nàahn gwo** 難過

safe **ngōn chyùhn** 安全

safety belt **ngōn chyùhn dáai** 安全帶

salary **sān séui** 薪水

sale, for **chēut sauh** 出售

sale (reduced prices) **daaih gáam ga** 大減價

sales assistant **sauh fo yùhn** 售貨員

salt **yìhm** 鹽

salty **hàahm** 鹹

same **yāt yeuhng** 一樣

same day **jīk yaht** 即日

sample **yeuhng bún** 樣本

sand **sā** 沙

sandals **lèuhng hàaih** 涼鞋

sanitary napkins **waih sāng gān** 衛生巾

satisfied, to satisfy **múhn jūk** 滿足

Saturday **Sīng kèih luhk** 星期六

sauce **jāp** 汁

sauce (chilli) **laaht jīu jeung** 辣椒醬

saucepan **pìhng dái wohk** 平底鑊

say, to **góng** 講

say hello **mahn hauh** 問候

say goodbye **douh biht** 道別

say sorry **douh hip** 道歉

say thank you **douh jeh** 道謝

scales **ching/bóng** 秤／磅

scan **sou miù** 掃描

scarce **kyut faht** 缺乏

scared **pa** 怕

scenery **jih yìhn fūng gíng** 自然風景

schedule **sìh gaan bíu/yaht chìhng bíu** 時間表／日程表

school **hohk haauh** 學校

scissors **gaau jín** 較剪

screwdriver **lòh sī pāi** 螺絲批

sea **hói** 海

seafood **hói sīn** 海鮮

search for, to **wáhn** 搵

season **gwai jit** 季節

seat **joh wái** 座位

second (in sequence) **daih yih** 第二

secret **bei maht** 秘密

secretary **bei syū** 秘書

secure, safe **ngōn chyùhn** 安全

see, to **tái gin** 睇見

seed **júng jí** 種子

seek, to **chàhm kàuh** 尋求

seem, to **chíh fùh** 似乎

See you later! **Yāt jahn gin!** 一陣見!

seldom **hóu síu** 好少

select, to **gáan** 揀

self **jih géi** 自己

selfie stick **jih paak gwan** 自拍棍

sell, to **maaih** 賣

send, to **sung** 送

seniors **jéung jé** 長者

sensible **mìhng ji** 明智

sentence **geui** 句

separate (couple) **fān sáu** 分手

separate, to **fān hōi** 分開

September **Gáu yuht** 九月

sequence, order **chi jeuih** 次序

serious (not funny) **yìhm sūk** 嚴肅

serious (severe) **yìhm juhng** 嚴重

servant **gūng yàhn** 工人

service **fuhk mouh** 服務

sesame oil **màh yàuh** 麻油

seven **chāt** 七

seventeen **sahp chāt** 十七

seventy **chāt sahp** 七十

several **géi (go)** 幾(個)

severe **yìhm laih** 嚴厲

sex, gender **sing biht** 性別

sex, sexual activity **jouh ngoi/oi** 做愛

shall, will **jēung yiu** 將要

shallow **chín** 淺

shame, disgrace **cháu/sāu gā** 醜／羞家

shame, what a shame **jān haih hó sīk** 真係可惜

shampoo **sái faat louh** 洗髮露

Shanghai **Seuhng Hói** 上海

shape **yìhng johng** 形狀

shark **sā yùh** 鯊魚

sharp **leih** 利

shave **tai sōu** 剃鬚

she, her **kéuih** 佢

sheet (for bed) **chòhng dāan** 床單

ship **syùhn** 船

shirt **sēut sāam** 恤衫

shit **sí** 屎

shiver, to **dá láahng jan** 打冷震

shoes **hàaih** 鞋

shop, store **pou táu** 舖頭

shopping, go **máaih yéh** 買嘢

short (concise) **dyún** 短

short (not tall) **ngái** 矮

short message service (SMS) **dyún seun** 短訊

shorts (short trousers) **dyún fu** 短褲

shorts (underpants) **dái fu** 底褲

shoulder **bok tàuh** 膊頭

shout, to **daaih sēng ngaai** 大聲嗌

show (live performance) **bíu yín** 表演

show, to **béi yàhn tái** 俾人睇

shower (for washing) **fā sá** 花洒

shower (of rain) **jaauh yúh** 驟雨

shower, to take a **chūng fā sá** 沖花洒

shrimp, prawn **sai hā** 細蝦

shut **sāan** 閂

sibling **hīng daih jí muih** 兄弟姊妹

sick, ill **behng jó** 病咗

sick to be (vomit) **ngáu tou** 嘔吐

side **pòhng bīn** 旁邊

sightseeing **tái fūng gíng** 睇風景

signature, to sign **chīm méng** 簽名

silent **jihng** 靜

silk **sī chàuh** 絲綢

silver **ngàhn** 銀

SIM card **chyúh jihk kāat** 儲值卡

similar **sēung chíh** 相似

simple (easy) **yùhng yih** 容易

simple (uncomplicated) **gáan dāan** 簡單

since **jih chùhng** 自從

sing, to **cheung gō** 唱歌

Singapore **Sān Ga Bō** 新加坡

Singaporean (in general) **Sān Ga Bō ge** 新加坡嘅

Singaporean (people) **Sān Ga Bō yàhn** 新加坡人

single (not married) **dāan sān** 單身

single (only one) **yāt go yàhn** 一個人

sir (term of address) **sīn sāang** 先生

sister (older) **jèh jē** 姐姐

sister (younger) **mùih múi** 妹妹

sister-in-law (older) **sóu** 嫂

sister-in-law (younger) **daih fúh** 弟婦

sit, to **chóh** 坐

sit down, to **chóh dāi** 坐低

situation, how things are **chìhng fong** 情況

six **luhk** 六

sixteen **sahp luhk** 十六

sixty **luhk sahp** 六十

size, large **daaih máh** 大碼

size, medium **jūng máh** 中碼

size, small **sai máh** 細碼

skewer **chyun sīu** 串燒

skilful **suhk lihn** 熟練

skin **pèih fū** 皮膚

skirt **kwàhn** 裙

sky **tīn hūng** 天空

skydiving **tiu saan** 跳傘

sleep, to **fan gaau** 瞓覺

sleeping bag **seuih dói** 睡袋

sleepy **ngáahn fan** 眼瞓

slender **sai chèuhng** 細長

slightly **sáau wàih** 稍為

slim **míuh tíuh** 苗條

slippers **tō háai** 拖鞋

slope **sāan bō** 山坡

slow **maahn** 慢

slowly **maahn máan déi** 慢慢地

small **sai** 細

smart **chūng mìhng** 聰明

smell, bad odor **chau meih** 臭味

smell, to **màhn** 聞

smile, to **siu** 笑

smoke **yīn** 煙

smoke (tobacco) **sihk yīn** 食煙

smooth (unproblematic) **seuhn leih** 順利

smooth (surfaces) **pìhng waaht** 平滑

smuggle, to **jáau sī** 走私

snake **sèh** 蛇

sneeze, to **dá hāt chī** 打乞嗤

snow **syut** 雪

snow, to **lohk syut** 落雪

snow peas **hòh lāan dáu** 荷蘭豆

so (degree) **gám yéung** 咁樣

so, therefore **só yíh** 所以

soap **fāan gáan** 番梘

soccer **jūk kàuh** 足球

socket (electric) **chaap tàuh** 插頭

socks **maht** 襪

soda water **sō dá séui** 梳打水

sofa, couch **sō fá** 梳化

soft **yúhn** 軟

software **yúhn gín** 軟件

soft drink **hei séui** 汽水

sold **maaih jó** 賣咗

soldier **sih bīng** 士兵

sold out **maaih saai** 賣晒

sole, only **wàih yāt** 唯一

solve, to **gáai kyut** 解決

some **yāt dī** 一啲

somebody **yáuh yàhn** 有人

something **yáuh dī yéh** (有啲)嘢

sometimes **yáuh sìh** 有時

somewhere **máuh chyu** 某處

son **jái** 仔

son-in-law **néuih sai** 女婿

song **gō(kūk)** 歌(曲)

soon **jauh faai** (就)快

sore, painful **tung** 痛

sorry, to feel regretful **hauh fui** 後悔

Sorry! **Deui m̀h jyuh!** 對唔住!

sort, type **júng leuih** 種類

sort out, deal with **gáai kyut** 解決

sound, noise **sēng yām** 聲音

sour **syūn** 酸

source **lòih yùhn** 來源

south **nàahm bīn/bihn** 南邊

south-east **dūng nàahm** 東南

south-west **sāi nàahm** 西南

souvenir **géi nihm bán** 紀念品

soy sauce **sāang chāu** 生抽

spacious **fut lohk** 闊落

speak, to **góng** 講

special **dahk biht** 特別

specialist (doctor) **jyūn fō yī sāng** 專科醫生

spectacles **ngáahn géng** 眼鏡

speech, to make a speech **yín góng** 演講

speed **chūk douh** 速度

speeding **hōi faai chē** 開快車

spell, to **chyun** 串

spend, to **sái chín** 洗錢

spices **hēung líu** 香料

spinach **bō choi** 菠菜

spine **bui jek gwāt** 背脊骨

spoiled (of children) **jung waaih jó** 縱壞咗

spoiled (of food) **waaih jó/sūk jó** 壞咗／縮咗

spoon **chìh gāng** 匙羹

sports **wahn duhng** 運動

spring (season) **chēun tīn** 春天

spring (of water) **kwong chyùhn séui** 礦泉水

spouse **pui ngáuh** 配偶

square (shape) **jing fōng yìhng** 正方形

square, town square **gwóng chèuhng** 廣場

stain **wū dím** 污點

stairs **làuh tāi** 樓梯

stall (of vendor) **tāan** 攤

stall, to (car) **séi fó** 死火

stamp (postage) **yàuh piu** 郵票

stand, to **kéih** 企

stand up, to **kéih héi sān** 企起身

star **sīng** 星

start, beginning **hōi chí** 開始

start, to **faat duhng** 發動

statement (police) **háu gūng** 口供

station **dihn chē jaahm** 電車站

stationery **màhn geuih** 文具

stay overnight, to **gwo yé** 過夜

steal, to **tāu** 偷

steamed **jīng ge** 蒸嘅

steel **gong** 鋼

step **bouh** 步

steps, stairs **làuh tāi kāp** 樓梯級

stick **tip** 貼

sticky **chī nahp nahp** 痴立立

stiff **ngaahng** 硬

stifling **muhn yiht** 悶熱

still, quiet **pìhng jihng** 平靜

stink, to **faat chau** 發臭

stomach, belly **tóuh** 肚

stomach ulcer **waih kwúi yèuhng** 胃潰瘍

stone **sehk tàuh** 石頭

stool, chair **dang** 凳

stop (bus, train) **jaahm** 站

stop, to **tìhng** 停

store, shop **pou táu** 舖頭

store, to **chyúh chòhng** 儲存

storm **dá fūng** 打風

story (building) **chàhng/láu** 層／樓

story (tale) **gú jái** 故仔

stove, cooker **lòuh tàuh** 爐頭

straight (not crooked) **jihk** 直

straight ahead **yāt jihk heui** 一直去

strange **kèih gwaai** 奇怪

stranger **sāang bóu yàhn** 生步人

street **gāai** 街

strength **lihk** 力

strict **yìhm gaak** 嚴格

strike, hit **dá** 打

string **síng** 繩

strong **kèuhng jong** 強壯

stubborn, determined **ngaahng géng** 硬頸

student **hohk sāang** 學生

study, learn **hohk** 學

stupid **bahn/chéun** 笨／蠢

style **fūng gaak** 風格

subtitle **jih mohk** 字幕

succeed, to (follow) **gai sìhng** 繼承

success **sìhng gūng** 成功

such **gám yéung** 噉樣

such as, for example **laih yùh** 例如

suddenly **dahk yìhn** 突然

sugar **tòhng** 糖

suggestion **tàih yíh** 提議

suit, business **sāi jōng** 西裝

suitable, fitting **ngāam sān** 啱身

suitcase **hàhng léih sēung/gīp** 行李箱／喼

summer **hah tīn** 夏天

sun **taai yèuhng** 太陽

Sunday **Sīng kèih yaht** 星期日

sunlight **yèuhng gwōng** 陽光

sunscreen lotion **taai yèuhng yàuh/ fòhng saai yàuh** 太陽油／防晒油

sunny **chìhng lóhng** 晴朗

sunrise **yaht chēut** 日出

sunset **yaht lohk** 日落

supermarket **chīu kāp síh chèuhng** 超級市場

suppose, to **gá dihng** 假定

sure **háng dihng/kok dihng** 肯定／確定

surface **bíu mihn** 表面

surface mail **pìhng yàuh** 平郵

surfboard **waaht séui báan** 滑水板

surname **sing** 姓

surprised **gīng kèih/gám dou yi ngoih** 驚奇／感到意外

surprising **lihng yàhn gám dou yi ngoih** 令人感到意外

surroundings **wàahn gíng** 環境

survive, to **sāng chyùhn** 生存

suspect, to **wàaih yìh** 懷疑

swallow, to **tān** 吞

sweat **hohn** 汗

sweat, to **chēut hohn** 出汗

sweet (taste) **tìhm** 甜

sweet, dessert **tìhm bán** 甜品

sweet and sour **tìhm syūn** 甜酸

sweetcorn **sūk máih** 粟米

sweets, candy **tóng** 糖

sweet drinks **tìhm jáu** 甜酒

swim, to **yàuh séui** 游水

swimming costume **wihng yī** 泳衣

swimming pool **yàuh wihng chìh** 游泳池

switch **jai** 掣

synthetic **yàhn jouh ge** 人造嘅

T

table **tói** 檯

tablecloth **tói bou** 檯布

tablets **yeuhk béng** 藥餅

tail **méih** 尾

take, to remove **ló jáu** 攞走

take care of, to **fuh jaak** 負責

talk, to **kīng gái** 傾偈

tall **gōu** 高

Taoism **Douh Gaau** 道教

tape, adhesive **gāau jí** 膠紙

tape, recording **luhk yām dáai** 錄音帶

taste **meih douh** 味道

taste, to (sample) **si meih** 試味

tasty **hóu sihk** 好食

taxi **dīk sí** 的士

taxi stand **dīk sí jaahm** 的士站

tea **chàh** 茶

tea, black **hùhng chàh** 紅茶

tea, with milk **náaih chàh** 奶茶

tea, Jasmine **hēung pín** 香片

teach, to **gaau** 教

teacher **gaau sī** 教師

tears **ngáahn leuih** 眼淚

teenager **chīng siu nìhn** 青少年

t-shirt **tī sēut** T恤

teeth **ngàh** 牙

telephone **dihn wá** 電話

telephone card **dihn wá kāat** 電話咭

telephone directory **dihn wá bóu** 電話簿

telephone number **dihn wá houh máh** 電話號碼

television **dihn sih** 電視

tell, to (a story) **góng** 講

tell, to **wah béi...jī** 話俾…知

temperature **wān douh** 溫度

temperature (body) **tái wān** 體溫

temple (Chinese) **míu** 廟

temporary **jaahm sìh** 暫時

ten **sahp** 十

ten million **chīn maahn** 千萬

tennis **móhng kàuh** 網球

tens of **géi sahp** 幾十

tense **gán jēung** 緊張

ten thousand **maahn** 萬

tent **jeung pùhng** 帳篷

tequila **lùhng sit làahn jáu** 龍舌蘭酒

terrible **hó pa** 可怕

test **si yihm** 試驗

test, to **chāak yihm** 測驗

testicles **gōu yún** 睾丸

Thai (in general) **Taai Gwok ge** 泰國嘅

Thai (language) **Taai Mán** 泰文

Thai (people) **Taai Gwok yàhn** 泰國人

Thailand **Taai Gwok** 泰國

thank you (for a service) **m̀h gōi** 唔該

thank you (for a gift) **dō jeh** 多謝

that, those **gó** 嗰

theater (drama) **kehk yún** 劇院

their, theirs **kéuih deih ge** 佢哋嘅

then **yìhn hauh** 然後

there **gó douh/gó syu** 嗰度／嗰處

therefore **yān chí** 因此

there is, there are **yáuh** 有

thermos **nyúhn séui wùh** 暖水壺

these **nī dī** 呢啲

they, them **kéuih deih** 佢哋

thick (of liquids) **nùhng** 濃

thick (of things) **háuh** 厚

thief **cháak/síu tāu** 賊／小偷

thigh **daaih téui** 大腿

thin (of liquids) **hēi** 稀

thin (of persons) **sau** 瘦

thing **yéh** 嘢

think, to ponder **séung/háau leuih** 想／考慮

think, to have an opinion **yihng wàih** 認為

third (in a series) **daih sāam** 第三

third, a **sāam fahn jī yāt** 三分之一

thirsty **háu hot** 口渴

thirty **sāam sahp** 三十

this **nī** 呢

though **sēui yìhn** 雖然

thoughts **séung faat** 想法

thousand **chīn** 千

thread **sin** 線

threaten, to **húng haak** 恐嚇

three **sāam** 三

throat **hàuh lùhng** 喉嚨

through, past **tūng gwo** 通過

throw, to **dám** 揼

throw away **dám jó** 揼咗

thunder **dá lèuih** 打雷

Thursday **Sīng kèih sei** 星期四

thus, so **yū sih** 於是

ticket **fēi/piu** 飛／票

ticket office **sauh piu chyu** 售票處

tidy **jíng chàih** 整齊

tidy up **sāu sahp** 收拾

tie, necktie **léhng tāai** 領呔

tie, to **bóng** 綁

tiger **lóuh fú** 老虎

tight **gán/jaak** 緊／窄

time **sìh gaan** 時間

time to time, from **gaan jūng** 間中

timetable **sìh gaan bíu** 時間表

tiny **sai síu** 細小

tip (gratuity) **tīp sí** 貼士

tired (sleepy) **ngáahn fan** 眼瞓

tired (worn out) **gwuih** 劫

title (of book, film) **bīu tàih** 標題

title (of person) **hàahm tàuh** 銜頭

to, toward **heung/deui** 向／對

toasted **hong** 烘

today **gām yaht** 今日

toe **geuk jí** 腳趾

tofu **dauh fuh** 豆腐

together **yāt chàih** 一齊

toilet **chi só/sái sáu gāan** 廁所／洗手間

toilet paper **chi jí** 廁紙

tomato **fāan ké** 番茄

tomorrow **tīng yaht** 聽日

tongue **leih** 脷

tonight **gām máahn** 今晚

too (also) **dōu haih** 都係

too (excessive) **taai** 太

too bad **taai chā** 太差

too much **taai dō** 太多

tool **gūng geuih** 工具

tooth **ngàh** 牙

toothache **ngàh tung** 牙痛

toothbrush **ngàh cháat** 牙刷

toothpaste **ngàh gōu** 牙膏

top **déng** 頂

top up **jāng jihk** 增值

topic **tàih muhk** 題目

torch, flashlight **dihn túng** 電筒

total **yāt guhng** 一共

touch, to **mó** 摸

tourist **léuih haak/yàuh haak** 旅客／遊客

toward (people/place) **heung** 向

towel **mòuh gān** 毛巾

tower **taap** 塔

town **síh jan** 市鎮

toy **wuhn geuih** 玩具

trade, exchange **gāau yihk** 交易

traditional **chyùhn túng** 傳統

traffic **gāau tūng** 交通

traffic lights **hùhng luhk dāng/gāau tūng dāng** 紅綠燈／交通燈

train **fó chē** 火車

train (direct/through train) **jihk tūng chē** 直通車

train station **fó chē jaahm** 火車站

training **fan lihn** 訓練

tram **dihn chē** 電車

tranquillizer **jang jihng jāi** 鎮靜劑

translate, to **fāan yihk** 翻譯

travel, to **léuih hàhng** 旅行

traveler **léuih haak** 旅客

tray **tok pún** 托盤

treat, a **tìhm táu** 甜頭

treat, to (behavior) **deui yàhn** 對人

treat, to (medically) **yī** 醫

tree **syuh** 樹

triangle **sāam gok yìhng** 三角形

trip, journey **léuih hàhng/léuih chìhng** 旅行／旅程

troops **gwān déui** 軍隊

trouble, troublesome **màh fàahn** 麻煩

trousers **fu** 褲

truck **fo chē** 貨車

true **jān** 真

trust, to **seun yahm** 信任

try, to **si** 試

try on (clothes) **si sān** 試身

Tuesday **Sīng kèih yih** 星期二

tunnel **seuih douh** 隧道

turn around, to **jyun** 轉

turn off, to **sāan/sīk** 閂／熄

turn on, to **hōi** 開

TV **dihn sih gēi** 電視機

twelve **sahp yih** 十二

twenty **yih sahp** 二十

twice **léuhng chi** 兩次

two (numeral) **yih** 二

two (measure) **léuhng** 兩

type, sort **júng leuih** 種類

type, to **dá jih** 打字

typhoon **dá fūng** 打風

typical **dín yìhng** 典型

U

ugly **cháu yéung** 醜樣

umbrella **jē** 遮

under **hah mihn** 下面

undergo, to **gīng gwo** 經過

underpants **dái fu** 底褲

undershirt **dái sāam** 底衫

understand **mìhng** 明

unfortunately **hóu m̀h hóu chói** 好唔好彩

unemployed **sāt yihp** 失業

uneven **lāp daht** 凹凸

unhappy **m̀h hōi sām** 唔開心

United Kingdom **Yīng Gwok** 英國

United States **Méih Gwok** 美國

university **daaih hohk** 大學

unleaded petrol **mòuh yùhn dihn yàuh** 無鉛電油

unless **chèuih fēi** 除非

unlimited local calls **mòuh haahn bún deih tūng wah** 無限本地通話

unlimited Wi-Fi **mòuh haahn séuhng móhng** 無限上網

unlucky **m̀h hóu chói** 唔好彩

until **jihk dou** 直到

up, upward **heung seuhng** 向上

upset, unhappy **m̀h hōi sām** 唔開心

upstairs **làuh seuhng** 樓上

urban **sìhng síh** 城市

urgent **gán gāp** 緊急

urinate, to **síu bihn** 小便

us **ngóh deih** 我哋

use, to **yuhng** 用

used to **jaahp gwaan** 習慣

useful **yáuh yuhng ge** 有用嘅

useless **móuh yuhng ge** 冇用嘅

usually **tūng sèuhng** 通常

V

vacation **ga kèih** 假期

vaccination **dá fòhng yihk jām** 打防疫針

vagina **yām douh** 陰道

vague **hàhm wùh** 含糊

valid **yáuh haauh** 有效

value (cost) **ga jihk** 價值

value, good **jihk dāk** 值得

value, to **juhng sih** 重視

vegetable **sō choi** 蔬菜

vegetarian **sihk jāai** 食齋

vehicle **chē** 車

via **louh gīng** 路經

video camera **sip luhk gēi** 攝錄機

visa **chīm jing** 簽証

Vietnam **Yuht Nàahm** 越南

Vietnamese (in general) **Yuht Nàahm ge** 越南嘅

Vietnamese (people) **Yuht Nàahm yàhn** 越南人

Vietnamese (language) **Yuht Nàahm wá** 越南話

view, panorama **fūng gíng** 風景

view, look at **tái** 睇

village **chyūn** 村

vinegar **chou** 醋

visa **chīm jing** 簽証

visit **chāam gūn** 參觀

visit, to pay a **fóng mahn** 訪問

vodka **fukh dahk gāa** 伏特加

voice **sēng yām** 聲音

vomit, to **ngáu** 嘔

vote, to **tàuh piu** 投票

W

wages **yàhn gūng** 人工

wait for, to **dáng** 等

waiter, waitress **sih ying sāng** 待應生

wake up **séng** 醒

wake someone up **giu séng** 叫醒

wakeboard **fā sīk waaht séui báan** 花式滑水板

walk, to **hàahng** 行

walking distance **hàahng dāk dou** 行得到

wall **chèuhng** 牆

wallet **ngàhn bāau** 銀包

want, to **yiu** 要

war, to make **dá jeung** 打仗

warm, warmth **nyúhn** 暖

warning, to warn **gíng gou** 警告

wash, to **sái** 洗

wash the dishes **sái wún** 洗碗

watch (wristwatch) **sáu bīu** 手錶

watch, to **tái** 睇

watch over, guard **tái jyuh** 睇住

water **séui** 水

waterfall **buhk bou** 瀑布

watermelon **sāi gwā** 西瓜

wave (in sea) **lohng** 浪

wave, to **jīu sáu** 招手

way, method **fōng faat** 方法

way, by way of **louh ging** 路徑

way in **yahp háu** 入口

way out **chēut háu** 出口

we, us **ngóh deih** 我哋

weak **yeuhk** 弱

wealthy **yáuh chín** 有錢

wear, to **jeuk** 著

weary **gwuih** 劫

weather **tīn hei** 天氣

wedding **fān láih** 婚禮

Wednesday **Sīng kèih sāam** 星期三

week **sīng kèih** 星期

weekend **jāu muht** 週末

weekly **múih go sīng kèih** 每個星期

weep, to **haam** 喊

weigh, to **ching/bong** 秤／磅

weigh out, to **ching chēut** 秤出

weight **chúhng leuhng** 重量

weight (body) **tái chúhng** 體重

weight, to gain **jāng bóng** 增磅

weight, to lose **gáam bóng/gáam fèih** 減磅／減肥

welcome, welcome, to **fūn yìhng** 歡迎

well (good) **hóu** 好

well-cooked, well-done **jyú suhk** 煮熟

Well done! **Jouh dāk hóu!** 做得好!

well-mannered **yáuh láih maauh** 有禮貌

well off, wealthy **yáuh chín** 有錢

Welsh (in general) **Wāi yíh sī ge** 威爾斯嘅

Welsh (people) **Wāi yíh sī yàhn** 威爾斯人

west **sāi bīn/bihn** 西邊

Westerner **Sāi yàhn** 西人

wet **sāp** 濕

wetsuit **chìhm séui yī** 潛水衣

what **māt yéh** 乜嘢

what for **dím gáai** 點解

what kind of **bīn júng** 邊種

what time **géi dím** 幾點

wheel **chē lūk** 車轆

when **géi sìh** 幾時

when, at the time **dōng/...ge sìh hauh** 當／…既時候

whenever **mòuh leuhn hòh sìh** 無論何時

where **bīn douh/bīn syu** 邊度／邊處

where to **heui bīn douh/heui bīn syu** 去邊度／去邊處

which one **bīn (go)** 邊(個)

while, during **hái...kèih gāan** 喺…期間

whisky **wāi sih géi** 威士忌

white **baahk sīk** 白色

who **bīn go/bīn wái** 邊個／邊位

whole, all of **chyùhn bouh** 全部

whole, to be complete **jíng go** 整個

Why? **Dím gáai?** 點解?

wicked **waaih sām chèuhng ge** 壞心腸嘅

wide **fut** 闊

width **fut douh** 闊度

widow **gwá fúh** 寡婦

widowed **yíh song ngáuh** 已喪偶

widower **gwāan fū** 鰥夫

wife **taai táai/lóuh pòh** 太太／老婆

Wi-Fi **mòuh sin séuhng móhng** 無線上網

wild **yéh sāng ge** 野生嘅

will, shall **jēung wúih** (將)會

win, to **yèhng** 贏

wind, breeze **fūng** 風

window (in house) **chēung** 窗

window (for paying, buying tickets) **chēung háu** 窗口

windsurfing **fūng fàahn** 風帆

wine **pòuh tòuh jáu** 葡萄酒

wine, red **hùhng jáu** 紅酒

wine, white **baahk jáu** 白酒

winner **dāk jéung yàhn** 得獎人

winter **dūng tīn** 冬天

wipe, to **maat gōn** 抹乾

wireless **mòuh sin** 無線

wise **chūng mìhng** 聰明

wish, to **hēi mohng** 希望

with, and **tùhng** 同

within reason **chìhng léih jī noih** 情理之內

without **móuh** 冇

witness **jing yàhn** 証人

witness, to **chān ngáahn gin dóu** 親眼見到

woman **néuih yán** 女人

wonderful **hóu gihk laak** 好極嘞

wonton noodles **wàhn tān mihn** 雲吞麵

wood **muhk tàuh** 木頭

wooden **muhk jai ge** 木製嘅

wool **yèuhng mòuh/lāang** 羊毛／冷

wool (for knitting) **lāang** 冷

work **gūng jok** 工作

work, to **jouh** 做

work, to function **héi jok yuhng** 起作用

world **sai gaai** 世界

worn out, tired **gwuih** 劼

worn out (clothes, machine) **chàhn gaau** 陳舊

worry, to **dāam sām** 擔心

worse **gang waaih/gang chā** 更壞／更差

worst **jeui waaih/jeui chā** 最壞／最差

worth, to be **jihk dāk** 值得

wound **sēung háu** 傷口

wrap, to **bāau** 包

wrist **sáu wún** 手腕

write, to **sé** 寫

writer **jok gā** 作家

wrong (false) **m̀h ngāam** 唔啱

wrong (mistaken) **cho** 錯

wrong (morally) **bāt douh dāk** 不道德

Y

yawn **dá haam louh** 打喊路

year **nìhn** 年

years old **seui** 歲

yell, to **daaih sēng giu** 大聲叫

yellow **wòhng sīk** 黃色

yes **haih** 係

yesterday **kàhm/chàhm yaht** 琴／尋日

yet: not yet **juhng meih** 仲未

you **néih** 你

you (plural) **néih deih** 你哋

You're welcome! **M̀h sái haak hei!** 唔駛客氣!

young **hauh sāang/nìhn hēng** 後生／年輕

youth (state of being young) **chīng chēun** 青春

youth (young person) **hauh sāang jái néui** 後生仔女

Z

zero **lìhng** 零

zoo **duhng maht yùhn** 動物園

"Books to Span the East and West"

Tuttle Publishing was founded in 1832 in the small New England town of Rutland, Vermont [USA]. Our core values remain as strong today as they were then—to publish best-in-class books which bring people together one page at a time. In 1948, we established a publishing outpost in Japan—and Tuttle is now a leader in publishing English-language books about the arts, languages and cultures of Asia. The world has become a much smaller place today and Asia's economic and cultural influence has grown. Yet the need for meaningful dialogue and information about this diverse region has never been greater. Over the past seven decades, Tuttle has published thousands of books on subjects ranging from martial arts and paper crafts to language learning and literature—and our talented authors, illustrators, designers and photographers have won many prestigious awards. We welcome you to explore the wealth of information available on Asia at **www.tuttlepublishing.com**.

Published by Tuttle Publishing, an imprint of Periplus Editions (HK) Ltd.

www.tuttlepublishing.com

Copyright © 2017 Periplus Editions (HK) Ltd.

Library of Congress Control Number: 2017959647

ISBN 978-0-8048-4708-7

28 27 26 25 24 23
10 9 8 7 6 5 4 3   2310CM
Printed in China

TUTTLE PUBLISHING® is a registered trademark of Tuttle Publishing, a division of Periplus Editions (HK) Ltd.

Distributed by

North America, Latin America & Europe
Tuttle Publishing
364 Innovation Drive
North Clarendon, VT 05759-9436 U.S.A.
Tel: 1 (802) 773-8930
Fax: 1 (802) 773-6993
info@tuttlepublishing.com
www.tuttlepublishing.com

Japan
Tuttle Publishing
Yaekari Building 3rd Floor 5-4-12 Osaki
Shinagawa-ku, Tokyo 141 0032
Tel: (81) 3 5437-0171
Fax: (81) 3 5437-0755
sales@tuttle.co.jp
www.tuttle.co.jp

Asia Pacific
Berkeley Books Pte. Ltd.
3 Kallang Sector #04-01
Singapore 349278
Tel: (65) 6741-2178
Fax: (65) 6741-2179
inquiries@periplus.com.sg
www.tuttlepublishing.com